Philosophical Introductions

FIRST EDITION

Philosophical Introductions

Introductory Readings in Philosophy

EDITED BY Dr. Michael K. Cundall, Jr.

North Carolina A&T State University

Bassim Hamadeh, CEO and Publisher

Kaela Martin, Project Editor

Celeste Paed, Associate Production Editor

Jess Estrella, Senior Graphic Designer

Alexa Lucido, Licensing Manager

Natalie Piccotti, Director of Marketing

Kassie Graves, Vice President of Editorial

Jamie Giganti, Director of Academic Publishing

cognella® | ACADEMIC PUBLISHING

3970 Sorrento Valley Blvd., Ste. 500, San Diego, CA 92121

TABLE OF CONTENTS

Philosophical Introductions

A Short and Funny Introduction to Philosophy

Note to my astute reader:

If you are bothering to read this introduction, thank you. I hope that you get a lot of meaningful somethings from this book and the class you're in. I know you're probably not here of your own accord. You likely have to take this course to meet some standards you never agreed to and are only really doing it so that you can graduate. So, I am going to do my best to point out some of the main ideas, some of the ways in which various cases are made, and hopefully give you more of the flavor of the writings you're reading. Believe it or not, if you try to pay attention to the writing for its style, its voice, and its humor, you're going to have a richer experience. This is something that I didn't pay enough attention to when I first started. If you're one of the very few who are reading this because you want to, I wholeheartedly invite you to take your time and try to enjoy the readings and the ideas in them. Whatever sort of reader, forced marcher, or volunteer, philosophy is an exciting and humbling undertaking; and if you stay with it and get through the headaches and difficult language that is sure to come, you will come out the other side a better person. You'll have been exposed to ideas and authors that have left deep impressions on the history of human thought as well as develop better reading and critical evaluation skills. But enough about you, let's talk about me!

I am one of those rare folks who knew at 14 what I wanted to do. I wanted to do philosophy. I know, my parents shook their heads too. If you'd have asked 14-year-old me if I expected to be writing philosophy articles and books, I would have laughed, but, as I learned, that's part of it. I still sort of chuckle at my writing this now. I mean, does the world need another introduction to philosophy text? Probably not. Am I going to write one that I believe is strong and tries to keep the cost of the text low? You bet. One of my reasons to take this project on was to make a text that was inexpensive and good. The project of philosophy, the answering of the "Why?" question, fascinated me at 14 and fascinates me still. I hope to introduce you to some of that fascination and enjoyment I receive, and maybe, just maybe, get you to enjoy it in some ways like I do. But, like almost any program of study or exercise routine, the work is going to be tough, demanding, but ultimately worth it. Long ago the patron saint of philosophers, Socrates, claimed, "The unexamined life is not worth living." You'll be meeting Socrates here shortly. If you carry through with the readings, if you make an honest and concerted effort to read the materials a couple of times (I still read articles two times or more), I promise you you'll emerge from your readings a better person. You'll have begun the long journey of life examination. That, among other things, is the universal promise of education. It's why parents and societies spend so much time, effort, energy, and money on education. It's one of the reasons I'm writing now.

So maybe you're asking yourself, astute reader, if there are already a bunch of introduction to philosophy texts out there, why should I use yours? Good question. One of the ways I think that my text is going to be different is that I am going to introduce humor as much as I can. Now before you get all excited, this isn't going to be a trip to a comedy club, or a read filled with LOL's page after page. LOLs aren't my goal. But smiles, small chuckles, irony, and wit are. Philosophy can be terribly, even wickedly funny at times. Socrates, for many, was master rhetorician, a clever and insightful philosopher, and pretty funny. So, what I need from you, astute reader, is that you relax a little bit when you read. Try and look at times for the wit present in what we read. I will do my best to point it out, but as you know, if I have to explain a joke, it's often no longer funny. If you're open to finding humor, trust me: The world is chock full of it.

There are a number of choices any author doing a sort of introductory text is presented with. Should the approach be topical, historical, a mixture? Should I treat it like a Jackson Pollock painting and just have at it and let the words fall where they may? Do you even care? Not likely on the last one, but the choices I make in writing this text, in presenting the ideas and authors within, will have irrevocable effects on your experience of philosophy. And since I am both an educator and a lover of philosophy, I want that experience to be engaging, challenging, and ultimately rewarding. I don't want to give you answers; I want to give you questions and, more importantly, the skills, abilities, confidence, and courage to work to answer them.

So, how is this book going to work? There are 15 chapters in total. Some will deal with topics; some will deal with a particular author's treatment of a topic. If you're interested to experience what I am hoping this class will teach you, you need look no further than the classic Platonic Dialogue, the Euthyphro. (You can find a translation of the Euthyphro on the web. Do a search for "Euythyphro" and you'll find it.) In this dialogue you will get an exposure to the Socratic Method. More importantly, you will be exposed to the rigorous and careful examination of thoughts and ideas Socrates was known for. He wants you to think hard about what you believe and if those beliefs are well-supported. It turns out that Socrates' partner in the dialogue, Euthyphro, most certainly does not. Reading this may spur you to confusion, may annoy you, and you may be frustrated that no acceptable definition of piety is offered. Often we learn more when we are not given a direct answer. But more importantly, you may now wonder what an argument in the philosophical sense is. You may wonder how one effectively supports your position. How do premises and conclusions relate? If those questions get to you, then you're well on your way to understanding the main point of this class. Given these readings, how do they teach you to be a better and more refined and more effective thinker?

Now many texts will then go on to give a thumbnail sketch of all the chapters, a sort of "tell-'em-what-you're-going-to-tell-'em" approach. But there isn't a need. You'll get to the content as it comes:

page by page. The chapters of the text are not arranged in any specific way. You could read Chapter 7 before chapter 2, or Chapter 11 right after Chapter 4. In his *Meditations on First Philosophy*, Descartes wonders what he can know and how he can go about finding out.

The readings are all self-contained, but can relate to each other if you care to look for commonalities. Some of these works you'll be reading have had numerous books, articles, dissertations, and coffeehouse chats dedicated to them. It's impossible to cover all the issues. I don't even come close to knowing them all. I will give you a basic outline of the ideas, some description of the main topics and how they relate to broader themes in philosophy, as well as some questions to think about at the end of each reading. Remember, it would be best if you read the primary material at least twice before every class. The first time through just gets you next to the material. If you can basically say what the main topic or two of the reading is, you're doing fine. The second time through the material, you should be looking to see how the main points are supported. What is the author using as evidence? Do you understand or agree with the argument of train of thoughts presented? Where are you confused? This is particularly important. Don't just reflexively say "All of it." That doesn't do you, or your teacher, any good. If you have a specific problem, write it down, note it in the text. Do whatever you can to locate the issue and then bring it up to your teacher. Trust me when I say this. If our students came in with specific questions like, "I don't understand what's happening on page 13," we would be ecstatic.

If you want the real answer on how to read this and any material for retention and understanding, here it is. Read and prepare anything as if you had to present it as a teacher the next day. If you're able to do that, you will have developed a level of familiarity with the material that will allow you to generate a broader and more in-depth understanding. Even if you get something wrong, which we all do, no matter how adept we are, you'll be able to understand why the mistake was made. This is a far more demanding form of reading, but one that will pay you huge dividends in this class and far after you leave college. Imagine going into your first meeting and demonstrating to your new colleagues how much you know of what's going on. You'll get that raise sooner rather than later.

Enough introductions. Let's get on into the material. It won't always be easy, and some of the stuff you simply won't get. I still don't get much of what a number of really well-known and respected philosophers have done, but I try when I can. I get frustrated at both myself and at them, but that's part of the goal of examination. I may not get it now, but I may yet get it. And even if I never come to a full understanding of someone like Heidegger (I never have made it past page 20 in *Being and Time*), I know that there are other things I do know well. You will get there soon, I promise. But let's get on with it.

Meditations 1–3

René Descartes and Donald A. Cress

Meditations on First Philosophy in Which the Existence   *17*
of God And the Distinction Between the Soul and the
Body are Demonstrated

Meditation One: Concerning Those Things That Can Be Called into Doubt

Several years have now passed since I first realized how numerous were the false opinions that in my youth I had taken to be true, and thus how doubtful were all those that I had subsequently built upon them. And thus I realized that once in my life I had to raze everything to the ground and begin again from the original foundations, if I wanted to establish anything firm and lasting in the sciences. But the task seemed enormous, and I was waiting until I reached a point in my life that was so timely that no more suitable time for undertaking these plans of action would come to pass. For this reason, I procrastinated for so long that I would henceforth be at fault, were I to waste the time that remains for carrying out the project by brooding over it. Accordingly, I have today suitably freed my mind of all cares, secured for myself a period of leisurely tranquillity, and am   *18* withdrawing into solitude. At last I will apply myself earnestly and unreservedly to this general demolition of my opinions.

Yet to bring this about I will not need to show that all my opinions are false, which is perhaps something I could never accomplish. But reason now persuades me that I should withhold my assent no less carefully from opinions that are not completely certain and indubitable than I would from those that are patently false. For this reason, it will suffice for the rejection of all of these opinions, if I find in each of them some reason for doubt. Nor therefore need I survey each opinion individually, a task that would be endless. Rather, because undermining the foundations will cause whatever has been built upon them to crumble of its own accord, I will attack straightaway those principles which supported everything I once believed.

Surely whatever I had admitted until now as most true I received either from the senses or through the senses. However, I have noticed that the senses are sometimes deceptive; and it is a mark of prudence never to place our complete trust in those who have deceived us even once.

But perhaps, even though the senses do sometimes deceive us when it is a question of very small and distant things, still there are many other matters concerning which one simply cannot doubt, even though they are derived from the very same senses: for example, that I am sitting here next to the fire, wearing my winter dressing gown, that I am holding this sheet of paper in my hands, and the like. But on what grounds could one deny that these hands and this entire body are mine? Unless perhaps I were to 19 liken myself to the insane, whose brains are impaired by such an unrelenting vapor of black bile that they steadfastly insist that they are kings when they are utter paupers, or that they are arrayed in purple robes when they are naked, or that they have heads made of clay, or that they are gourds, or that they are made of glass. But such people are mad, and I would appear no less mad, were I to take their behavior as an example for myself.

This would all be well and good, were I not a man who is accustomed to sleeping at night, and to experiencing in my dreams the very same things, or now and then even less plausible ones, as these insane people do when they are awake. How often does my evening slumber persuade me of such ordinary things as these: that I am here, clothed in my dressing gown, seated next to the fireplace—when in fact I am lying undressed in bed! But right now my eyes are certainly wide awake when I gaze upon this sheet of paper. This head which I am shaking is not heavy with sleep. I extend this hand consciously and deliberately, and I feel it. Such things would not be so distinct for someone who is asleep. As if I did not recall having been deceived on other occasions even by similar thoughts in my dreams! As I consider these matters more carefully, I see so plainly that there are no definitive signs by which to distinguish being awake from being asleep. As a result, I am becoming quite dizzy, and this dizziness nearly convinces me that I am asleep.

Let us assume then, for the sake of argument, that we are dreaming and that such particulars as these are not true: that we are opening our eyes, moving our head, and extending our hands. Perhaps we do not even have such hands, or any such body at all. Nevertheless, it surely must be admitted that the things seen during slumber are, as it were, like painted images, which could only have been produced in the likeness of true things, and that therefore at least these general things—eyes, head, hands, and the whole body—are not imaginary things, but are true and exist. For indeed when painters themselves wish to represent sirens and satyrs by *20* means of especially bizarre forms, they surely cannot assign to them utterly new natures. Rather, they simply fuse together the members of various animals. Or if perhaps they concoct something so utterly novel that nothing like it has ever been seen before (and thus is something utterly fictitious and false), yet certainly at the very least the colors from which they fashion it ought to be true. And by the same token, although even these general things—eyes, head, hands and the like—could be imaginary, still one has to admit that at least certain other things that are even more simple and universal are true. It is from these components, as if from true colors, that all those images of things that are in our thought are fashioned, be they true or false.

This class of things appears to include corporeal nature in general, together with its extension; the shape of extended things; their quantity, that is, their size and number; as well as the place where they exist; the time through which they endure, and the like.

Thus it is not improper to conclude from this that physics, astronomy, medicine, and all the other disciplines that are dependent upon the consideration of composite things are doubtful, and that, on the other hand, arithmetic, geometry, and other such disciplines, which treat of nothing but the simplest and most general things and which are indifferent as to whether these things do or do not in fact exist, contain something certain and indubitable. For whether I am awake or asleep, two plus three make five, and a square does not have more than four sides. It does not seem possible that such obvious truths should be subject to the suspicion of being false.

Be that as it may, there is fixed in my mind a certain opinion of long *21* standing, namely that there exists a God who is able to do anything and by whom I, such as I am, have been created. How do I know that he did not bring it about that there is no earth at all, no heavens, no extended thing, no shape, no size, no place, and yet bringing it about that all these things appear to me to exist precisely as they do now? Moreover, since I judge that others sometimes make mistakes in matters that they believe they know most perfectly, may I not, in like fashion, be deceived every time I add two and three or count the sides of a square, or perform an even simpler operation, if that can be imagined? But perhaps God has not willed that I be deceived in this way, for he is said to be supremely good. Nonetheless, if it were repugnant to his goodness to have created me such that I be deceived all the time, it would also seem foreign to that same goodness to permit me to be deceived even occasionally. But we cannot make this last assertion.

Perhaps there are some who would rather deny so powerful a God than believe that everything else is uncertain. Let us not oppose them; rather, let us grant that everything said here about God is fictitious. Now they suppose that I came to be what I am either by fate, or by chance, or by a connected chain of events, or by some other way. But because being deceived and being mistaken appear to be a certain imperfection, the less powerful they take the author of my origin to be, the more probable it will be that I am so imperfect that I am always deceived. I have nothing to say in response to these arguments. But eventually I am forced to admit that there is nothing among the things I once believed to be true which it is not permissible to doubt—and not out of frivolity or lack of forethought, but for valid and considered reasons. Thus I must be no less careful to 22 withhold assent henceforth even from these beliefs than I would from those that are patently false, if I wish to find anything certain.

But it is not enough simply to have realized these things; I must take steps to keep myself mindful of them. For long-standing opinions keep returning, and, almost against my will, they take advantage of my credulity, as if it were bound over to them by long use and the claims of intimacy. Nor will I ever get out of the habit of assenting to them and believing in them, so long as I take them to be exactly what they are, namely, in some respects doubtful, as has just now been shown, but nevertheless highly probable, so that it is much more consonant with reason to believe them than to deny them. Hence, it seems to me I would do well to deceive myself by turning my will in completely the opposite direction and pretend for a time that these opinions are wholly false and imaginary, until finally, as if with prejudices weighing down each side equally, no bad habit should turn my judgment any further from the correct perception of things. For indeed I know that meanwhile there is no danger or error in following this procedure, and that it is impossible for me to indulge in too much distrust, since I am now concentrating only on knowledge, not on action.

Accordingly, I will suppose not a supremely good God, the source of truth, but rather an evil genius, supremely powerful and clever, who has directed his entire effort at deceiving me. I will regard the heavens, the air, the earth, colors, shapes, sounds, and all external things as nothing but the bedeviling hoaxes of my dreams, with which he lays snares for my credulity. I will regard myself as not having hands, or eyes, or flesh, or blood, or any senses, but as nevertheless falsely believing that I possess all these things. I will remain resolute and steadfast in this meditation, and even if it is not within my power to know anything true, it certainly is within my power to take care resolutely to withhold my assent to what is false, lest this deceiver, however powerful, however clever he may be, have any effect on me. But this undertaking is arduous, and a certain laziness brings me back to my customary way of living. I am not unlike a prisoner who enjoyed an imaginary freedom during his sleep, but, when he later begins to suspect that he is dreaming, fears being awakened and nonchalantly conspires with these pleasant illusions. In just the same way, I fall back of my own accord into my old opinions, and dread being awakened, lest the toilsome wakefulness which follows upon a peaceful rest must be spent thenceforward not in the light but among the inextricable shadows of the difficulties now brought forward.

Meditation Two: Concerning the Nature of the Human Mind: That It Is Better Known Than the Body

Yesterday's meditation has thrown me into such doubts that I can no longer ignore them, yet I fail to see how they are to be resolved. It is as if I had suddenly fallen into a deep whirlpool; I am so tossed about that I can neither touch bottom with my foot, nor swim up to the top. Nevertheless I will work my way up and will once again attempt the same path I entered upon yesterday. I will accomplish this by putting aside everything that admits of the least doubt, as if I had discovered it to be completely false. I will stay on this course until I know something certain, or, if nothing else, until I at least know for certain that nothing is certain. Archimedes sought but one firm and immovable point in order to move the entire earth from

23

24

one place to another. Just so, great things are also to be hoped for if I succeed in finding just one thing, however slight, that is certain and unshaken.

Therefore I suppose that everything I see is false. I believe that none of what my deceitful memory represents ever existed. I have no senses whatever. Body, shape, extension, movement, and place are all chimeras. What then will be true? Perhaps just the single fact that nothing is certain.

But how do I know there is not something else, over and above all those things that I have just reviewed, concerning which there is not even the slightest occasion for doubt? Is there not some God, or by whatever name I might call him, who instills these very thoughts in me? But why would I think that, since I myself could perhaps be the author of these thoughts? Am I not then at least something? But I have already denied that I have any senses and any body. Still I hesitate; for what follows from this? Am I so tied to a body and to the senses that I cannot exist without them? But I have persuaded myself that there is absolutely nothing in the world: no sky, no earth, no minds, no bodies. Is it then the case that I too do not exist? But doubtless I did exist, if I persuaded myself of something. But there is some deceiver or other who is supremely powerful and supremely sly and who is always deliberately deceiving me. Then too there is no doubt that I exist, if he is deceiving me. And let him do his best at deception, he will never bring it about that I am nothing so long as I shall think that I am something. Thus, after everything has been most carefully weighed, it must finally be established that this pronouncement "I am, I exist" is necessarily true every time I utter it or conceive it in my mind.

But I do not yet understand sufficiently what I am—I, who now necessarily exist. And so from this point on, I must be careful lest I unwittingly mistake something else for myself, and thus err in that very item of knowledge that I claim to be the most certain and evident of all. Thus, I will meditate once more on what I once believed myself to be, prior to embarking upon these thoughts. For this reason, then, I will set aside whatever can be weakened even to the slightest degree by the arguments brought forward, so that eventually all that remains is precisely nothing but what is certain and unshaken.

What then did I use to think I was? A man, of course. But what is a man? Might I not say a "rational animal"? No, because then I would have to inquire what "animal" and "rational" mean. And thus from one question I would slide into many more difficult ones. Nor do I now have enough free time that I want to waste it on subtleties of this sort. Instead, permit me to focus here on what came spontaneously and naturally into my thinking whenever I pondered what I was. Now it occurred to me first that I had a face, hands, arms, and this entire mechanism of bodily members: the very same as are discerned in a corpse, and which I referred to by the name "body." It next occurred to me that I took in food, that I walked about, and that I sensed and thought various things; these actions I used to attribute to the soul. But as to what this soul might be, I either did not think about it or else I imagined it a rarified I-know-not-what, like a wind, or a fire, or ether, which had been infused into my coarser parts. But as to the body I was not in any doubt. On the contrary, I was under the impression that I knew its nature distinctly. Were I perhaps tempted to describe this nature such as I conceived it in my mind, I would have described it thus: by "body," I understand all that is capable of being bounded by some shape, of being enclosed in a place, and of filling up a space in such a way as to exclude any other body from it; of being perceived by touch, sight, hearing, taste, or smell; of being moved in several ways, not, of course, by itself, but by whatever else impinges upon it. For it was my view that the power of self-motion, and likewise of sensing or of thinking, in no way belonged to the nature of the body. Indeed I used rather to marvel that such faculties were to be found in certain bodies.

But now what am I, when I suppose that there is some supremely powerful and, if I may be permitted to say so, malicious deceiver who deliberately tries to fool me in any way he can? Can I not affirm that I possess at least a small measure of all those things which I have already said belong to the nature of the body? I focus my attention on them, I think about them, I review them again, but nothing comes to mind. I am tired of repeating this to no purpose. But what about those things I ascribed to the soul? What about being nourished or moving about? Since I now do not have a body, these are surely nothing but fictions. What about sensing? Surely this too does not take place without a body; and I seemed to have sensed in my dreams many things that I later realized I did not sense. What about thinking? Here I make my discovery: thought exists; it alone cannot be separated from me. I am; I exist—this is certain. But for how long? For as long as I am thinking; for perhaps it could also come to pass that if I were to cease all thinking I would then utterly cease to exist. At this time I admit nothing that is not necessarily true. I am therefore precisely nothing but a thinking thing; that is, a mind, or intellect, or understanding, or reason—words of whose meanings I was previously ignorant. Yet I am a true thing and am truly existing; but what kind of thing? I have said it already: a thinking thing.

What else am I? I will set my imagination in motion. I am not that concatenation of members we call the human body. Neither am I even some subtle air infused into these members, nor a wind, nor a fire, nor a vapor, nor a breath, nor anything I devise for myself. For I have supposed these things to be nothing. The assumption still stands; yet nevertheless I am something. But is it perhaps the case that these very things which I take to be nothing, because they are unknown to me, nevertheless are in fact no different from that "me" that I know? This I do not know, and I will not quarrel about it now. I can make a judgment only about things that are known to me. I know that I exist; I ask now who is this "I" whom I know? Most certainly, in the strict sense the knowledge of this "I" does 28 not depend upon things of whose existence I do not yet have knowledge. Therefore it is not dependent upon any of those things that I simulate in my imagination. But this word "simulate" warns me of my error. For I would indeed be simulating were I to "imagine" that I was something, because imagining is merely the contemplating of the shape or image of a corporeal thing. But I now know with certainty that I am and also that all these images—and, generally, everything belonging to the nature of the body—could turn out to be nothing but dreams. Once I have realized this, I would seem to be speaking no less foolishly were I to say: "I will use my imagination in order to recognize more distinctly who I am," than were I to say: "Now I surely am awake, and I see something true; but since I do not yet see it clearly enough, I will deliberately fall asleep so that my dreams might represent it to me more truly and more clearly." Thus I realize that none of what I can grasp by means of the imagination pertains to this knowledge that I have of myself. Moreover, I realize that I must be most diligent about withdrawing my mind from these things so that it can perceive its nature as distinctly as possible.

But what then am I? A thing that thinks. What is that? A thing that doubts, understands, affirms, denies, wills, refuses, and that also imagines and senses.

Indeed it is no small matter if all of these things belong to me. But why should they not belong to me? Is it not the very same "I" who now doubts almost everything, who nevertheless understands something, who affirms that this one thing is true, who denies other things, who desires to know more, who wishes not to be deceived, who imagines many things even against my will, who also notices many things which appear to come from the senses? What is there in all of this that is not every bit as true as the fact that I exist—even if I am always asleep or even if my creator makes every effort to mislead me? Which of these things is distinct from my thought? Which of them can be said to be separate from myself? For it is so obvious that it is I who doubt, I who understand, and I who will, that there is nothing by which it could be explained more clearly. But indeed it is also the same "I" who imagines; for although perhaps, as I supposed before, absolutely nothing that I imagined is true, still the very power of imagining really does exist, and constitutes a part of my thought. Finally, it is this same "I" who senses or who is cognizant of bodily things as if through the senses. For example, I now see a light, I hear a noise, I feel heat. These things are false, since I am asleep. Yet I certainly do seem to see, hear, and feel warmth. This cannot be false. Properly speaking, this is what in me is called "sensing." But this, precisely so taken, is nothing other than thinking.

From these considerations I am beginning to know a little better what I am. But it still seems (and I cannot resist believing) that corporeal things—whose images are formed by thought, and which the senses themselves examine—are much more distinctly known than this mysterious "I" which does not fall within the imagination. And yet it would be strange indeed were I to grasp the very things I consider to be doubtful, unknown, and foreign to me more distinctly than what is true, what is known—than, in short, myself. But I see what is happening: my mind loves to wander and does not yet permit itself to be restricted within the confines of truth. So be it then; let us just this once allow it completely free rein, so that, a little while later, when the time has come to pull in the reins, the mind may more readily permit itself to be controlled.

Let us consider those things which are commonly believed to be the most distinctly grasped of all: namely the bodies we touch and see. Not bodies in general, mind you, for these general perceptions are apt to be somewhat more confused, but one body in particular. Let us take, for instance, this piece of wax. It has been taken quite recently from the honeycomb; it has not yet lost all the honey flavor. It retains some of the scent of the flowers from which it was collected. Its color, shape, and size are manifest. It is hard and cold; it is easy to touch. If you rap on it with your knuckle it will emit a sound. In short, everything is present in it that appears needed to enable a body to be known as distinctly as possible. But notice that, as I am speaking, I am bringing it close to the fire. The remaining traces of the honey flavor are disappearing; the scent is vanishing; the color is changing; the original shape is disappearing. Its size is increasing; it is becoming liquid and hot; you can hardly touch it. And now, when you rap on it, it no longer emits any sound. Does the same wax still remain? I must confess that it does; no one denies it; no one thinks otherwise. So what was there in the wax that was so distinctly grasped? Certainly none of the aspects that I reached by means of the senses. For whatever came under the senses of taste, smell, sight, touch or hearing has now changed; and yet the wax remains.

Perhaps the wax was what I now think it is: namely that the wax itself never really was the sweetness of the honey, nor the fragrance of the flowers, nor the whiteness, nor the shape, nor the sound, but instead was a body that a short time ago manifested itself to me in these ways, and now does so in other ways. But just what precisely is this thing that I thus 31 imagine? Let us focus our attention on this and see what remains after we have removed everything that does not belong to the wax: only that it is something extended, flexible, and mutable. But what is it to be flexible and mutable? Is it what my imagination shows it to be: namely, that this piece of wax can change from a round to a square shape, or from the latter to a triangular shape? Not at all; for I grasp that the wax is capable of innumerable changes of this sort, even though I am incapable of running through these innumerable changes by using my imagination. Therefore this insight is not achieved by the faculty of imagination. What is it to be extended? Is this thing's extension also unknown? For it becomes greater in wax that is beginning to melt, greater in boiling wax, and greater still as the heat is increased. And I would not judge correctly what the wax is if I did not believe that it takes on an even greater variety of dimensions than I could ever grasp with the imagination. It remains then for me to concede that I do not grasp what this wax is through the imagination; rather, I perceive it through the mind alone. The point I am making refers to this particular piece of wax, for the case of wax in general is clearer still. But what is this piece of wax which is perceived only by the mind? Surely it is the same piece of wax that I see, touch, and imagine; in short it is the same piece of wax I took it to be from the very beginning. But I need to realize that the perception of the wax is neither a seeing, nor a touching, nor an imagining. Nor has it ever been, even though it previously seemed so; rather it is an inspection on the part of the mind alone. This inspection can be imperfect and confused, as it was before, or clear and distinct, as it is now, depending on how closely I pay attention to the things in which the piece of wax consists.

But meanwhile I marvel at how prone my mind is to errors. For although I am considering these things within myself silently and without words, *32* nevertheless I seize upon words themselves and I am nearly deceived by the ways in which people commonly speak. For we say that we see the wax itself, if it is present, and not that we judge it to be present from its color or shape. Whence I might conclude straightaway that I know the wax through the vision had by the eye, and not through an inspection on the part of the mind alone. But then were I perchance to look out my window and observe men crossing the square, I would ordinarily say I see the men themselves just as I say I see the wax. But what do I see aside from hats and clothes, which could conceal automata? Yet I judge them to be men. Thus what I thought I had seen with my eyes, I actually grasped solely with the faculty of judgment, which is in my mind.

But a person who seeks to know more than the common crowd ought to be ashamed of himself for looking for doubt in common ways of speaking. Let us then go forward and inquire when it was that I perceived more perfectly and evidently what the piece of wax was. Was it when I first saw it and believed I knew it by the external sense, or at least by the so-called common sense, that is, the power of imagination? Or do I have more perfect knowledge now, when I have diligently examined both what the wax is and how it is known? Surely it is absurd to be in doubt about this matter. For what was there in my initial perception that was distinct? What was there that any animal seemed incapable of possessing? But indeed when I distinguish the wax from its external forms, as if stripping it of its clothing, and look at the wax in its nakedness, then, even though there can be still an error in my judgment, nevertheless I cannot perceive it thus without a human mind.

But what am I to say about this mind, that is, about myself? For as *33* yet I admit nothing else to be in me over and above the mind. What, I ask, am I who seem to perceive this wax so distinctly? Do I not know myself not only much more truly and with greater certainty, but also much more distinctly and evidently? For if I judge that the wax exists from the fact that I see it, certainly from this same fact that I see the wax it follows much more evidently that I myself exist. For it could happen that what I see is not truly wax. It could happen that I have no eyes with which to see anything. But it is utterly impossible that, while I see or think I see (I do not now distinguish these two), I who think am not something. Likewise, if I judge that the wax exists from the fact that I touch it, the same outcome will again obtain, namely that I exist. If I judge that the wax exists from the fact that I imagine it, or for any other reason, plainly the same thing follows. But what I note regarding the wax applies to everything else that is external to me. Furthermore, if my perception of the wax seemed more distinct after it became known to me not only on account of sight or touch, but on account of many reasons, one has to admit how much more distinctly I am now known to myself. For there is not a single consideration that can aid in my perception of the wax or of any other body that fails to make even more manifest the nature of my mind. But there are still so many other things in the mind itself on the basis of which my knowledge of it can be rendered more distinct that it hardly seems worth enumerating those things which emanate to it from the body.

34   But lo and behold, I have returned on my own to where I wanted to be. For since I now know that even bodies are not, properly speaking, perceived by the senses or by the faculty of imagination, but by the intellect alone, and that they are not perceived through their being touched or seen, but only through their being understood, I manifestly know that nothing can be perceived more easily and more evidently than my own mind. But since the tendency to hang on to long-held beliefs cannot be put aside so quickly, I want to stop here, so that by the length of my meditation this new knowledge may be more deeply impressed upon my memory.

Meditation Three: Concerning God, That He Exists

I will now shut my eyes, stop up my ears, and withdraw all my senses. I will also blot out from my thoughts all images of corporeal things, or rather, since the latter is hardly possible, I will regard these images as empty, false and worthless. And as I converse with myself alone and look more deeply into myself, I will attempt to render myself gradually better known and more familiar to myself. I am a thing that thinks, that is to say, a thing that doubts, affirms, denies, understands a few things, is ignorant of many things, wills, refrains from willing, and also imagines and senses. For as I observed earlier, even though these things that I sense or imagine may perhaps be nothing at all outside me, nevertheless I am certain that these modes of thinking, which are cases of what I call sensing and
35   imagining, insofar as they are merely modes of thinking, do exist within me.

In these few words, I have reviewed everything I truly know, or at least what so far I have noticed that I know. Now I will ponder more carefully to see whether perhaps there may be other things belonging to me that up until now I have failed to notice. I am certain that I am a thinking thing. But do I not therefore also know what is required for me to be certain of anything? Surely in this first instance of knowledge, there is nothing but a certain clear and distinct perception of what I affirm. Yet this would hardly be enough to render me certain of the truth of a thing, if it could ever happen that something that I perceived so clearly and distinctly were false. And thus I now seem able to posit as a general rule that everything I very clearly and distinctly perceive is true.

Be that as it may, I have previously admitted many things as wholly certain and evident that nevertheless I later discovered to be doubtful. What sort of things were these? Why, the earth, the sky, the stars, and all the other things I perceived by means of the senses. But what was it about these things that I clearly perceived? Surely the fact that the ideas or thoughts of these things were hovering before my mind. But even now I do not deny that these ideas are in me. Yet there was something else I used to affirm, which, owing to my habitual tendency to believe it, I used to think was something I clearly perceived, even though I actually did not perceive it at all: namely, that certain things existed outside me, things from which those ideas proceeded and which those ideas completely resembled. But on this point I was mistaken; or rather, if my judgment was a true one, it was not the result of the force of my perception.

But what about when I considered something very simple and easy in the areas of arithmetic or geometry, for example that two plus three make five, and the like? Did I not intuit them at least clearly enough so as to affirm them as true? To be sure, I did decide later on that I must doubt these things, but that was only because it occurred to me that some God could perhaps have given me a nature such that I might be deceived even about matters that seemed most evident. But whenever this preconceived opinion about the supreme power of God occurs to me, I cannot help admitting that, were he to wish it, it would be easy for him to cause me to err even in those matters that I think I intuit as clearly as possible with the eyes of the mind. On the other hand, whenever I turn my attention to those very things that I think I perceive with such great clarity, I am so completely persuaded by them that I spontaneously blurt out these words: "let anyone who can do so deceive me; so long as I think that I am

36

something, he will never bring it about that I am nothing. Nor will he one day make it true that I never existed, for it is true now that I do exist. Nor will he even bring it about that perhaps two plus three might equal more or less than five, or similar items in which I recognize an obvious contradiction." And certainly, because I have no reason for thinking that there is a God who is a deceiver (and of course I do not yet sufficiently know whether there even is a God), the basis for doubting, depending as it does merely on the above hypothesis, is very tenuous and, so to speak, metaphysical. But in order to remove even this basis for doubt, I should at the first opportunity inquire whether there is a God, and, if there is, whether or not he can be a deceiver. For if I am ignorant of this, it appears I am never capable of being completely certain about anything else.

However, at this stage good order seems to demand that I first group
37 all my thoughts into certain classes, and ask in which of them truth or falsity properly resides. Some of these thoughts are like images of things; to these alone does the word "idea" properly apply, as when I think of a man, or a chimera, or the sky, or an angel, or God. Again there are other thoughts that take different forms: for example, when I will, or fear, or affirm, or deny, there is always some thing that I grasp as the subject of my thought, yet I embrace in my thought something more than the likeness of that thing. Some of these thoughts are called volitions or affects, while others are called judgments.

Now as far as ideas are concerned, if they are considered alone and in their own right, without being referred to something else, they cannot, properly speaking, be false. For whether it is a she-goat or a chimera that I am imagining, it is no less true that I imagine the one than the other. Moreover, we need not fear that there is falsity in the will itself or in the affects, for although I can choose evil things or even things that are utterly non-existent, I cannot conclude from this that it is untrue that I do choose these things. Thus there remain only judgments in which I must take care not to be mistaken. Now the principal and most frequent error to be found in judgments consists in the fact that I judge that the ideas which are in me are similar to or in conformity with certain things outside me. Obviously, if I were to consider these ideas merely as certain modes of my thought, and were not to refer them to anything else, they could hardly give me any subject matter for error.

Among these ideas, some appear to me to be innate, some adventitious,
38 and some produced by me. For I understand what a thing is, what truth

is, what thought is, and I appear to have derived this exclusively from my very own nature. But say I am now hearing a noise, or looking at the sun, or feeling the fire; up until now I judged that these things proceeded from certain things outside me, and finally, that sirens, hippogriffs, and the like are made by me. Or perhaps I can even think of all these ideas as being adventitious, or as being innate, or as fabrications, for I have not yet clearly ascertained their true origin.

But here I must inquire particularly into those ideas that I believe to be derived from things existing outside me. Just what reason do I have for believing that these ideas resemble those things? Well, I do seem to have been so taught by nature. Moreover, I do know from experience that these ideas do not depend upon my will, nor consequently upon myself, for I often notice them even against my will. Now, for example, whether or not I will it, I feel heat. It is for this reason that I believe this feeling or idea of heat comes to me from something other than myself, namely from the heat of the fire by which I am sitting. Nothing is more obvious than the judgment that this thing is sending its likeness rather than something else into me.

I will now see whether these reasons are powerful enough. When I say here "I have been so taught by nature," all I have in mind is that I am driven by a spontaneous impulse to believe this, and not that some light of nature is showing me that it is true. These are two very different things. For whatever is shown me by this light of nature, for example, that from the fact that I doubt, it follows that I am, and the like, cannot in any way be doubtful. This is owing to the fact that there can be no other faculty that I can trust as much as this light and which could teach that these things are not true. But as far as natural impulses are concerned, in the 39 past I have often judged myself to have been driven by them to make the poorer choice when it was a question of choosing a good; and I fail to see why I should place any greater faith in them than in other matters.

Again, although these ideas do not depend upon my will, it does not follow that they necessarily proceed from things existing outside me. For just as these impulses about which I spoke just now seem to be different from my will, even though they are in me, so too perhaps there is also in me some other faculty, one not yet sufficiently known to me, which produces these ideas, just as it has always seemed up to now that ideas are formed in me without any help from external things when I am asleep.

And finally, even if these ideas did proceed from things other than myself, it does not therefore follow that they must resemble those things.

Indeed it seems I have frequently noticed a vast difference in many respects. For example, I find within myself two distinct ideas of the sun. One idea is drawn, as it were, from the senses. Now it is this idea which, of all those that I take to be derived from outside me, is most in need of examination. By means of this idea the sun appears to me to be quite small. But there is another idea, one derived from astronomical reasoning, that is, it is elicited from certain notions that are innate in me, or else is fashioned by me in some other way. Through this idea the sun is shown to be several times larger than the earth. Both ideas surely cannot resemble the same sun existing outside me; and reason convinces me that the idea that seems to have emanated from the sun itself from so close is the very one that least resembles the sun.

40   All these points demonstrate sufficiently that up to this point it was not a well-founded judgment but only a blind impulse that formed the basis of my belief that things existing outside me send ideas or images of themselves to me through the sense organs or by some other means.

But still another way occurs to me for inquiring whether some of the things of which there are ideas in me do exist outside me: insofar as these ideas are merely modes of thought, I see no inequality among them; they all seem to proceed from me in the same manner. But insofar as one idea represents one thing and another idea another thing, it is obvious that they do differ very greatly from one another. Unquestionably, those ideas that display substances to me are something more and, if I may say so, contain within themselves more objective reality than those which represent only modes or accidents. Again, the idea that enables me to understand a supreme deity, eternal, infinite, omniscient, omnipotent, and creator of all things other than himself, clearly has more objective reality within it than do those ideas through which finite substances are displayed.

Now it is indeed evident by the light of nature that there must be at least as much [reality] in the efficient and total cause as there is in the effect of that same cause. For whence, I ask, could an effect get its reality, if not from its cause? And how could the cause give that reality to the effect, unless it also possessed that reality? Hence it follows that something cannot come into being out of nothing, and also that what is more perfect
41   (that is, what contains in itself more reality) cannot come into being from what is less perfect. But this is manifestly true not merely for those effects whose reality is actual or formal, but also for ideas in which only objective reality is considered. For example, not only can a stone which did not exist

previously not now begin to exist unless it is produced by something in which there is, either formally or eminently, everything that is in the stone; nor heat be introduced into a subject which was not already hot unless it is done by something that is of at least as perfect an order as heat—and the same for the rest—but it is also true that there can be in me no idea of heat, or of a stone, unless it is placed in me by some cause that has at least as much reality as I conceive to be in the heat or in the stone. For although this cause conveys none of its actual or formal reality to my idea, it should not be thought for that reason that it must be less real. Rather, the very nature of an idea is such that of itself it needs no formal reality other than what it borrows from my thought, of which it is a mode. But that a particular idea contains this as opposed to that objective reality is surely owing to some cause in which there is at least as much formal reality as there is objective reality contained in the idea. For if we assume that something is found in the idea that was not in its cause, then the idea gets that something from nothing. Yet as imperfect a mode of being as this is by which a thing exists in the intellect objectively through an idea, nevertheless it is plainly not nothing; hence it cannot get its being from nothing.

Moreover, even though the reality that I am considering in my ideas is merely objective reality, I ought not on that account to suspect that there is no need for the same reality to be formally in the causes of these ideas, *42* but that it suffices for it to be in them objectively. For just as the objective mode of being belongs to ideas by their very nature, so the formal mode of being belongs to the causes of ideas, at least to the first and preeminent ones, by their very nature. And although one idea can perhaps issue from another, nevertheless no infinite regress is permitted here; eventually some first idea must be reached whose cause is a sort of archetype that contains formally all the reality that is in the idea merely objectively. Thus it is clear to me by the light of nature that the ideas that are in me are like images that can easily fail to match the perfection of the things from which they have been drawn, but which can contain nothing greater or more perfect.

And the longer and more attentively I examine all these points, the more clearly and distinctly I know they are true. But what am I ultimately to conclude? If the objective reality of any of my ideas is found to be so great that I am certain that the same reality was not in me, either formally or eminently, and that therefore I myself cannot be the cause of the idea, then it necessarily follows that I am not alone in the world, but that something else, which is the cause of this idea, also exists. But if no such idea is found in me, I will have no argument whatsoever to make me certain of the existence of anything other than myself, for I have conscientiously reviewed all these arguments, and so far I have been unable to find any other.

Among my ideas, in addition to the one that displays me to myself 43 (about which there can be no difficulty at this point), are others that represent God, corporeal and inanimate things, angels, animals, and finally other men like myself.

As to the ideas that display other men, or animals, or angels, I easily understand that they could be fashioned from the ideas that I have of myself, of corporeal things, and of God—even if no men (except myself), no animals, and no angels existed in the world.

As to the ideas of corporeal things, there is nothing in them that is so great that it seems incapable of having originated from me. For if I investigate them thoroughly and examine each one individually in the way I examined the idea of wax yesterday, I notice that there are only a very few things in them that I perceive clearly and distinctly: namely, size, or extension in length, breadth, and depth; shape, which arises from the limits of this extension; position, which various things possessing shape have in relation to one another; and motion, or alteration in position. To these can be added substance, duration, and number. But as for the remaining items, such as light and colors, sounds, odors, tastes, heat and cold and other tactile qualities, I think of these only in a very confused and obscure manner, to the extent that I do not even know whether they are true or false, that is, whether the ideas I have of them are ideas of things or ideas of non-things. For although a short time ago I noted that falsity properly so called (or "formal" falsity) is to be found only in judgments, nevertheless there is another kind of falsity (called "material" falsity) which is found in ideas whenever they represent a non-thing as if 44 it were a thing. For example, the ideas I have of heat and cold fall so far short of being clear and distinct that I cannot tell from them whether cold is merely the privation of heat or whether heat is the privation of cold, or whether both are real qualities, or whether neither is. And because ideas can only be, as it were, of things, if it is true that cold is merely the absence of heat, then an idea that represents cold to me as something real and positive will not inappropriately be called false. The same holds for other similar ideas.

Assuredly I need not assign to these ideas an author distinct from myself. For if they were false, that is, if they were to represent non-things, I know by the light of nature that they proceed from nothing; that is, they are in me for no other reason than that something is lacking in my nature, and that my nature is not entirely perfect. If, on the other hand, these ideas are true, then because they exhibit so little reality to me that I cannot distinguish it from a non-thing, I see no reason why they cannot get their being from me.

As for what is clear and distinct in the ideas of corporeal things, it appears I could have borrowed some of these from the idea of myself: namely, substance, duration, number, and whatever else there may be of this type. For instance, I think that a stone is a substance, that is to say, a thing that is suitable for existing in itself; and likewise I think that I too am a substance. Despite the fact that I conceive myself to be a thinking thing and not an extended thing, whereas I conceive of a stone as an extended thing and not a thinking thing, and hence there is the greatest diversity between these two concepts, nevertheless they seem to agree with one another when considered under the rubric of substance. Furthermore, I perceive that I now exist and recall that I have previously existed for some time. And I have various thoughts and know how many of them there are. It is in doing these things that I acquire the ideas of duration *45* and number, which I can then apply to other things. However, none of the other components out of which the ideas of corporeal things are fashioned (namely extension, shape, position, and motion) are contained in me formally, since I am merely a thinking thing. But since these are only certain modes of a substance, whereas I am a substance, it seems possible that they are contained in me eminently.

Thus there remains only the idea of God. I must consider whether there is anything in this idea that could not have originated from me. I understand by the name "God" a certain substance that is infinite, independent, supremely intelligent and supremely powerful, and that created me along with everything else that exists—if anything else exists. Indeed all these are such that, the more carefully I focus my attention on them, the less possible it seems they could have arisen from myself alone. Thus, from what has been said, I must conclude that God necessarily exists.

For although the idea of substance is in me by virtue of the fact that I am a substance, that fact is not sufficient to explain my having the idea of an infinite substance, since I am finite, unless this idea proceeded from some substance which really was infinite.

Nor should I think that I do not perceive the infinite by means of a true idea, but only through a negation of the finite, just as I perceive rest and darkness by means of a negation of motion and light. On the contrary, I clearly understand that there is more reality in an infinite substance than there is in a finite one. Thus the perception of the infinite is somehow prior in me to the perception of the finite, that is, my perception of God is prior to my perception of myself. For how would I understand that I 46 doubt and that I desire, that is, that I lack something and that I am not wholly perfect, unless there were some idea in me of a more perfect being, by comparison with which I might recognize my defects?

Nor can it be said that this idea of God is perhaps materially false and thus can originate from nothing, as I remarked just now about the ideas of heat and cold, and the like. On the contrary, because it is the most clear and distinct and because it contains more objective reality than any other idea, no idea is in and of itself truer and has less of a basis for being suspected of falsehood. I maintain that this idea of a being that is supremely perfect and infinite is true in the highest degree. For although I could perhaps pretend that such a being does not exist, nevertheless I could not pretend that the idea of such a being discloses to me nothing real, as was the case with the idea of cold which I referred to earlier. It is indeed an idea that is utterly clear and distinct; for whatever I clearly and distinctly perceive to be real and true and to involve some perfection is wholly contained in that idea. It is no objection that I do not comprehend the infinite or that there are countless other things in God that I can in no way either comprehend or perhaps even touch with my thought. For the nature of the infinite is such that it is not comprehended by a being such as I, who am finite. And it is sufficient that I understand this very point and judge that all those things that I clearly perceive and that I know to contain some perfection—and perhaps even countless other things of which I am ignorant—are in God either formally or eminently. The result is that, of all the ideas that are in me, the idea that I have of God is the most true, the most clear and distinct.

But perhaps I am something greater than I myself understand. Perhaps all these perfections that I am attributing to God are somehow in me 47 potentially, although they do not yet assert themselves and are not yet actualized. For I now observe that my knowledge is gradually being increased, and I see nothing standing in the way of its being increased more and more to infinity. Moreover, I see no reason why, with my knowledge thus increased, I could not acquire all the remaining perfections of God. And, finally, if the potential for these perfections is in me already, I see no reason why this potential would not suffice to produce the idea of these perfections.

Yet none of these things can be the case. First, while it is true that my knowledge is gradually being increased and that there are many things in me potentially that are not yet actual, nevertheless, none of these pertains to the idea of God, in which there is nothing whatever that is potential. Indeed this gradual increase is itself a most certain proof of imperfection. Moreover, although my knowledge may always increase more and more, nevertheless I understand that this knowledge will never by this means be actually infinite, because it will never reach a point where it is incapable of greater increase. On the contrary, I judge God to be actually infinite, so that nothing can be added to his perfection. Finally, I perceive that the objective being of an idea cannot be produced by a merely potential being (which, strictly speaking, is nothing), but only by an actual or formal being.

Indeed there is nothing in all these things that is not manifest by the light of nature to one who is conscientious and attentive. But when I am less attentive, and the images of sensible things blind the mind's eye, I do not so easily recall why the idea of a being more perfect than me necessarily proceeds from a being that really is more perfect. This being the case, it   *48* is appropriate to ask further whether I myself who have this idea could exist, if such a being did not exist.

From what source, then, do I derive my existence? Why, from myself, or from my parents, or from whatever other things there are that are less perfect than God. For nothing more perfect than God, or even as perfect as God, can be thought or imagined.

But if I got my being from myself, I would not doubt, nor would I desire, nor would I lack anything at all. For I would have given myself all the perfections of which I have some idea; in so doing, I myself would be God! I must not think that the things I lack could perhaps be more difficult to acquire than the ones I have now. On the contrary, it is obvious that it would have been much more difficult for me (that is, a thing or substance that thinks) to emerge out of nothing than it would be to acquire the knowledge of many things about which I am ignorant (these items of knowledge being merely accidents of that substance). Certainly, if I got this greater thing from myself, I would not have denied myself at least those things that can be had more easily. Nor would I have denied myself any of those other things that I perceive to be contained in the idea of God, for surely none of them seem to me more difficult to bring about. But if any of them were more difficult to bring about, they would certainly also seem more difficult to me, even if the remaining ones that I possess I got from myself, since it would be on account of them that I would experience that my power is limited.

Nor am I avoiding the force of these arguments, if I suppose that perhaps I have always existed as I do now, as if it then followed that no author of my existence need be sought. For because the entire span of one's life can be divided into countless parts, each one wholly independent of the rest, it does not follow from the fact that I existed a short time ago that I must exist now, unless some cause, as it were, creates me all over again at this moment, that is to say, which preserves me. For it is obvious to one who pays close attention to the nature of time that plainly the same force and action are needed to preserve anything at each individual moment that it lasts as would be required to create that same thing anew, were it not yet in existence. Thus conservation differs from creation solely by virtue of a distinction of reason; this too is one of those things that are manifest by the light of nature.

Therefore I must now ask myself whether I possess some power by which I can bring it about that I myself, who now exist, will also exist a little later on. For since I am nothing but a thinking thing—or at least since I am now dealing simply and precisely with that part of me which is a thinking thing—if such a power were in me, then I would certainly be aware of it. But I observe that there is no such power; and from this very fact I know most clearly that I depend upon some being other than myself.

But perhaps this being is not God, and I have been produced either by my parents or by some other causes less perfect than God. On the contrary, as I said before, it is obvious that there must be at least as much in the cause as there is in the effect. Thus, regardless of what it is that eventually is assigned as my cause, because I am a thinking thing and have within me a certain idea of God, it must be granted that what caused me is also a thinking thing and it too has an idea of all the perfections which I attribute to God. And I can again inquire of this cause whether it got its existence from itself or from another cause. For if it got its existence from itself, it is evident from what has been said that it is itself God, because, having the power of existing in and of itself, it unquestionably also has the power of actually possessing all the perfections of which it has in itself an idea—that is, all the perfections that I conceive to be in God. However, if it got its existence from another cause, I will once again inquire in similar fashion about this other cause: whether it got its existence from itself or from another cause, until finally I arrive at the ultimate cause, which will be God. For it is apparent enough that there can be no infinite regress here, especially since I am not dealing here merely with the cause that once produced me, but also and most especially with the cause that preserves me at the present time.

Nor can one fancy that perhaps several partial causes have concurred in bringing me into being, and that I have taken the ideas of the various perfections I attribute to God from a variety of causes, so that all of these perfections are found somewhere in the universe, but not all joined together in a single being—God. On the contrary, the unity, the simplicity, that is, the inseparability of all those features that are in God is one of the chief perfections that I understand to be in him. Certainly the idea of the unity of all his perfections could not have been placed in me by any cause from which I did not also get the ideas of the other perfections; for neither could some cause have made me understand them joined together and inseparable from one another, unless it also caused me to recognize what they were.

Finally, as to my parents, even if everything that I ever believed about them were true, still it is certainly not they who preserve me; nor is it they who in any way brought me into being, insofar as I am a thinking thing. Rather, they merely placed certain dispositions in the matter which I judged to contain me, that is, a mind, which now is the only thing I take myself to be. And thus there can be no difficulty here concerning my 51 parents. Indeed I have no choice but to conclude that the mere fact of my existing and of there being in me an idea of a most perfect being, that is, God, demonstrates most evidently that God too exists.

All that remains for me is to ask how I received this idea of God. For I did not draw it from the senses; it never came upon me unexpectedly, as is usually the case with the ideas of sensible things when these things present themselves (or seem to present themselves) to the external sense organs. Nor was it made by me, for I plainly can neither subtract anything from it nor add anything to it. Thus the only option remaining is that this idea is innate in me, just as the idea of myself is innate in me.

To be sure, it is not astonishing that in creating me, God should have endowed me with this idea, so that it would be like the mark of the craftsman impressed upon his work, although this mark need not be something distinct from the work itself. But the mere fact that God created me makes it highly plausible that I have somehow been made in his image and likeness, and that I perceive this likeness, in which the idea of God is contained, by means of the same faculty by which I perceive myself.

That is, when I turn the mind's eye toward myself, I understand not only that I am something incomplete and dependent upon another, something aspiring indefinitely for greater and greater or better things, but also that the being on whom I depend has in himself all those greater things—not merely indefinitely and potentially, but infinitely and actually, and thus that he is God. The whole force of the argument rests on the fact that

52   I recognize that it would be impossible for me to exist, being of such a nature as I am (namely, having in me the idea of God), unless God did in fact exist. God, I say, that same being the idea of whom is in me: a being having all those perfections that I cannot comprehend, but can somehow touch with my thought, and a being subject to no defects whatever. From these considerations it is quite obvious that he cannot be a deceiver, for it is manifest by the light of nature that all fraud and deception depend on some defect.

But before examining this idea more closely and at the same time inquiring into other truths that can be gathered from it, at this point I want to spend some time contemplating this God, to ponder his attributes and, so far as the eye of my darkened mind can take me, to gaze upon, to admire, and to adore the beauty of this immense light. For just as we believe by faith that the greatest felicity of the next life consists solely in this contemplation of the divine majesty, so too we now experience that from the same contemplation, although it is much less perfect, the greatest pleasure of which we are capable in this life can be perceived.

The Problem of Evil

Richard M. Gale

T he widespread existence of evil is the greatest challenge to the rationality of belief in the God of traditional theism, who has every perfection to an unlimited extent, among which are being omnipotent (all-powerful), omniscient (all-knowing), omni-benevolent (all-good), and sovereign (all-determining). One form that this challenge takes is an argument that attempts to deduce a contradiction from the existence of both God and evil, but the more popular form is an inductive argument that infers from the known evils of the world that it is improbable that God exists or, more weakly, that the probability of his existence is lowered by these evils. The theist responds to the deductive argument by offering a defense in which it is shown how it is possible for God to have a morally exonerating excuse for permitting or causing these evils. There are two ways in which the theist counters the inductive argument. One is to give a *theodicy*, which is a defense coupled with some evidence that the possible excusing condition articulated in the defense actually obtains. The other is *theistic skepticism*, which holds that we humans are incapable of understanding God's reasons for permitting evil.

The Deductive Argument

The aim of this argument, which was first given by J. L. Mackie (1982: 150–76), is to hang the theist by her own rope. From an initial set of premises accepted by the theist, namely, that there exists an omnipotent and omni-benevolent God and that evil exists, it is deduced that evil does not exist, thereby resulting in the contradiction that evil exists and that evil does not exist. In order to deduce that evil does not exist, it must be assumed that an omnipotent being can bring about anything and that an omni-benevolent being will prevent and eliminate every evil it can. The theist challenges both of these assumptions. An omnipotent God can bring about only everything that it is consistent for him to bring about and an omni-benevolent being prevents and eliminates every *unjustified* evil, that is, every evil for which there is not a morally exonerating excuse. Thus, from the initial set of premises it can be deduced only that unjustified evil does not exist. But that evil exists and that unjustified evil does not exist is not a contradiction.

This manner of rebutting Mackie's argument, however, leaves us with the resident problem of explaining how a being who has all of God's unlimited perfections could be morally justified in bringing about or permitting an evil. The excuses that we are familiar with do not seem applicable to God, given that he is omni-competent. The lack-of-power excuse for failing to eliminate or prevent an evil ('I wasn't strong enough to lift the car that you were pinned under') cannot be available to an omnipotent being. And the excusable-ignorance excuse ('How could I have known that saying "Niagara Falls" would send him into a homicidal rage?') could not apply to an omniscient being. And since God is sovereign over everything, he cannot be excused because of a lack of opportunity ('I couldn't have saved him from dying from the rattler's bite because I did not have the needed anti-venom serum or I wasn't there').

The theist is prepared to offer a number of possible excuses for God's causing or permitting evil. There is the cover-all compensation-in-an-afterlife defense. It is essential that the worldly suffering and afterlife compensation form an integral unity. It won't do for God to say, 'I caused you five units of worldly suffering; so I will give you ten units of pleasure in an afterlife.' For why didn't he just create the pleasures *sans* the suffering? A number of responses make use of creedal doctrines of different theistic religions, an example of which is the merited-punishment defense according to which the evils that befall us result from the first generation of humans freely rebelling against God, with their ruin being inherited by all of their descendants. Peter van Inwagen has extended this defense so that it covers chance, gratuitous evils: those that are necessary neither for the realization of an outweighing good nor the prevention of an even greater evil (in Howard-Snyder 1996). Through these evils God makes it clear that man cannot live apart from him. Eleonore Stump has espoused a defense that is a close cousin to van Inwagen's in that it too is based on original sin (Stump 1985). Natural evils, that is, those that cannot be attributed to the improper use of free will by finite persons, help to realign our wills so that they will again be directed toward serving God by reminding us that we are unable to make it on our own. Marilyn McCord Adams has developed a redemptive suffering defense that is based upon the value of martyrdom, which then is extrapolatable to some, but not all, other types of suffering (Adams 1989). Through being successfully tested in her faith, the martyr builds a closer relation of trust with her God. Furthermore, through suffering she gets a vision into the inner life of God incarnate on the cross. This defense, as well as Stump's, has a limited application since it does not apply to the suffering of animals and the very young.

Many who give these creedal-based defenses take them to be theodicies as well, since they are prepared to argue that the Scriptures upon which they are based are true revelations, which is a matter that falls outside the purview of this essay. A major challenge to these strained defenses is that they seem to depict God as petty, wrathful, and vindictive, which is inconsistent with his being a God of love, a God that is eminently worthy of worship and adoration. Such a God, it is contended, is worthy only of a prudence-based fear and obedience.

The Free Will Defense

The most important defense is the free will defense (FWD), whose aim is to articulate a possible justification for God's creating persons who sometimes freely go morally wrong, thereby resulting in moral evil. There are several different versions of it (e.g., Plantinga 1974). The following is a generic brand FWD that captures what is common to them.

1. It is God's intention to create the best overall situation or the best world that he can. Intention premise

2. A world containing free persons who freely perform both right and wrong actions, but for the most part go right, is better than any possible world devoid of free persons. Normative premise

3. God cannot cause or determine in any way what a created person freely does. Incompatibilist premise

4. It is logically possible that God is contingently unable to create free persons who always go right. God-could-be-unlucky premise

Premise (1) results from God's being omnibenevolent. A consequence of the normative premise, (2), is that God is morally excused from permitting some moral evil if this is the price that he must pay for there to exist any free persons at all. The incompatibilist premise, (3), requires that a free action be determined wholly by the agent and thus not by something external to the agent, such as prior causes or even the will of God, which can be explicitly formulated as:

> *L.* A free act is not sufficiently caused by anything external to the agent.

Without this premise the proponent of the FWD would have no response to the objection of the causal or theological compatibilist, such as Augustine and Leibniz, who contend that God could have determined that every created free person always freely goes right by either, respectively, a suitable determination of the initial state of the universe and the causal laws or simply willing in his own inimitable supernatural way that they do.

Each version of the FWD will tell a different story about how the God-could-be-unlucky premise, (4), could be realized, of how it is possible that God be frustrated in his endeavor to create a universe containing moral good (good that results from the use of creaturely free will) *sans* moral evil. They differ with respect to whether God has *middle knowledge*, that is, foreknowledge of what would result from his creating various types of free persons in this or that possible world. Alvin Plantinga's version gives God middle knowledge but has created free persons who, not God, determine what they freely do (Plantinga 1974). The created free persons alone take 'the fall,' the blame, for the moral evil they wrought. Although God is responsible for the moral evils wrought by the free persons he creates, since he could have prevented these evils simply by not creating any free persons, he is not blameworthy for them, since he, unlike the created free persons, has a morally exonerating excuse for permitting these evils based on the great value of there being free persons.

The other two versions of the FWD deny God middle knowledge, having him create free persons without knowing what will result. Herein God's benevolence is exonerated because of excusable ignorance. And, if it is charged that he acts recklessly in creating free persons without knowing in advance what will result, the answer is that it is well worth the gamble, given the great value of free will. The Robert M. Adams's version bases God's ignorance on there not being any fact of the matter, and therefore nothing to be known, about what would result from his creating various kinds of free persons (1979). The Richard Swinburne version holds that there are such facts but denies that God can access them (Swinburne 1979). Each of these three versions will be discussed in turn.

According to Plantinga's version, God cannot both create free beings and determine what they freely do, since this would violate L. What he must do, therefore, is to create persons who are free with respect to certain actions and then leave it up to them what they freely do. This requires that God creates incomplete or diminished persons. To see how this works, we must begin with a *possible free person*, which is a maximal and compossible set of abstract properties and contains the property of being free with respect to at least one morally significant action, A, that is, the property of either freely doing A or freely refraining from doing A. Alternatively, you can think of a possible free person as a compossible set of abstract propositions that completely describes the life of such a free person, everything that she does and undergoes, including her free actions. The set of properties is compossible in that it is logically possible that a single person instantiates all of them, and it is maximal because for every property that could be possessed by a person either it or its complement is included in the set, the complement of the property P being non-P.

Each possible free person contains a *diminished possible free person*, which is its largest proper subset of properties that is such that for any action A, it neither includes or entails freely doing A; nor does it include or entail freely refraining from doing A. A property H includes or entails another property G just in case it is logically impossible that H be instantiated and G not be. The property of being red, for example, includes or entails the property of being colored since it is impossible for an object to be red but not be colored. A diminished possible free person is a 'freedom-neutral' set of properties.

For every possible free person containing the property of freely doing A, there is a numerically distinct possible person that includes all of the same properties save for its including the property of freely refraining from doing A instead. Let us call such a pair of possible free persons an 'incompatible pair.' Whenever you freely perform an action, you instantiate one member of such a pair to the exclusion of the other. For any incompatible pair, God will be contingently unable to actualize one person in the pair. Let our specimen incompatible pair be P and P_1, who include all of the same properties save for P's including freely doing A and P_1's instead including freely refraining from doing A.

The question is: What would result if God were to instantiate diminished person, DP, that is common to P and P_1? Would the concrete instantiator of this diminished person or set of freedom-neutral properties freely do *A* or freely refrain? Plainly, it must do one or the other, since it has the disjunctive property of either freely doing *A* or freely refraining from doing *A*. Thus, it is either true that

> *F*. If *DP* were instantiated, the instantiator would freely do *A*.

or true that

> *F**. If *DP* were instantiated, the instantiator would freely refrain from doing *A*.

Let us call these free will subjunctive conditional propositions '*F*-conditionals.' An *F*-conditional has an antecedent that reports the instantiation of a diminished possible free person and consequent that reports the performance of a free action by the instantiator. If *F* is true, then were God to instantiate *DP*, it would result in *P* being actualized; whereas, if *F** is true, were God to actualize *DP*, it would result in P_1 being actualized. Since *F* and *F** are logically incompatible, it follows that if *F* is true, God is unable to actualize P_1, and if *F** is true, God is unable to actualize *P*. But necessarily one of them is true and therefore necessarily true that God cannot actualize *P* or cannot actualize P_1.

At the outset let us confine ourselves to possible persons that include the property of being free with respect to only one action, such as persons *P* and P_1 above. What we establish then can be generalized to more complex possible persons. Any incompatible pair of such simplified persons is a Dr Jekyll and Mr Hyde pair, the former being the one that contains the property of freely doing *A* (which we'll suppose is the morally right thing to do), the latter the property of freely refraining from doing *A* (which is the morally wrong thing to do). God might not be able to actualize *P*, the Dr Jekyll member of the pair, since *F* could be false. But what could be true for this particular Dr Jekyll and Mr Hyde pair could be true for all of them. Every incompatible pair of this sort could be such that it is true that if God were to instantiate the diminished possible person common to both, the instantiator would freely do the morally wrong alternative. Under such unfortunate circumstances, God can actualize only Hydes, and therefore will not attempt to instantiate any of these simple possible free persons, assuming that his brand of benevolence requires that there be a favorable balance of moral good over moral evil.

The result can be generalized so as to apply to more rich possible persons that contain the property of being free in respect to more than one action. It could still be the case for every such person that it is true that if God were to actualize its diminished person, the instantiator would freely go wrong with respect to at least one of these actions, which shows that it is possible that God cannot actualize a possible world in which all free persons always freely go right.

At this point, Plantinga can complete his FWD by claiming that in the possible world in which the truth-values of the *F*-conditionals preclude God from actualizing any Dr Jekylls or, more generally, possible persons containing the property of always freely doing what is right, he is excused for creating persons who sometimes freely go wrong provided that for the most part they freely go right. The *F*-conditionals are God's kryptonite. They have brute, contingent truth-values that are not determined by God and limit his power in a similar way to that in which fate limits the powers of the Greek gods.

In both cases there is a force or power above and beyond the control of the individual that limits its powers to do what it wants. The idea that God must be lucky, that he must be dealt a favorable poker hand of *F*-conditional facts, if he is to be able to create a universe containing moral good *sans* moral evil, strikes some as blasphemous, as a radical distortion of the orthodox concept of God's omnipotence. While Plantinga's account of omnipotence is not every theist's cup of tea, certainly not that of the great medieval theists, it might be the cup of tea that will prove most digestible and healthy for theism in its effort to construct an adequate defense for God's permitting moral evil.

Numerous objections have been made to Plantinga's FWD, but each one admits of a response. The first claims, contra the normative premise, that it would be better for God to create a world containing conscious automata who are programmed by God always to go morally right than a world containing persons who freely perform both right and wrong actions. Plainly, this is not the normative intuition of the theist, who places a much greater value upon free will than does this objection. And since it is the internal consistency of theism that is challenged by the deductive argument from evil, it should be the theist's normative intuition that is operative.

There are a number of objections to the 'God-can-do-more' variety that have been advanced by Robert M. Adams (1979). All of them are subject to the following dilemma. If God goes so far as to ensure that all created persons always go right, he negates their freedom; and, if he doesn't go this far, he leaves it open that he will be thwarted by the contingent truth-values of the relevant *F*-conditionals. Yet another objection is based on God's having the power to step in just in the nick of time when he foresees, on the basis of his middle knowledge, that someone will freely go wrong, by either preventing this wrong choice or causally quarantining the culprit from the surrounding world after she has made her wrong choice so that no innocent persons are harmed. But, if he does the former, he negates the culprit's free will by denying her the power to choose other than the right alternative; and, if he does the latter, he has failed to bestow significant freedom on her since she lacks the freedom to act.

There is an opposite objection to the God-can-do-more variety, namely, that God cannot consistently do as much as is required by Plantinga's FWD. It could be argued that God, in virtue of having middle knowledge, has a freedom-canceling control over created persons; and, therefore, the buck of moral blame for moral evils cannot stop with them but must reach through to God, which destroys the FWD's attempt to show how God can escape blame, although not responsibility, for these evils. The reason for this is that if a person foreknows what will result from his doing something, he causes this result. Thus, God, in virtue of having middle knowledge of what will result from his actualizing a diminished possible person, causes the actions of the created persons. And, since God causally determines all of this person's actions, he has a freedom-canceling control over her.

This objection can be overcome by going with either one of the other two versions of the FWD, since each denies that God has such foreknowledge. On the Adams version, God lacks this foreknowledge because the *F*-conditionals are neither true nor false, since there is nothing in reality that could make them true. Thus, there is no fact of the matter to be known by God in advance. For the Swinburne version, the *F*-conditionals are either true or false, but God lacks middle knowledge of them. This seems to be a blatant violation of God's omniscience, since he does not know every true proposition. Swinburne models God's omniscience on his omnipotence. Just as God can bring about anything that it is consistent for him to bring about, he knows every true proposition that it is consistent for him to know. The reason why it would be inconsistent for God to know the truth of *F*-conditionals in advance of his creative choices is that this would preclude his being able to create free persons, but it is essential to God that he can create free persons.

The Inductive Argument

The inductive argument, which has been championed by William Rowe, begins with the fact that there are numerous terrible evils, *E*, for which we are unable to find any good that would justify God, were he to exist, in permitting *E* (in Howard-Snyder 1996). From this failure to find such goods it is inductively inferred that there probably are no goods that would justify God's permitting *E*. And, since God cannot coexist with unjustified evil, it follows that probably God does not exist. A weaker version of the inductive argument holds that *E* lowers the probability that God exists over what it is relative to our background knowledge, *K*, alone; that is

$$P \text{ (God exists/There are evils } E \text{ and } K) < P \text{ (God exists/}K).$$

K includes everything that we know that is not relevant to determining the truth of either that God exists or that there are evils *E*.

There also is an *abductive* or inference to the best explanation version of the inductive argument that goes back to Hume and finds a contemporary defender in Paul Draper (in Howard-Snyder 1996). It contends that the known evils and goods of the world are more probable, more to be expected, on the hypothesis that God does not exist than it is by the hypothesis that God exists.

The theist has a battery of responses to these inductive arguments. One is to point out that a proposition's probability can vary across different reference classes. The probability that Feike can swim relative to the proposition that he is Frisian is quite low but can be much higher relative to the proposition that many people believe that they have seen him swim. Similarly, the proposition that God exists relative to the conjunction of *K* and that there are evils *E* could be quite low but be quite high when all of the arguments for the existence of God are added to this conjunction. And, if it is probable that God exists relative to the agglomeration of these arguments, then it also is probable that for each evil specified in *E*, there is a God-justifying reason. In fact, if among them is a knock-down ontological argument, we can be certain that there is and thus that there are evils *E* does not even lower the probability that God exists. It was because Leibniz thought he had such an argument that he confined himself in his misnamed book, *The Theodicy* (1952), to sketching some possible *defenses* for God's allowing evil without making any effort to give evidence for their actually obtaining. Augustine did likewise.

Another response is to give a theodicy for E, the most impressive of which is John Hick's free-will-cum-soul-building one (Hick 1966). It is based on the reasonable axiological intuition that it is better to achieve some desirable state through one's own free endeavoring than to be in this state from the very beginning or have it imposed on one by some external power. God could have created human beings in a state of perfection, but it is better that he created them in an imperfect state so that they could freely bring about their own moral progress in approximating this ideal state, which, for the Christian, is union or a communal relation with God. God does not merely allow but actually causes natural evils so as to give persons the opportunity to freely develop certain desirable character traits, such as sympathy, charity, courage, patience, and the like. If it be objected that this would license a finite father breaking his son's legs so as to afford him an opportunity for soul-building, the reply is that this confounds the role of God as the designer of the entire scheme of things with that of created person, which is that of promoting good and fighting evil. Thus, the fact that God is permitted to do things that a human being is not does not result from his being subject to a different moral code than are humans but to the different roles they play.

Hick's theodicy does not apply to all known cases of evil. The baby who succumbs to leukemia or the deer that dies painfully in a forest fire is not afforded an opportunity by these evils to engage in soul building. To handle these recalcitrant cases Hick has supplemented his theodicy with a compensation-in-an-afterlife one. But the latter is nothing more than a defense, since the evidential credentials for it are very thin.

But by far the most favored response among sophisticated contemporary theorists, most notably Alston, Plantinga, Wykstra, and van Inwagen, is that of theistic skepticism (in Howard-Snyder 1996). Because our imaginative and cognitive powers are so radically limited, we are not warranted in inferring that there are not or probably are not God-justifying reasons for evils E. Theistic skepticism involves our inability, first, to access the divine mind so as to determine the different sorts of reasons that God could have for permitting evil and, second, to determine whether some purported God-justifying reason applies to a given case of evil. The former will be called 'reason skepticism' and the latter 'application skepticism.' Defenders of theistic skepticism invariably supplement it with some speculation about possible defenses or theodicies for E. This is fitting, since the believer must have some target for her faith, however sketchy and evidentially unsupported it is.

Rowe's argument mistakenly assumes that we are up to divining every possible God-justifying reason for permitting evil. As Stephen Wykstra has put it, God's reasons are 'noseeums' for us (in Russell and Wykstra 1988). If you carefully inspect a room and fail to detect a zebra, it is reasonable for you inductively to infer that there is no zebra in the room. But if you were trying to detect an ammonia molecule in the room, your failure to find it by unaided observation would not justify your inference that no ammonia molecule is in the room. The divine mind is the ultimate noseeum for us, regardless of what instruments of detection we employ. Our minds are to God's as a one-month-old baby's is to an adult's mind.

Many objections have been lodged against theistic skepticism. One is that it precludes the theist from employing teleological arguments, although not ontological and cosmological arguments; for, if the bad things about the world should not be evidence against the existence of God, the good things should not count in favor of his existence. Teleological arguments turn into two-edge swords. Maybe the good aspects of the world that these arguments appeal to are produced by a malevolent deity so as to highlight evil or because they are necessary for the realization of an outweighing evil, and so on for all the other demonodicies.

The most serious problem for theistic skepticism, which is raised by Bruce Russell, is that it seems to require that we become complete moral skeptics (Russell and Wykstra 1988). Should we be horrified at a child being brutally tortured and raped? Should we have tried to prevent it or take steps to prevent similar incidents in the future? Who knows?! For all we can tell, it might be a blessing in disguise or serve some God-justifying reason that is too deep for us to access. The result of this moral skepticism is paralysis of the will, since we can have no reason for acting, given that we are completely in the dark whether the consequences of our action is good or bad.

Another objection concerns whether theistic skepticism allows for there to be a meaningful personal love relation with God. The problem is whether we humans can have such a relation with a being whose mind so completely transcends ours, who is so inscrutable with respect to his values, reasons, and intentions.

Making God so inscrutable also raises a threat that theism thereby will turn out to be falsified or, if not falsified, rendered meaningless. Several atheists, including Michael Scriven and Theodore Drange, have used the hiddenness of God as the basis for an argument against his existence (Scriven 1966; Drange 1998). There is, they say, a presumption of atheism so that no news is bad news. Numerous quotations from the Bible are assembled in which it is said that God's intention in creating men was so that they would come to know of his existence and worship, obey, and enter into a communal loving relation with him. Thus, if we do not have good evidence that God exists because he has chosen to remain hidden, this constitutes good evidence against his existence.

By not allowing known evils E to count against God's existence, not even allowing it to lower the probability that he exists, the skeptical theist might be draining the theistic hypothesis of all meaning. E is itself a staggering array of evils, many of the most horrifying sort. If E is not the least bit probability-lowering, then it would appear that for theistic skeptics no amount of evil would be. Even if the world were a living hell in which each sentient being's life was one of unrelenting suffering of the worst sort, it would not count as evidence against God's existence; it would not lower the probability of his existence one bit. This seems highly implausible and calls into question the very meaningfulness of the claim that God exists. And this is so whether or not we accept the notorious verifiability theory of meaningfulness, which Plantinga likes to have die the death of self-reference by pointedly asking whether it is applicable to itself. We can recognize that something has gone wrong even if we cannot come up with a good theoretical explanation of why it is wrong.

We have yet to consider one rather obvious way for theists to meet the challenge of evil: settle for a finite God, as do process theologians like Alfred North Whitehead (1979) and Charles Hartshorne (1964a; 1964b). There are many ways to achieve this, since God has many omni-perfections that can be tinkered with. No theist wants to downgrade his omnibenevolence, since this would preclude God from playing the role of an eminently worship-worthy being.

The most obvious omni-perfection to downgrade is omnipotence, which brings us back to the Demiurge of Plato's *Timaeus*. Like a sculptor who is given a block of marble to work with that limits what he can create because it has a nature of its own, this god is given stuff to work with that limits what he can create. But if God is not all-powerful, how powerful is he? Does not this account of God's excuse for allowing evil run into the same unfalsifiability-in-principle problem as did theistic skepticism? No matter how much evil there is, the response is that he is just not *that* powerful, which resembles the punch-line of the famous shaggy dog joke, 'Yes, he was a shaggy dog, but he wasn't *that* shaggy.'

[...]

References

Adams, M. M. (1989) 'Horrendous suffering and the goodness of God,' *Aristotelian Society Supplementary Volume* 63: 297–310.

Adams, R. M. (1979) 'Middle knowledge and the problem of evil,' *American Philosophical Quarterly* 14: 109–17.

Drange, T. M. (1998) *Nonbelief and Evil: Two Arguments for the Nonexistence of God*, Amherst, NY: Prometheus.

Hartshorne, C. (1964a) *Man's Vision of God and the Logic of Theism*, Hamden, CT: Archon.

——— (1964b) *The Divine Relativity: A Social Conception of God*, New Haven, CT: Yale University Press.

Hick, J. (1966) *Evil and the God of Love*, New York: Harper & Row.

Howard-Snyder, D. (ed.) (1996) *The Evidential Argument from Evil*, Bloomington, IN: Indiana University Press.

Leibniz, G. F. W. (1952) *Theodicy*, ed. A. Farrer, trans. E. M. Huggard, New Haven, CT: Yale University Press.

Mackie, J. L. (1982) *The Miracle of Theism: Arguments For and Against the Existence of God*, Oxford: Clarendon Press.

Plantinga, A. (1974) *God, Freedom and Evil*, Grand Rapids, MI: Eerdmans.

——— (1979) 'The probabilistic argument from evil,' *Philosophical Studies* 35: 1–53.

Russell, B. and S. Wykstra (1988) 'The inductive argument from evil: a dialogue,' *Philosophical Topics* 16: 133–60.

Scriven, M. (1966) *Primary Philosophy*, New York: McGraw Hill.

Stump, E. (1985) 'The problem of evil,' *Faith and Philosophy* 2: 392–424.

Swinburne, R. (1979) *The Existence of God*, Oxford: Clarendon Press.

Whitehead, A. N. (1979) *Process and Reality*, corr. edn, New York: Free Press.

Further Reading

Gale, R. M. (2007) *On the Philosophy of Religion*, Belmont, CA: Wadsworth. (A full and balanced discussion of the problem of evil.)

Howard-Snyder, D. (ed.) (1996) *The Evidential Argument from Evil*, Bloomington, IN: Indiana University Press. (This volume contains important essays by Alston, Draper, Plantinga, Rowe, Russell, van Inwagen, and Wykstra.)

Lewis, C. S. (1940) *The Problem of Pain*, London: Geoffrey Bles. (An especially good book for the novice because it is clearly and cogently written.)

Forgiveness and Apology

What, When, Why?

Charles L. Griswold

Human life teems with temptations, one of which is to think that the people who do grave harm to others are fundamentally different from us. We reserve a special vocabulary for them: "beasts," "monsters," "inhuman." Yet that outlook is a self-protective delusion. As Primo Levi somewhat shockingly remarks of the concentration camp guards at Auschwitz:

> "These were not monsters. I didn't see a single monster in my time in the camp. Instead I saw people like you and I who were acting in that way because there was Fascism, Nazism in Germany. Were some form of Fascism or Nazism to return, there would be people, like us, who would act in the same way, everywhere. And the same goes for the victims, for the particular behaviour of the victims about which so much has been said, mostly typically by young Israelis who object 'but we would never act that way'. They're right. They would not act that way. But if they had been born forty years earlier, they would have. They would have behaved exactly as the deported Jews—and, it's worth adding, the deported Russians and Italians and the rest" ("Interview with Primo Levi (1979)," in *The Voice of Memory: Interviews 1961–1987* [New York: The New Press, 2001]).

One must distinguish between degrees of wrongdoing, to be sure. Yet honesty requires recognizing that Levi's point applies to each of us. The disturbing fact is that even those who commit terrible wrongs are by and large not "beasts," but rather all too human—characteristically and predictably human, one might even argue. Look into your heart and recall the last time you treated another badly. Nearly everyone has wronged another. Remember too your response to the last time you felt mistreated or insulted. Nearly everyone has suffered the bitter injustice of wrongdoing. We have all struggled not to retaliate in kind.

What a struggle it is to resist the cycle of retaliation! Revenge impulsively surges in response to wrong, and becomes perversely delicious to those possessed by it. The agony of our predicament is as ancient as it is well established, and Homer's Achilles articulates it incomparably well:

> Why, I wish that strife would vanish away from among gods and mortals, and gall, which makes a man grow angry for all his great mind, that gall of anger that swarms like smoke inside of a man's heart and becomes a thing sweeter to him by far than the dripping of honey (*Iliad* 18.107-110, trans. R. Lattimore).

Vengefulness, resentment and moral hatred cloud judgment but seem sweet to the one they possess, transforming a peaceful character into a connoisseur of violence. Personal and national credos proudly anchor themselves in tales of unfairness and the glories of retaliation. Oceans of blood and mountains of bones are their testament. It is an addictive cycle.

Forgiveness is and should be of intense concern to us in ordinary life, both as individuals and as communities. Not surprisingly, the discussions of forgiveness, apology, and reconciliation in theology, literature, political science, sociology, and psychology are innumerable. In a development of great importance, Truth and Reconciliation Commissions have been forging powerful new approaches to ancient conflicts. Groundbreaking work in conflict resolution, international law, the theory of reparations, and political theory pays ever more attention to forgiveness and the related concepts of pardon, excuse, mercy, pity, apology, and reconciliation. Yet, every position taken in theory or practice with regard to these notions assumes that it has understood them accurately. In particular, a defensible analysis of forgiveness in both its interpersonal and political dimension is crucial; for how else are we to know that when we say we forgive, or apologize, or reconcile, we are doing what we claim, and not something else?

At first blush, the answer to the question "what is forgiveness?" seems perfectly straightforward. To forgive is to stop hating the person or persons who have injured you. Notice that even this commits to a criterion: if you still hate someone, you have not forgiven them. But have you forgiven them if you've stopped hating them no matter what the reason? Say you forgot all about them or the injury caused to you (you took the latest bliss drug, or had brain surgery that deleted that part of your memory, or possess a remarkable ability to repress from consciousness emotions you do not like). Since forgiving is not forgetting, it must be the case that it requires remembering; so that too is a criterion. And if you stop hating, while not forgetting, but still take revenge, you haven't forgiven: so revenge too must be forsworn, if forgiveness is to take place.

Resentment or moral hatred may rightly be felt; indeed, we would surely think ill of a person who responded to injustice with indifference. One *should* feel angry in response to wrongdoing; it can be a warranted emotion that expresses self-respect, a respect for moral principle, and the resolve to defend oneself. Consequently, if forgiveness requires that resentment be forsworn, it cannot be in spite of the fact that the anger is still warranted. It must be because the anger is no longer warranted. And what would provide a reason that makes it no longer warranted?

Answers to this question diverge at the deepest level, but here is mine: the victim's anger at the offender should be forsworn first and foremost because the offender has taken certain steps that render continued anger inappropriate. What are those steps? Ideally, they will include acknowledgment of responsibility for having done the wrong; repudiation in deed and word of oneself as the wrongdoer, and a commitment to become the sort of person who does not do such things; the expression of regret to the victim for the specific wrong done by the offender; and finally, some sort of narrative accounting for how one came to do wrong, how the wrong-doing does not express the totality of one's character, and how one is changing for the better. This last provision will help the victim answer such questions as "who is that person who could injure me thus, that I should trust with my forgiveness, and be reconciled with?"

In the face of such steps taken by the offender, a victim who categorically refused to embark on the road to forgiveness, and thus to forswear moral hatred, would betray an ethical shortcoming of his or her own—assuming, of course, that the wrong is not in principle unforgivable. For the wrongdoer has supplied just the *right* sorts of reasons for rendering the victim's anger.

To come off fully, however, forgiveness also requires steps on the part of the victim. We have already named several of these: giving up revenge; letting go of moral hatred; and remembering the relevant facts about the injury. Additionally, the victim should re-envision or re-frame his or her view of the offender, such that the latter is no longer conceived of as the monster whose sum and substance is wrong-doing, but instead as one-like-us, as redeemable. Moving past one's vengefulness and anger for reasons such as these will also mean reframing one's view of oneself. For one must begin to see one's injury, terrible though it may have been, as a chapter of one's life, not as defining who one is. So the victim's narrative of self too must change. As anybody knows who has struggled to recover from moral injury, this can be a difficult challenge to meet. And the final step is one we applaud instinctively: the victim, far from withholding the expression of forgiveness, explicitly addresses it to the offender.

Then all that can be done to repair the breach has been accomplished. Importantly, forgiveness has not collapsed into either excuse or condonation, if both parties meet all of these conditions. A theory of forgiveness fails if it cannot distinguish forgiveness from excuse or condonation. To excuse is not to hold the perpetrator responsible, whereas forgiveness does not absolve the offender of responsibility even while—and here is its wonder—somehow allowing both parties to repair their moral relationship. To condone is to sanction (if implicitly) or even to enable continued wrongdoing, just as happens when, say, an abused spouse "forgives" the offender every morning for beating her the night before, thereby encouraging more of the same misbehavior. If that counted as forgiveness, then forgiveness would no longer be a virtue.

I disagree with the idea of "unconditional forgiveness."

In thinking of forgiveness along these lines, my view—though secular—parallels that of the Medieval philosopher Maimonides (consider his discussion of repentance in the opening four chapters of Treatise 5 of *The Book of Knowledge,* Book I of his *Mishneh Torah),* and differs from those theories (which I would think of as congenial to a Christian framework) according to which forgiveness is a "gift" and requires no steps at all from the offender. According to theories of the latter sort, the victim undertakes forgiveness for his or her own sake—in particular, to shed the painful and toxic emotion of retributive hatred. Call this the "unconditional" or "unilateral" conception of forgiveness. Its inspiration is the insight that the victim is not dependent on the offender in order to forgive; perhaps the victim depends on the grace of God, but in any case, may forgive without the offender showing the slightest contrition, taking any responsibility, or apologizing. Countless books both in the Christian theological tradition and in the self-help literature talk about the "work" of forgiveness as being purely internal in this sense: it's all about your overcoming moral hatred for the sake of your own spiritual, moral, and psychological well-being. When achieved, forgiveness thus understood often sounds as though it is a gift, or a release from debt, bestowed upon the offender; the offender is presented with it, for the victim's own sake as it were, even though the offender may have done nothing to "earn" it.

As examples of the position I am disagreeing with, consider two relatively recent books. The first is Colin C. Tipping's Radical Forgiveness: Making Room for the Miracle (Global 13 Publications, Inc., 2002). The author's "Four Steps to Forgiveness" program is solely about the victim's moving beyond his or her anger; nowhere in the book are we told that the victim's "radical forgiveness" is dependent on the offender taking any steps. Indeed, on page fifty-four we read: "Radical Forgiveness has no limits whatsoever and is completely unconditional. If Radical Forgiveness cannot forgive Hitler, it can forgive nobody. Like unconditional love, it's all or nothing."

Similarly, in *The Process of Forgiveness* (Continuum, 1996), Father William A. Meninger argues that, "It is extremely important from the very beginning to understand that the primary consideration and motivation for forgiveness is ourselves. We forgive others, in the first place, for our own sake." Specifically, he writes that we forgive others for "our own happiness." The five stages of forgiveness he delineates in chapters nine through thirteen overwhelmingly assume or emphasize that the power to forgive lies entirely in the hands of the victim (perhaps with the help of God); the offender is not required to take any steps. Thus in speaking of the successful completion of the final stage of the "process," viz. that of "wholeness" or our own "healing," Meninger remarks:

> Your injurers are also free—at least, as far as you are concerned. The perpetrators still have to deal with their part in their transgression, but they don't owe you anything. You are not dependent on what someone else does for you just as you are no longer dependent on what someone else did to you. You can now freely release them of all personal debts. It is quite another question as to whether or not you allow them to make amends for their own personal needs, the requirements of justice, or the promptings of love.

This in turn is to lead to the recognition that the offender is a "child of God with his/her own sorrows, sins, pains, wounds, regrets, and needs," just as you are *qua* victim. And we are encouraged to consider initiating "reconciliation" with the offender, perhaps by writing "a forgiving letter," even if the letter is not actually sent, though it might be—again, all this in spite of the absence of the slightest emendatory steps on the part of the offender (p. 71).

I disagree with the idea of "unconditional forgiveness." To my mind that view collapses forgiveness into either excuse or condonation, precisely because it demands nothing of the offender. While neither of the two texts I've just mentioned deploy the metaphor of gift-giving to characterize the unilateral forgiveness bestowed by the victim on the offender, given that the metaphor seems so natural a way to express the unilateral waiving of the "debt" as well as the one-sided way in which the wrong-doer is released from the victim's vengeful anger, it is worth noting that the metaphor does not perfectly cohere with the view that forgiveness is unilateral. For gifts, too, come with expectations of reciprocity attached.

Putting aside issues of metaphor and theology and returning to the most important point, I argue that the view of forgiveness as unilateral occludes a fundamental feature of the context. The original context was from the start bilateral and, in that way, social, involving at least two people (the offender and victim). The situation to which forgiveness responds represents a rupture of a basic interpersonal moral relationship (even where the parties to it did not previously know one another) and forgiveness inherits the basic features of that situation. Forgiveness is other-directed; except in cases of self-forgiveness, it is another person who is the target of this moral and affective relation. Ideally, forgiveness preserves, rather than dismisses, the relevant features of that original context. My view does that, whereas the rival view that champions the primacy of unilateral and unconditional forgiveness dispenses with it. That competing view is literally ego-centric; by contrast, mine requires reciprocity, and is responsive to moral ideals that the other ignores in part.

I am not arguing, I hasten to add, that absent the conditions for forgiveness, the victim ought to hold onto vengeful anger; there may be self-regarding reasons to give it up, and any number of therapeutic steps or stages may be required to achieve that end. But not every manner of giving up moral anger or revenge counts as forgiveness.

But what, then, of forgiving the dead and the unrepentant? The one cannot and the other will not take the steps I have set out. Is forgiveness therefore impossible under those circumstances? Does this not mean that the victim is doubly injured—first by the original injustice, and second by being unable to forgive since the offender does not take the required steps?

Such non-ideal or imperfect cases of forgiveness *may* fall below the threshold of what can count as forgiveness, in which case we must with regret conclude that forgiveness there is impossible. What is that threshold? Three conditions must be met for it to be crossed: the victim must be willing to lower his or her pitch of resentment to the degree appropriate to the injury, and to forswear revenge; the offender must take minimal steps to qualify for forgiveness, namely to take responsibility and apologize; and the injury must be humanly forgivable. Between that threshold, and perfected forgiveness, lies a spectrum of cases.

Forgiveness in the political realm is another, related matter. "Political forgiveness," as it is often called, is not so much a kind of forgiveness as it is part of the same family of notions. It shares some characteristics in common with forgiveness, but not others. For that reason, I would denominate it "political apology," a phrase that refers to the offering and receiving of apology in a political context. What is the difference between political apology and forgiveness? First, one or both of the parties concerned may be corporate or state entities, rather than individuals. This means that some, or the entirety, of the moral transaction is conducted by representation or substitution: so-and-so, speaking for entity X (say, the United States government, or a corporation), apologizes to so-and-so, speaking for Y (say, another nation, or consumers in a particular state).

For example, consider the U.S. government's apology to Japanese Americans for their internment during the Second World War. The Civil Liberties Act of 1988 explicitly apologizes for the government's wrongdoing. It specifies what the wrongs were and to whom they were done, citing the documentary work of the Commission on Wartime Relocation and Internment of Civilians—in effect, a sort of Truth Commission (its report is entitled *Personal Justice Denied*). The Act explains that, "For these fundamental violations of the basic civil liberties and constitutional rights of these individuals of Japanese ancestry, the Congress apologizes on behalf of the Nation," and details further steps to be taken, including restitution (the amounts to be determined subsequently) and the funding of a public education program. Interestingly, it also declares as one of its purposes "to make more credible and sincere any declaration of concern by the United States over violations of human rights committed by other nations." In signing the bill into law, President Reagan is quoted as saying, "Yet no payment can make up for those lost years. So, what is most important in this bill has less to do with property than with honor. For here we admit a wrong." President Clinton's letter of some five years letter, accompanying reparation payments, also was explicit, succinct, and unambiguous in its apology.

This is an example of a successful political apology in the political realm. Notice that the forswearing of revenge and violence is certainly a precondition of the transaction, but not the forswearing of any particular person's resentment, especially not by those involved in the current discursive exchange. Neither the spokesperson for the relevant body (in this case, the U.S. government), nor for the recipient(s) of the apology, may have any personal feelings about the harm involved; the apology or receipt thereof does not require them to do so; and the individuals offering the apology may bear no responsibility, personally, for the wrongs. Not all those receiving the apology, furthermore, may have themselves suffered the wrong for which the apology is offered; they may accept the apology on behalf of someone else. In the context of political apology, that is, the exchange requires to one degree or another a fair amount of symbolism and representation.

This is not to say that the exchange is morally vacuous—on the contrary. Genuine apology in the political realm, while neither the same as forgiveness nor a modulation thereof, embodies substantive moral ideals. These include the ideals of truth telling; the taking of responsibility; the call to address others respectfully; the possibility of a future that does not simply reiterate the past; and the importance of promoting peace. The reconciliation that successful apology brings about—consisting in respectful non-interference and the willingness to cooperate with each other, for example—may seem to be a superficial achievement in comparison with reconciliation understood as deep reunion, love, and harmony. But compared to ongoing violent conflict and ferocious retaliation, it is heaven on earth. Furthermore, the reconciling ideals of political apology are substantive and noble, even though they are not intended to satisfy the soul's deepest yearnings. I would not argue that political apology is the magic key that unlocks the secrets of reconciliation at the political level. And yet, the part that political apology may play in civic reconciliation is neither trivial nor dispensable, and a community in which it is commended and practiced is an accomplishment as difficult as it is rare.

But what of self-forgiveness? Of forgiveness by God, or indeed, of forgiving God? Or of such notions as amnesty, pity, mercy, clemency, pardon? Are they imperfect forms of forgiveness or, like political apology, simply part of the same family of concepts? I attempt to answer these complicated questions in my book on forgiveness (from which the present essay is drawn). But by way of conclusion we may briefly consider this further question: why forgiveness? What makes it morally good?

Utilitarian considerations provide a first answer: without forgiveness, human life is worse off. Egoist considerations provide a second answer: without forgiveness, my life is worse off. But there is a third reason, one that cuts deeper: forgiveness is a virtue, and expresses a commendable trait of character. And what makes that characteristic itself valuable? The answer brings us back to the ideals that articulate the moral good, namely those of truth-telling, responsibility-taking, spiritual and moral growth, reconciliation, and love. Given the moral imperfection endemic to the world as we have it, these may seem to be merely ideal, abstract, and irrelevant in practice. But that is not so. We necessarily measure our actions according to some conception of the good. Our success or failure, both in discerning accurately the nature of the good, and in living up to that conception, decisively mold the moral character of our lives. These are practical ideals, and we ignore them at our peril.

Free Will and Determinism

Richard Kenneth Atkins

It has been already sufficiently proved that the soul is nothing more than the body considered relatively to some of its functions more concealed than others. … Consequently, it is subjected to the influence of those material and physical causes which give impulse to the body. … Thus man is a being purely physical; in whatever manner he is considered, he is connected to universal nature, and submitted to the necessary and immutable laws that she imposes on all the beings she contains. … Man's life is a line that nature commands him to describe upon the surface of the earth, without his ever being able to swerve from it, even for an instant. He is born without his own consent; his organization does in nowise depend upon himself; his ideas come to him involuntarily; his habits are in the power of those who cause him to contract them; he is unceasingly modified by causes, whether visible or concealed, over which he has no control. … Nevertheless, in despite of the shackles by which he is bound, it is pretended he is a free agent, or that independent of the causes by which he is moved, he determines his own will, and regulates his own condition.

—Baron Paul Henri Thiry d'Holbach (1723–1789 CE),
The System of Nature

The Philosopher

As can be judged from his name, Baron d'Holbach was a baron. He was rich. Filthy rich. D'Holbach was born in Landau, on the border between France and Germany. His mother was the daughter of the local tax collector. His father grew grapes for wine. However, his parents didn't raise him. Rather, d'Holbach's uncle raised him in Paris. His uncle was a millionaire who gained his wealth by speculating in the stock exchange.

Here's a timeline of d'Holbach's life from 1749 to 1755:

1749: D'Holbach marries his second cousin.
1753: D'Holbach's father-in-law and uncle die. He inherits lots of money.
1754: D'Holbach's wife dies.
1755: With special dispensation from the Pope, d'Holbach marries the younger sister of his deceased wife.

In Paris' high society, d'Holbach gained a reputation, but not for his questionable marital decisions. He became famous for the parties he threw. The food was magnificent. The wine was the best. When you're filthy rich, you can afford it.

D'Holbach also formed a *salon*, a gathering of like-minded people for the purpose of discussing philosophy, politics, or other intellectual topics. He invited only the smartest people in France to join. Among them were Denis Diderot and Jean le Rond d'Alembert (1713–1784 CE and 1717–1783 CE, respectively, editors and contributors to the *Encyclopédie*, a forerunner to our encyclopedias), Étienne Bonnot de Condillac and Jean Jacques Rousseau (1715–1780 CE and 1712–1778 CE, respectively, two of the leading philosophers in France), and the Marquis de Condorcet (1743–1794 CE, an important mathematician and political scientist). D'Holbach would also support these thinkers with generous, anonymous gifts. Philosophers outside of France also made their ways to d'Holbach's parties. Among them were David Hume (1711–1776 CE, a Scottish philosopher), Adam Smith (1723–1790 CE, economist and author of *The Wealth of Nations*), and Edward Gibbon (1737–1794 CE, historian and author of *The History of the Decline and Fall of the Roman Empire*).

The lesson to be learned here is that great thinkers never decline good food and good wine when another person is paying.

One peculiar fact about d'Holbach is that his reputation as a great and generous man never declined. However, he published books that endorsed atheism, determinism, and materialism. He denied God exists, he thought that we are governed by immutable natural laws and have no free will, and he argued that there is no spiritual, immaterial realm of being. Had the people of France known this, d'Holbach surely would have come under heavy criticism. He would have been ostracized from high society. Also, it's unlikely the Pope would have given him a special dispensation to marry to his dead wife's younger sister.

Fortunately for d'Holbach, no one did know these things. He published all of his highly contentious books anonymously. As a result, he was able to preserve his standing among Paris' elite and even in the Catholic Church. Moreover, his secret was carefully guarded. Not until the early eighteen hundreds did it become widely known that he was the author of these books.

D'Holbach died in 1789, just before the French Revolution. Ironically, he was buried at the Church of Saint Roch, Paris. However, the exact location of his grave is no longer known.

The Puzzle

What is d'Holbach's puzzling argument? It's as follows:

(1)   Humans are wholly part of nature.

(2)   Every event in nature is necessitated—or determined—by prior events, conditions, and the laws of nature.

(3)   If humans are wholly part of nature and every natural event is determined, then all of our actions are determined.

(4)   If all of our actions are determined, then none of our actions is done freely.

(5)   Therefore, none of our actions is done freely; we have no free will.

Once again, this is a deductively valid argument. If we accept the premises, then we must accept the conclusion. There are no two ways about it. If the premises are true, then we have to admit that free will is just an illusion. Our actions are not freely chosen; we *had* to do them.

Above, I noted that d'Holbach was an atheist, determinist, and materialist. Here, we see his commitments to determinism and materialism come to the fore. Premise (1) expresses his commitment to materialism. We're wholly material beings. We don't have immaterial souls. We're not spiritual beings. We're physical beings who are wholly part of the natural order.

Premise (2) expresses d'Holbach's commitment to the view that regular and immutable laws govern all of nature. This view is often called *determinism*, the theory that prior events, conditions, and the laws of nature necessitate every event in the universe. Those events could not have been otherwise; they were necessary.

We can hardly deny that the conclusion of d'Holbach's argument is surprising. After all, it certainly seems as though we act freely. Indeed, if I don't have a free will, what explains the fact that I deliberate? Why would I weigh the pros and cons of various options if I couldn't freely choose among them? For example, just this morning I was trying to decide whether or not I should kick my downstairs neighbor's yappy dog. I thought of all the pros it would bring: great pleasure and a quieter home life. I also thought of all the cons it would bring: a lawsuit and a visit from the police. Ultimately, I decided not to do it. But why weigh the options at all if I have no free choice in the matter?

Another reason to think we have a free will is that we are morally responsible for our actions. But can we really be held morally responsible for our actions if we ultimately have no free choice in the matter, if we have no free will? For example, people who commit crimes while sleepwalking are not freely choosing to commit those crimes. Hence, sleepwalking has been used as a successful defense in murder trials. Murdering sleepwalkers don't freely choose to commit murder. They have no control over their actions, and so they're not guilty. Wouldn't the same be true for all our actions if we admit that they are necessitated, that they *had* to happen?

These—deliberation and moral responsibility—are two reasons to reject the conclusion of d'Holbach's argument. However, we can't reject an argument just because we disagree with the conclusion. That's because with valid arguments the premises *require* us to accept the conclusion. So, if we reject the conclusion, we must also reject one of the premises. But which one shall we reject? Before addressing that question, let's look at what can be said in favor of the premises themselves.

The Premises

Premise (1)

Humans are wholly part of nature. We don't have immaterial souls. Our mental lives—what we think, what we feel, and what we decide to do—depend on our brains, not on an immaterial soul really distinct from our brains.

Why think that's true? One reason is that if a neurosurgeon opens up our heads and starts poking around in our brains, we'll start to have different sorts of mental experiences. The same is true if we suffer a stroke or other brain trauma. What best explains this fact? The fact that our mental lives depend on our brains, not on an immaterial soul.

Another reason to think premise (1) is true is that drugs affect our brains chemically. Yet, whether it's LSD, alcohol, or antidepressants, drugs also affect our moods, our thoughts, and our experiences. What's the best way to explain this correlation of chemical interaction to mental experience? Our mental lives depend on our bodies. All of our experiences, all of our thoughts, all of our beliefs, attitudes, and emotions depend on the white and grey matter that sloshes around in our skulls.

A third reason to endorse (1) is the development of humans themselves. When we're young, our bodies are growing and developing. Corresponding with that physical growth and development is mental growth and development. Yet when we're old, our bodies are weakening and declining. Corresponding with that weakening and declining is mental decline and, sometimes, senility. What best explains this parallelism? The fact that our mental lives are really a result of, depend on, our bodies.

That last argument isn't simply supported by observations of the ways bodies look and people behave. It's supported by studies of the way the brain develops. When we're young, our brains are highly plastic. That is, our brains form new neural connections quickly and easily. When we're old, those neural connections do not form so quickly and easily. So, there's a scientific basis for the saying that you can't teach an old dog new tricks. It's true of dogs and it's true of humans. And what explains this best? The fact that our mental lives depend on our brains, not immaterial souls separate from our brains. In short, we're physical beings through and through.

Premise (2)

In our first puzzle I mentioned Isaac Newton's (1643–1727 CE) discoveries of the laws of motion and gravity. Newton's law of gravity is able to explain the orbit of the earth around the sun, the tides, and the fact that objects fall when dropped. That's quite impressive.

Also, Newton's formulae enable us to predict what will happen. We can foresee where the sun will be, when the tides will ebb and flow, and how quickly objects accelerate when dropped. Moreover, nature never really veers from these laws. They are regular. They don't change.

D'Holbach was very impressed with Newton's discoveries. If what Newton discovered is true of the motions of the planets and oceans, why isn't it true of the whole of nature? Isn't it plausible to suppose that such immutable laws govern all of nature, not merely the planets and oceans? For millennia, humans trod the earth observing instances of gravitational attraction: the sun rising and setting, the tides rising, apples falling, etc. Newton showed that all of these occurrences are explained by, and are governed by, natural laws. Similarly, maybe all of the activities we observe today—handsome young men helping old ladies across the street, kittens yawning while watching tennis, courageous soldiers stabbing their mortal enemies to death, lovers gazing deeply into each other's eyes, and my kicking the neighbor's yappy dog—can be explained naturally. Maybe they, too, are governed by natural laws and necessitated by those natural laws in conjunction with the current state of the universe.

Such a view is what premise (2) endorses: every event in nature is necessitated by prior events, conditions, and the laws of nature. Consider, for example, a dropped pencil falling. The event of the pencil falling had to happen. Prior events (me letting go of the pencil), prior conditions (there is not, for example, a sudden gust of wind that might blow the pencil upward), and the laws of nature (most notably, the law of gravity) necessitate that the dropped pencil will fall. That's what *had* to happen.

In Puzzle One, I already mentioned two possible responses to this claim. First, the natural laws might change, so they're not immutable. Second, the natural laws admit a degree of indeterminacy such that they're not perfectly regularly. I'll take these up in the "Possible Responses" section below. As we shall see then, even if these claims are true it does not imperil d'Holbach's argument.

Premise (3)

Premise (3) follows directly from premises (1) and (2). First, premise (1) states that we're wholly part of nature. So, all of our actions occur in nature. There is nothing outside of the natural order that could cause our actions. Second, premise (2) states that every natural event is necessitated by prior events, conditions, and the laws of nature. Since our actions occur in nature and as part of the natural order of things, it follows that our actions must also be necessitated by prior events, conditions, and the laws of nature. In other words, if we're wholly part of nature and determinism is true then even our actions must be the necessary result of prior events, conditions, and the laws of nature.

Similar considerations apply to our supposedly free actions. When I kick my neighbor's yappy dog (I haven't done it, but *when* I do) it will be necessitated by prior events (hearing the yappy dog when I'm trying to sleep), conditions (no police officer being in the vicinity, since I would otherwise fear being arrested), and the laws of nature (the psychological laws that govern my hatred of yappy dogs, the laws that govern motion, etc.).

Premise (4)

Plausibly, when a person acts freely, when a person acts on the basis of her free will, she could have done otherwise. For example, if I leave a party of my own free will, it implies that I could have stayed. I wasn't required to leave. Rather, I opted to leave. I freely chose to leave. An action is free only if the agent could have done otherwise, only if there were some alternative possibilities open to the agent.

In contrast, if I leave a party under police escort I could not do otherwise than leave the party. I am forced to leave the party. Had I tried to stay, I would have been pepper-sprayed, tased, cuffed, and carried out the front door. Thus, I do not leave the party freely.

In like manner, if our actions are necessitated then we could not do otherwise. It would be like leaving a party by police escort. The prior events, conditions, and laws of nature make it such that we cannot do otherwise. That's why premise (4) is plausible. If all of our actions are necessitated by prior events, conditions, and the laws of nature, then we could never act otherwise than we do. If we could never act otherwise than we do, then we have no free will, no action is done freely. Therefore, if all of our actions are necessitated by prior events, conditions, and the laws of nature, then none of our actions are free.

That's an argument for premise (4), but it's not the only one. Perhaps the most famous defense of (4) is Peter van Inwagen's (b. 1942 CE). He presents us with an argument called the *consequence argument.* To understand the argument, the first things we need to get a handle on are the phrases "necessary that" and "necessary in a way opposed to free will that." The first phrase refers to what must be the case logically or metaphysically. The second phrase refers to things that must be the case not because they are logically or metaphysically necessary but because no person has control over them. We might call this *unactionable necessity* (as opposed to logical or metaphysical necessity) because we are unable to undertake any action to change it.

To illustrate the difference, two examples are useful. First, it is *necessary that* squares have four sides. It is also *necessary in a way opposed to free will that* squares have four sides, for there is no action I could undertake to change it. Second, although it is *not necessary that* the Andromeda galaxy be at least 400 light years away from the Milky Way galaxy, it is *necessary in a way opposed to free will.* We have no choice over the matter.

The next things we need to understand van Inwagen's argument are two logical principles. The first principle is called the *alpha principle.* The alpha principle says that if something is *necessary* then we can also conclude that *it is necessary in a way opposed to free will.* To state it in an argument form, where S is a sentence, the alpha principle states:

> It is necessary that: S.
>
> Therefore, it is necessary in a way opposed to free will that: S.

To use our first example, it is necessary that squares have four sides. So, we can conclude that it is necessary in a way opposed to free will that squares have four sides. There is nothing we can do to change that fact.

The second principle is the *beta principle*. The beta principle is a lot like modus ponens, discussed in our first and third puzzles. Modus ponens, recall, has this form, where S and S′ are sentences:

> If S, then S′.
>
> S.
>
> Therefore, S′.

All the beta principle does is put "It is necessary in a way opposed to free will that:" in front of those premises. The beta principle in argument form is this:

> It is necessary in a way opposed to free will that: If S, then S′.
>
> It is necessary in a way opposed to free will that: S.
>
> Therefore, it is necessary in a way opposed to free will that: S′.

For example, it is necessary in a way opposed to free will that: if Pluto orbits the sun, then Pluto moves. Moreover, it is necessary in a way opposed to free will that: Pluto orbits the sun. Therefore, it is necessary in a way opposed to free will that: Pluto moves.

With these two principles in place we can show that the theory of determinism entails that we have no free will. In other words, we can show that (4) is true. How so? First, we need to define two variables:

> Let U = The state of the universe 1 million years ago *and* the laws of nature.
>
> Let K = I kick my neighbor's yappy dog.

Now we move on to the argument. Determinism says that every event (for example, kicking my neighbor's yappy dog, K) is necessitated by prior events and conditions—even the state of the universe 1 million years ago—and the laws of nature (U). In other words, it affirms:

(6) It is necessary that: If U, then K.

Using the alpha principle, we can now conclude that:

(7) It is necessary in a way opposed to free will that: If U, then K.

It is also true, however, that the state of the universe 1 million years ago and the laws of the universe are necessary in a way opposed to free will. After all, I have no control over them and, as far as I can tell, no other person does. They are unactionably necessary. Hence, we can affirm:

(8) It is necessary in a way opposed to free will that: U.

Now, using the beta principle on (7) and (8), we can conclude:

(9) It is necessary in a way opposed to free will that: K.

But what does the argument from (6)–(9) show? Since we merely *assumed* that (6) was true, it shows that *if* (6) is true, *then* (9) is true. That is to say, it shows that:

(10)   If (6) it is necessary that: if U, then K, then (9) it is necessary in a way opposed to free will that: K.

Now recall that (6) is just the theory of determinism. Also, K could stand for any action whatsoever: kicking my neighbor's yappy dog; leaving a party; punching a stranger. So, all (10) is really saying is that:

(4)   If all of our actions are determined, then none of our actions is done freely.

And here we have a second argument for premise (4). If we accept both determinism and the alpha and beta principles, then we have to deny that we have free will.

I should note here that the consequence argument is still vigorously debated. Practically all of the debate centers around the beta principle, since the alpha principle is extremely plausible. Many philosophers now think that the beta principle, as originally stated by van Inwagen, is false. However, some philosophers also believe that it can be suitably altered to salvage the argument. The jury remains out.

Possible Responses

Whenever we encounter a philosophical puzzle we have just two options. The first is to reject one of the premises. The second is to accept the conclusion. ([…], all of our puzzles are valid, so we cannot reject an argument on the grounds that the premises do not really entail the conclusion.)

I've already stated that premise (3) follows directly from premises (1) and (2), assuming that human actions are events. That assumption is uncontroversial. So, we're not really in a position to reject (3). Thus, our only viable options are to accept the conclusion, reject premise (1), reject premise (2), or reject premise (4).

Philosophers who accept the conclusion are called *hard determinists*. They claim that determinism and free will are incompatible and settle for determinism.

Philosophers who reject either premise (1) or premise (2) are called *libertarians*. Like determinists, libertarians think that determinism and free will are incompatible. Unlike hard determinists, libertarians settle for freedom of the will.

Philosophers who reject (4) are called *compatibilists* or, sometimes, *soft determinists*. As might be guessed, they get their name because they think that determinism and free will are compatible, unlike hard determinists and libertarians.

Accept the Conclusion

Maybe d'Holbach is correct. Perhaps we have no free will. What would that mean for us today? Probably it means nothing at all. We would keep doing what we do. We would still punish criminals.

We would still hold each other morally responsible. We would still act and talk as though we have some free choice in what we decide to do.

Accepting the conclusion of d'Holbach's argument probably won't cause mass upheaval (at any rate, if it did, the mass upheaval would have been determined), but it can be quite disillusioning. We like to think we have some power over our lives. We like to think we can control our futures to some degree. But if d'Holbach's argument is sound, it turns out that what we like to think isn't what is true. And that's disappointing.

Yet disappointment and disillusionment have nothing to do with the soundness of d'Holbach's argument. We can't *philosophically* reject his argument just because it's disappointing and disillusioning. What we need is a good philosophical reason to reject one of the premises. Can we come up with one? Let's start with the two libertarian options: to reject premise (1) or to reject premise (2).

Reject Premise (1)

We might deny that we are wholly part of nature. Perhaps we have souls, souls that are really distinct from our bodies and so not subject to the laws of nature.

One reason to think this is true—that we have souls really distinct from our bodies and not subject to the laws of nature—is that many religions claim it is true. Those religions claim, for example, that when we die we go to heaven (or hell). We leave our bodies and exist in an immaterial world. The thing that survives, that continues to exist in an immaterial world, is our soul. Oftentimes, it has been thought that the afterlife is one of disembodiment. Rather than a material, embodied existence, in the afterlife our souls enjoy a disembodied, immaterial existence. So, if we're religious, we might deny (1) based on our beliefs.

Unfortunately, this view faces some very serious problems. First, how is it possible for an immaterial soul to interact with a material body? If we try to preserve freedom of the will by claiming that we have an immaterial soul that causes our bodies to act in certain ways, *how* does this happen? After all, immaterial souls don't have any *material*. They can't cause a body to move in the way that I cause my pen to move as I write. Immaterial souls don't even have a spatial location. Because they're immaterial, they are literally nowhere. But if they're *nowhere*, how do they cause motion *somewhere*?

A second problem with this strategy is that the religious texts of the major monotheistic religions (Judaism, Christianity, and Islam) do *not* claim we have a disembodied existence after death. Much to the contrary, all of those texts describe the afterlife as bodily. True, some of them say we have spiritual bodies. But a spiritual body is still a body. Yet, if we are bodily, physical beings, then we are part of nature. In fact, our word "physical" is derived from the Greek word *physis* (pronounced *foo-sis*), which means *nature*. So, the afterlife described in religious texts is not a disembodied and immaterial existence.

This raises a question: Why do some religious people teach that we have immaterial souls that go to heaven (or hell) after our deaths? Mainly it's because at some point in their existence those religions incorporated the ideas and arguments of early Greek philosophers like Plato into their theology. In his

"Phaedo," Plato (429–347 BCE) presents several arguments showing that humans have immaterial souls that are separate from their bodies. None of his arguments is very good, so I won't rehearse them here. Nonetheless, as religious thinkers began incorporating those ideas and arguments into their views, they concluded that we have immaterial souls that go to heaven after we die.

I should point out here that later religious thinkers (I dare say better ones)—for example, al-Ghazali (1058–1111 CE), mentioned in our sixth puzzle, and Thomas Aquinas (1225–1274 CE), mentioned in our first puzzle—deny that we have disembodied afterlives.

A third problem is that this view is not supported by our best science, as indicated in our discussion of premise (1) above. Our very best science affirms that our mental lives depend on our brains. Moreover, as we saw in Puzzle Six, it's generally not a good idea to endorse a position that runs contrary to our very best science. So, rejecting premise (1) on religious grounds is probably not the best strategy for responding to d'Holbach's argument.

If we cannot reject (1) on religious grounds, perhaps we can reject it on philosophical grounds. To be sure, many philosophers have offered arguments for the conclusion that the soul and body are separable. As I just mentioned, Plato is one such philosopher. Another philosopher is René Descartes (1596–1650 CE). However, none of the arguments for this view has much going for it. So, without further ado, let's turn to our next line of response.

Reject Premise (2)

Another line of response is to deny that every event in nature is necessitated by prior events, conditions, and the laws of nature. Someone who opts for this line of response might try one of two different strategies. The first one is hopeless. The second is promising.

Strategy One: Indeterminism: First is the hopeless strategy. It is widely admitted nowadays that nature is not entirely governed by necessary, regular, and immutable laws. D'Holbach and Newton knew nothing of quantum physics. But quantum physics tells us that there is a degree of randomness in nature, as discussed in Puzzle One. If that's true, not everything is determined. Nature is, to some degree, indeterminate, random.

The reason that this strategy is hopeless is that indeterminacy still does not make room for freedom of the will. An action that is random is no freer than an action that is necessitated. Suppose, for example, that I suffer from a neurological condition that *randomly* causes me to kick yappy dogs. Sure, I might end up kicking my neighbor's yappy dog. But would we say that I have freely chosen to kick his yappy dog? When the cause of my action *really is* my neurological condition, when my yappy-dog kicking really is *random, I* do not act freely.

The upshot of this is that d'Holbach's argument can be modified slightly so as to accommodate the insights of quantum physics. We can do so as follows:

(1a) Humans are wholly part of nature.

(2a) Every event in nature is either (i) determined or (ii) random.

(3a) If humans are wholly part of nature and every event in nature is either (i) determined or (ii) random, then all of our actions are either (i') determined or (ii') random.

(4a) If (i') our actions are determined, then our actions are not freely done, and if (ii') our actions are random, then they are not freely done.

(5a) Therefore, none of our actions is freely done; we have no free will.

In short, admitting that nature is to some degree indeterminate, random, doesn't help us respond to d'Holbach's puzzle.

One last note on this: I also previously mentioned (in Puzzle One) the possibility that the laws of nature are not immutable. Perhaps they are changing. However, we have no control over the laws of nature. So, even if they are changing, all of our actions remain necessitated by prior events, conditions, and the *laws of nature as they stand at the time of the action.*

Strategy Two: Agent Causation: It should be noted that all the libertarian has to do in order to deny premise (2) is to show that there is just one action in each of our lives that is not necessitated by prior events, conditions, and the laws of nature. Libertarianism makes no claim as to *how many* of our actions are free.

Now suppose that you are playing roulette. You are trying to decide whether you will put your chips on red or black. Which should you choose? (Assume that you really want to play, so you do have to choose.) There is simply no reason to favor red over black or vice versa. On any spin of the wheel the ball is as likely to land on red as it is on black. So, you decide on black.

Notice that here it is up to *you*, the agent, to decide. You recognize that there are reasons to choose red. You recognize that there are reasons to choose black. However, neither of those reasons determines that you should choose one over the other. And yet, since you want to play, you must choose one over the other. It is now up to you, the agent, to make a decision. You are free to choose one or the other.

Your freedom in this case stems from the fact that there is nothing to determine you choosing one over the other but you are determined to choose. What is more, situations like this arise when the probability is not objective (see Puzzle One for a discussion of objective and subjective probability). For example, suppose you are deciding whether or not to call up John and ask him on a date. Obviously, you will either call him or not. You have some good reasons to call him. For example, you've seen him staring at you in class and you really think he is dreamy and his lips are so full and. ... Well, you get the picture. Also, you have some good reasons not to call him. For example, you would be so embarrassed if he said no, and you might get flustered if his mom answers the phone, and you heard a rumor that he wasn't a good kisser anyway.

Now, it is possible that both sets of reasons are equally strong. It is not implausible to suppose that those reasons, while not quantifiable as objective probabilities, do not decisively favor one action over the other. Nevertheless, *you*, the agent, have to decide. You will either call him or not.

It is here that we begin to glimpse the agent causation view of free will, a view given recent development by Timothy O'Connor (b. 1965 CE) but originated by Thomas Reid (1710–1796 CE).

On this view, it is true that humans are the result of a variety of causes. For example, your parents made sweet, sweet love. You were nourished and grew into the person you are. You had a variety of experiences—being teased, being turned down for dates, being hit on by strange men—that have informed your beliefs and desires.

Even though we are the result of a variety of causes, we are also agents. We decide on certain courses of actions. Sometimes those decisions are determined by our beliefs and desires. We want to play roulette. We want to eat a bowl of ice cream. We want to go swimming.

Yet at other times those decisions are not determined by our beliefs and desires. We are torn. We have equally strong reasons for different courses of action. We want to play roulette, but we must decide between red and black. We want to eat ice cream, but we must decide between mint chocolate chip and rocky road. We want to go swimming, but we must decide between the pool and the ocean. In this case, it is up to us, the agents, to make a choice. And when we do so, we choose freely.

Reject Premise (4)

Premise (4) states that if all of our actions are necessitated by prior events, conditions, and the laws of nature, then we have no free will. That may sound right to you: How could we freely do an action if it was necessitated by what came before it, if we could not have done otherwise? After all, the view that an action is free only if one could have done otherwise has significant appeal.

Moreover, we commonly suppose that having a free will means not being determined to act by something else. We take *acting freely* and *being determined* to be opposites. But is this the right way to think of free will? Perhaps it's not. In what follows, we'll look at two other ways of thinking about freedom of the will.

Strategy One: Classic Compatibilism: David Hume (1711–1776 CE) argues that free will and determinism are not opposites. Rather, the opposite of free will is constraint. The opposite of determinism is randomness or indeterminacy. Thus, on Hume's view, an action is free just because (i) we desire to do it and (ii) we are not constrained from doing it. Because we desire to do it, the action is still determined. It is determined by our desires. Yet because we are not constrained in doing it, our action is free.

Consider, for example, these three scenarios:

> *Scenario One:* I kick a yappy dog because I want to and no one stops me.
>
> *Scenario Two:* I kick a yappy dog just because a mad scientist has hooked me up to a yappy-dog-kicking machine.
>
> *Scenario Three:* I don't kick a yappy dog, even though I want to, because the police hold me back.

Notice, first, that in all three cases what happens is determined. In the first case, it is determined by my desire to kick the dog. In the second case, it is determined by the yappy-dog-kicking machine. In the third case, it is determined by the police restraining me.

Notice also, however, that in the first scenario my action is free whereas in the second and third scenarios I do not act freely. In the second, I do not desire to kick the yappy dog. Rather, I kick the yappy dog just because I am hooked up to a yappy-dog-kicking machine. In the third, because I am constrained, I do not refrain from kicking the dog freely.

This sounds like a pretty good position to take. It allows us to have our cake and eat it too. On the one hand, we get to endorse determinism because our actions are necessitated by prior events, conditions, and the laws of nature. On the other hand, we also get to endorse the claim that we have a free will. That's because all it means to act freely is to desire to do it and not be constrained from doing it.

Unfortunately, there are two problems with this view. The first problem is that the position implies that animals have free wills too. Animals, after all, desire to do the actions they do. Also, they are not externally constrained in doing them. However, it seems strange to claim that animals have free wills. For example, when I see a snail slithering toward blades of grass, I do not think it is acting freely. It is just doing what snails do.

The second problem is that if classic compatibilism is true it follows that no one can do otherwise. However, we tend to think that free will requires that we be able to do otherwise. The classic compatibilist has not addressed this issue.

Strategy Two: Real-Self Compatibilism: As just indicated in the discussion of animals, something is missing in the story of classic compatibilism. But what is it? In answering that question, it is helpful to begin with the other objection, the one about being able to do otherwise.

Harry Frankfurt (b. 1929 CE) has called into question the claim that an action is free only if we can do otherwise. To see how, let's extend the second scenario above, the one about me being hooked up to a yappy-dog-kicking machine. Imagine that a mad scientist really wants me to kick my neighbor's yappy dog. He would much prefer that I do it myself. Nonetheless, he wants to be sure that I really will do it. After all, I have been known to waver when it comes to kicking yappy dogs.

To make sure I kick my neighbor's yappy dog, the mad scientist has (unknown to me) hooked me up to a yappy-dog-kicking machine. The machine is such that *if I show no signs of wavering* in kicking my neighbor's yappy dog it does nothing. However, *if I do show signs of wavering* in kicking my neighbor's yappy dog the machine will trigger and cause me to kick it. Notice that no matter what happens there is only one possibility: I will kick my neighbor's yappy dog.

Now suppose further that I kick my neighbor's dog and *do not waver*. In that case, I have acted freely. I have done what I planned to do all along. Also, the machine did not trigger.

So, here is a case where I do act freely. However, there were no other possibilities. I was going to kick the dog no matter what. Acting freely does not require that we be able to do otherwise than we do.

Moreover, if we change things in this story just a little bit, we can begin to see what Frankfurt thinks is missing from classic compatibilism. For now suppose that I did waver but that the yappy-dog-kicking machine triggered. In that case, my action would not have been consistent with what *I really* wanted to do, with what my real self wants to do.

Here we finally get to Frankfurt's view. When I kick my neighbor's yappy dog and do *not* waver, I have a *first-order desire* (to kick the yappy dog) and a *second-order volition* (to follow through). In this case, my first-order desire and my second-order volition *mesh*. So, I act freely.

In contrast, when I kick my neighbor's yappy dog because of the machine, I still have a first-order desire to do so but I lack a second-order volition. It is because I lack the second-order volition that I begin to waver. In this case, even though I kick the yappy dog, my first-order desire and my second-order volition *do not mesh*. So, I do not act freely.

Notice, nonetheless, that in both cases my action is determined. In the first case, it is determined by my first-order desire and second-order volition. In the second case, it is determined by the yappy-dog-kicking machine. Thus, on Frankfurt's view free will is compatible with determinism.

To make Frankfurt's position clearer, it is helpful to have recourse to his own example. Imagine the following two drug addicts:

> *The Unwilling Addict:* The unwilling addict has a first-order desire to do drugs and a second-order volition not to do drugs. However, because of the strength of his first-order desire, he takes the drugs.

> *The Willing Addict:* The willing addict has a first-order desire to do drugs and a second-order volition to continue doing drugs. He takes the drugs.

Which addict acts freely? According to Frankfurt, it is the willing addict. That is because the willing addict's first-order desire meshes with his second-order volition. In contrast, the unwilling addict does not act freely. His first-order desire and second-order volition do not mesh.

Moreover, we are now in a position to see how Frankfurt's version of compatibilism can explain why animals do not have free wills. Animals lack second-order volitions. They merely act on their first-order desires. As such, action on their first-order desires cannot mesh (or fail to mesh) with their second-order volitions.

Unfortunately, there is a problem with Frankfurt's position. It is that the meshing of my first-order desires and second-order volitions might itself be a consequence of outside manipulation. Imagine, for example, that the yappy-dog-kicking machine works by causing me to have a second-order volition. In that case, my first-order desire and second-order volition *do* mesh. Frankfurt must then admit that I act freely even though my action was caused by the yappy-dog-kicking machine. However, that is implausible.

In conclusion, if we want to have our cake and eat it too, if we want to retain a commitment to determinism and yet make room for free will, Hume and Frankfurt have surely brought us some way in showing how it may be done. However, it is not clear that they have brought us far enough.

References

Al-Ghazali. *Incoherence of the Philosophers*. Trans. Sabih Ahmad Kamali. Lahore: Pakistan Philosophical Congress, 1958.

Descartes, René. *Meditations on First Philosophy*. In *The Philosophical Writings of Decartes*. Vol. 2. Trans. John Cottingham, Robert Stoothoff, and Dugald Murdoch. Cambridge: Cambridge UP, 1984.

D'Holbach, Baron Paul Henri Thiry. *The System of Nature*. Trans. H. D. Robinson. J.P. Mendum, 1889.

Frankfurt, Harry. "Alternate Possibilities and Moral Responsibility." *Journal of Philosophy*. 66: 829–39, 1969.

Frankfurt, Harry. "Freedom of the Will and the Concept of a Person." *Journal of Philosophy*. 68: 5–20, 1971.

Hume, David. *An Enquiry Concerning Human Understanding*. 2nd ed. Ed. Eric Steinberg. Indianapolis: Hackett, 1993.

Newton, Isaac. *The Principia: Mathematical Principles of Natural Philosophy*. Trans. I. Bernard Cohen and Anne Whitman. Berkeley: University of California Press, 1999.

O'Connor, Timothy. *Persons and Causes: The Metaphysics of Free Will*. New York: Oxford UP, 2000.

Plato. "Phaedo." In *Complete Works*. Trans. G. M. A. Grube. Eds. John M. Cooper and D. S. Hutchinson. Indianapolis: Hackett, 1997.

Reid, Thomas. *Essays on the Active Powers of Man*. Edinburgh: Bell and Robinson, 1788.

Thomas Aquinas. *Summa Theologiae*. Vol. 11. Trans. Timothy Suttor. London: Eyre and Spottiswoode Limited, 1970.

Van Inwagen, Peter. *An Essay on Free Will*. Oxford: Clarendon Press, 1983.

Book II

Virtue of Character

Aristotle

....

1

[How a Virtue of Character Is Acquired]

Virtue, then, is of two sorts, virtue of thought and virtue of character. 15
Virtue of thought arises and grows mostly from teaching; that is why it
needs experience and time. Virtue of character [i.e., of *ēthos*] results from
habit [*ethos*]; hence its name 'ethical', slightly varied from 'ethos'.*

§2 Hence it is also clear that none of the virtues of character arises in
us naturally. For if something is by nature in one condition, habituation 20
cannot bring it into another condition. A stone, for instance, by nature
moves downwards, and habituation could not make it move upwards,
not even if you threw it up ten thousand times to habituate it; nor could
habituation make fire move downwards, or bring anything that is by
nature in one condition into another condition. §3 And so the virtues
arise in us neither by nature nor against nature. Rather, we are by nature 25
able to acquire them, and we are completed through habit.*

§4 Further, if something arises in us by nature, we first have the
capacity for it, and later perform the activity. This is clear in the case of the
senses; for we did not acquire them by frequent seeing or hearing, but we 30
already had them when we exercised them, and did not get them by exer-
cising them. Virtues, by contrast, we acquire, just as we acquire crafts, by
having first activated them. For we learn a craft by producing the same *1103a*
product that we must produce when we have learned it; we become
builders, for instance, by building, and we become harpists by playing
the harp. Similarly, then, we become just by doing just actions, temperate *1103b*
by doing temperate actions, brave by doing brave actions.

§5 What goes on in cities is also evidence for this. For the legislator makes the citizens good by habituating them, and this is the wish of every legislator; if he fails to do it well he misses his goal.* Correct habituation distinguishes a good political system from a bad one.

§6 Further, the sources and means that develop each virtue also ruin it, just as they do in a craft. For playing the harp makes both good and bad harpists, and it is analogous in the case of builders and all the rest; for building well makes good builders, and building badly makes bad ones. §7 Otherwise no teacher would be needed, but everyone would be born a good or a bad craftsman.

It is the same, then, with the virtues. For what we do in our dealings with other people makes some of us just, some unjust; what we do in terrifying situations, and the habits of fear or confidence that we acquire, make some of us brave and others cowardly. The same is true of situations involving appetites and anger; for one or another sort of conduct in these situations makes some temperate and mild, others intemperate and irascible. To sum it up in a single account: a state [of character] results from [the repetition of] similar activities.*

§8 That is why we must perform the right activities, since differences in these imply corresponding differences in the states.* It is not unimportant, then, to acquire one sort of habit or another, right from our youth. On the contrary, it is very important, indeed all-important.

2

[Habituation]

Our present discussion does not aim, as our others do, at study; for the purpose of our examination is not to know what virtue is, but to become good, since otherwise the inquiry would be of no benefit to us.* And so we must examine the right ways of acting; for, as we have said, the actions also control the sorts of states we acquire.

§2 First, then, actions should accord with the correct reason.* That is a common [belief], and let us assume it. We shall discuss it later, and say what the correct reason is and how it is related to the other virtues.

§3 But let us take it as agreed in advance that every account of the actions we must do has to be stated in outline, not exactly. As we also said at the beginning, the type of accounts we demand should accord with the subject matter; and questions about actions and expediency, like questions about health, have no fixed answers.*

§4 While this is the character of our general account, the account of particular cases is still more inexact. For these fall under no craft or profession; the agents themselves must consider in each case what the opportune action is, as doctors and navigators do.* §5 The account we offer, then, in our present inquiry is of this inexact sort; still, we must try to offer help.*

§6 First, then, we should observe that these sorts of states naturally tend to be ruined by excess and deficiency. We see this happen with strength and health—for we must use evident cases [such as these] as witnesses to things that are not evident.* For both excessive and deficient exercise ruin bodily strength, and, similarly, too much or too little eating or drinking ruins health, whereas the proportionate amount produces, increases, and preserves it.

§7 The same is true, then, of temperance, bravery, and the other virtues. For if, for instance, someone avoids and is afraid of everything, standing firm against nothing, he becomes cowardly; if he is afraid of nothing at all and goes to face everything, he becomes rash. Similarly, if he gratifies himself with every pleasure and abstains from none, he becomes intemperate; if he avoids them all, as boors do, he becomes some sort of insensible person. Temperance and bravery, then, are ruined by excess and deficiency, but preserved by the mean.*

§8 But these actions are not only the sources and causes both of the emergence and growth of virtues and of their ruin; the activities of the virtues [once we have acquired them] also consist in these same actions.* For this is also true of more evident cases; strength, for instance, arises from eating a lot and from withstanding much hard labor, and it is the strong person who is most capable of these very actions. §9 It is the same with the virtues. For abstaining from pleasures makes us become temperate, and once we have become temperate we are most capable of abstaining from pleasures. It is similar with bravery; habituation in disdain for frightening situations and in standing firm against them makes us become brave, and once we have become brave we shall be most capable of standing firm.

3

[The Importance of Pleasure and Pain]

5 But we must take someone's pleasure or pain following on his actions to be a sign of his state.* For if someone who abstains from bodily pleasures enjoys the abstinence itself, he is temperate; if he is grieved by it, he is intemperate.* Again, if he stands firm against terrifying situations and enjoys it, or at least does not find it painful, he is brave; if he finds it painful, he is cowardly. For virtue of character is about pleasures and pains.*

1104b10   For pleasure causes us to do base actions, and pain causes us to abstain from fine ones. §2 That is why we need to have had the appropriate upbringing—right from early youth, as Plato says*—to make us find enjoyment or pain in the right things; for this is the correct education.

§3 Further, virtues are concerned with actions and feelings; but every 15 feeling and every action implies pleasure or pain;* hence, for this reason too, virtue is about pleasures and pains. §4 Corrective treatments also indicate this, since they use pleasures and pains; for correction is a form of medical treatment, and medical treatment naturally operates through contraries.

§5 Further, as we said earlier, every state of soul is naturally related to 20 and about whatever naturally makes it better or worse; and pleasures and pains make people base, from pursuing and avoiding the wrong ones, at the wrong time, in the wrong ways, or whatever other distinctions of that sort are needed in an account. These [bad effects of pleasure and pain] are the reason why people actually define the virtues as ways of being 25 unaffected and undisturbed [by pleasures and pains].* They are wrong, however, because they speak of being unaffected without qualification, not of being unaffected in the right or wrong way, at the right or wrong time, and the added qualifications.

§6 We assume, then, that virtue is the sort of state that does the best actions concerning pleasures and pains, and that vice is the contrary state.

30 §7 The following will also make it evident that virtue and vice are about the same things. For there are three objects of choice—fine, expedient, and pleasant—and three objects of avoidance—their contraries, shameful, harmful, and painful.* About all these, then, the good person is 35 correct and the bad person is in error, and especially about pleasure. For 1105a pleasure is shared with animals, and implied by every object of choice, since what is fine and what is expedient appear pleasant as well.

§8 Further, pleasure grows up with all of us from infancy on. That is why it is hard to rub out this feeling that is dyed into our lives. We also estimate actions [as well as feelings]—some of us more, some less—by pleasure and pain. §9 For this reason, our whole discussion must be about these; for good or bad enjoyment or pain is very important for our actions.

§10 Further, it is more difficult to fight pleasure than to fight spirit—and Heracleitus tells us [how difficult it is to fight spirit].* Now both craft and virtue are in every case about what is more difficult, since a good result is even better when it is more difficult. Hence, for this reason also, the whole discussion, for virtue and political science alike, must consider pleasures and pains; for if we use these well, we shall be good, and if badly, bad.

§11 To sum up: Virtue is about pleasures and pains; the actions that are its sources also increase it or, if they are done badly, ruin it; and its activity is about the same actions as those that are its sources.

4

[Virtuous Actions versus Virtuous Character]

Someone might be puzzled, however, about what we mean by saying that we become just by doing just actions and become temperate by doing temperate actions.* For [one might suppose that] if we do grammatical or musical actions, we are grammarians or musicians, and, similarly, if we do just or temperate actions, we are thereby just or temperate.

§2 But surely actions are not enough, even in the case of crafts;* for it is possible to produce a grammatical result by chance, or by following someone else's instructions. To be grammarians, then, we must both produce a grammatical result and produce it grammatically—that is to say, produce it in accord with the grammatical knowledge in us.

§3 Moreover, in any case, what is true of crafts is not true of virtues.* For the products of a craft determine by their own qualities whether they have been produced well; and so it suffices that they have the right qualities when they have been produced.* But for actions in accord with the virtues to be done temperately or justly it does not suffice that they themselves have the right qualities.* Rather, the agent must also be in the right state when he does them. First, he must know [that he is doing virtuous actions]; second, he must decide on them, and decide on them for themselves; and, third, he must also do them from a firm and unchanging state.

1105b As conditions for having a craft, these three do not count, except for the bare knowing.* As a condition for having a virtue, however, the knowing counts for nothing, or [rather] for only a little, whereas the other two conditions are very important, indeed all-important. And we achieve
5 these other two conditions by the frequent doing of just and temperate actions.

§4 Hence actions are called just or temperate when they are the sort that a just or temperate person would do. But the just and temperate person is not the one who [merely] does these actions, but the one who also does them in the way in which just or temperate people do them.

10 §5 It is right, then, to say that a person comes to be just from doing just actions and temperate from doing temperate actions; for no one has the least prospect of becoming good from failing to do them.

§6 The many, however, do not do these actions. They take refuge in arguments, thinking that they are doing philosophy, and that this is the
15 way to become excellent people. They are like a sick person who listens attentively to the doctor, but acts on none of his instructions. Such a course of treatment will not improve the state of the sick person's body; nor will the many improve the state of their souls by this attitude to philosophy.*

5

[Virtue of Character: Its Genus]

1105b20 Next we must examine what virtue is. Since there are three conditions arising in the soul—feelings, capacities, and states—virtue must be one of these.*

§2 By feelings I mean appetite, anger, fear, confidence, envy, joy, love, hate, longing, jealousy, pity, and in general whatever implies pleasure or
25 pain. By capacities I mean what we have when we are said to be capable of these feelings—capable of being angry, for instance, or of being afraid* or of feeling pity. By states I mean what we have when we are well or badly off in relation to feelings.* If, for instance, our feeling is too intense or slack, we are badly off in relation to anger, but if it is intermediate, we are well off; the same is true in the other cases.

§3 First, then, neither virtues nor vices are feelings. For we are called 30
excellent or base insofar as we have virtues or vices, not insofar as we
have feelings. Further, we are neither praised nor blamed insofar as we
have feelings; for we do not praise the angry or the frightened person,
and do not blame the person who is simply angry, but only the person 1106a
who is angry in a particular way. We are praised or blamed, however,
insofar as we have virtues or vices.* §4 Further, we are angry and afraid
without decision; but the virtues are decisions of some kind, or [rather]
require decision.* Besides, insofar as we have feelings, we are said to be 5
moved; but insofar as we have virtues or vices, we are said to be in some
condition rather than moved.

§5 For these reasons the virtues are not capacities either; for we are
neither called good nor called bad, nor are we praised or blamed, insofar
as we are simply capable of feelings. Further, while we have capacities 10
by nature, we do not become good or bad by nature; we have discussed
this before.*

§6 If, then, the virtues are neither feelings nor capacities, the remaining
possibility is that they are states. And so we have said what the genus of
virtue is.

6

[Virtue of Character: Its Differentia]

But we must say not only, as we already have, that it is a state, but also 15
what sort of state it is.*

§2 It should be said, then, that every virtue causes its possessors to be
in a good state and to perform their functions well.* The virtue of eyes,
for instance, makes the eyes and their functioning excellent, because it
makes us see well; and similarly, the virtue of a horse makes the horse 20
excellent, and thereby good at galloping, at carrying its rider, and at
standing steady in the face of the enemy. §3 If this is true in every case, *1106a*
the virtue of a human being will likewise be the state that makes a human
being good and makes him perform his function well.

§4 We have already said how this will be true, and it will also be evident 25
from our next remarks, if we consider the sort of nature that virtue has.*

In everything continuous and divisible we can take more, less, and
equal, and each of them either in the object itself or relative to us; and
the equal is some intermediate between excess and deficiency. §5 By the 30

intermediate in the object I mean what is equidistant from each extremity; this is one and the same for all. But relative to us the intermediate is what is neither superfluous nor deficient; this is not one, and is not the same for all.*

§6 If, for instance, ten are many and two are few, we take six as intermediate in the object, since it exceeds [two] and is exceeded [by ten] by an equal amount, [four]. §7 This is what is intermediate by numerical proportion. But that is not how we must take the intermediate that is relative to us. For if ten pounds [of food], for instance, are a lot for someone to eat, and two pounds a little, it does not follow that the trainer will prescribe six, since this might also be either a little or a lot for the person who is to take it—for Milo [the athlete] a little, but for the beginner in gymnastics a lot; and the same is true for running and wrestling. §8 In this way every scientific expert avoids excess and deficiency and seeks and chooses what is intermediate—but intermediate relative to us, not in the object.

§9 This, then, is how each science produces its product well, by focusing on what is intermediate and making the product conform to that.* This, indeed, is why people regularly comment on well-made products that nothing could be added or subtracted; they assume that excess or deficiency ruins a good [result], whereas the mean preserves it. Good craftsmen also, we say, focus on what is intermediate when they produce their product. And since virtue, like nature, is better and more exact than any craft, it will also aim at what is intermediate.*

§10 By virtue I mean virtue of character; for this is about feelings and actions, and these admit of excess, deficiency, and an intermediate condition. We can be afraid, for instance, or be confident, or have appetites, or get angry, or feel pity, and in general have pleasure or pain, both too much and too little, and in both ways not well. §11 But having these feelings at the right times, about the right things, toward the right people, for the right end, and in the right way, is the intermediate and best condition, and this is proper to virtue. §12 Similarly, actions also admit of excess, deficiency, and an intermediate condition.

Now virtue is about feelings and actions, in which excess and deficiency are in error and incur blame, whereas the intermediate condition is correct and wins praise,* which are both proper to virtue. §13 Virtue, then, is a mean, insofar as it aims at what is intermediate.

§14 Moreover, there are many ways to be in error—for badness is proper to the indeterminate, as the Pythagoreans pictured it, and good to the determinate. But there is only one way to be correct. That is why error is easy and correctness is difficult, since it is easy to miss the target and difficult to hit it. And so for this reason also excess and deficiency are proper to vice, the mean to virtue; 'for we are noble in only one way, but bad in all sorts of ways.'* 35

§15 Virtue, then, is a state that decides, consisting in a mean, the mean 1107a relative to us, which is defined by reference to reason, that is to say, to the reason by reference to which the prudent person would define it.* It is a mean between two vices, one of excess and one of deficiency.

§16 It is a mean for this reason also: Some vices miss what is right because they are deficient, others because they are excessive, in feelings 5 or in actions, whereas virtue finds and chooses what is intermediate.

§17 That is why virtue, as far as its essence and the account stating what it is are concerned, is a mean, but, as far as the best [condition] and the good [result] are concerned, it is an extremity.

§18 Now not every action or feeling admits of the mean.* For the 10 names of some automatically include baseness—for instance, spite, shamelessness, envy [among feelings], and adultery, theft, murder, among actions.* For all of these and similar things are called by these names because they themselves, not their excesses or deficiencies, are base. Hence in doing these things we can never be correct, but must invariably be in error. We 15 cannot do them well or not well—by committing adultery, for instance, with the right woman at the right time in the right way. On the contrary, it is true without qualification that to do any of them is to be in error.

§19 [To think these admit of a mean], therefore, is like thinking that unjust or cowardly or intemperate action also admits of a mean, an excess 20 and a deficiency. If it did, there would be a mean of excess, a mean of deficiency, an excess of excess and a deficiency of deficiency. §20 On the contrary, just as there is no excess or deficiency of temperance or of bravery (since the intermediate is a sort of extreme), so also there is no mean of these vicious actions either, but whatever way anyone does them, he is in error. For in general there is no mean of excess or of deficiency, 25 and no excess or deficiency of a mean.

7

[The Particular Virtues of Character]

However, we must not only state this general account but also apply it to the particular cases. For among accounts concerning actions, though the 30 general ones are common to more cases, the specific ones are truer, since actions are about particular cases, and our account must accord with these.* Let us, then, find these from the chart.*

1107b §2 First, then, in feelings of fear and confidence the mean is bravery. The excessively fearless person is nameless (indeed many cases are nameless), and the one who is excessively confident is rash. The one who is excessive in fear and deficient in confidence is cowardly.

5 §3 In pleasures and pains—though not in all types, and in pains less than in pleasures*—the mean is temperance and the excess intemperance. People deficient in pleasure are not often found, which is why they also lack even a name; let us call them insensible.

10 §4 In giving and taking money the mean is generosity, the excess wastefulness and the deficiency ungenerosity. Here the vicious people have contrary excesses and defects; for the wasteful person is excessive in spending and deficient in taking, whereas the ungenerous person is excessive in taking and deficient in spending. §5 At the moment we are

15 speaking in outline and summary, and that is enough; later we shall define these things more exactly.

§6 In questions of money there are also other conditions. Another mean is magnificence; for the magnificent person differs from the generous by being concerned with large matters, while the generous person

20 is concerned with small. The excess is ostentation and vulgarity, and the deficiency is stinginess. These differ from the vices related to generosity in ways we shall describe later.

§7 In honor and dishonor the mean is magnanimity, the excess something called a sort of vanity, and the deficiency pusillanimity. §8 And

25 just as we said that generosity differs from magnificence in its concern with small matters, similarly there is a virtue concerned with small honors, differing in the same way from magnanimity, which is concerned with great honors. For honor can be desired either in the right way or more or less than is right. If someone desires it to excess, he is called an

30 honor-lover, and if his desire is deficient he is called indifferent to honor, but if he is intermediate he has no name. The corresponding conditions have no name either, except the condition of the honor-lover, which is called honor-loving.

This is why people at the extremes lay claim to the intermediate area. Moreover, we also sometimes call the intermediate person an honor-lover, and sometimes call him indifferent to honor; and sometimes we praise the honor-lover, sometimes the person indifferent to honor.* 1108a §9 We will mention later the reason we do this; for the moment, let us speak of the other cases in the way we have laid down.

§10 Anger also admits of an excess, deficiency, and mean. These are 5 all practically nameless; but since we call the intermediate person mild, let us call the mean mildness. Among the extreme people, let the excessive person be irascible, and his vice irascibility, and let the deficient person be a sort of inirascible person, and his deficiency inirascibility.

§11 There are also three other means, somewhat similar to one 10 another, but different. For they are all concerned with common dealings in conversations and actions, but differ insofar as one is concerned with *1108a* truth telling in these areas, the other two with sources of pleasure, some of which are found in amusement, and the others in daily life in general. Hence we should also discuss these states, so that we can better observe 15 that in every case the mean is praiseworthy, whereas the extremes are neither praiseworthy nor correct, but blameworthy. Most of these cases are also nameless, and we must try, as in the other cases also, to supply names ourselves, to make things clear and easy to follow.

§12 In truth-telling, then, let us call the intermediate person truthful, 20 and the mean truthfulness; pretense that overstates will be boastfulness, and the person who has it boastful; pretense that understates will be self-deprecation, and the person who has it self-deprecating.

§13 In sources of pleasure in amusements let us call the intermediate person witty, and the condition wit; the excess buffoonery and the person 25 who has it a buffoon; and the deficient person a sort of boor and the state boorishness.

In the other sources of pleasure, those in daily life, let us call the person who is pleasant in the right way friendly, and the mean state friendliness. If someone goes to excess with no [ulterior] aim, he will be ingratiating; if he does it for his own advantage, a flatterer. The deficient person, unpleasant 30 in everything, will be a sort of quarrelsome and ill-tempered person.

§14 There are also means in feelings and about feelings. Shame, for instance, is not a virtue, but the person prone to shame as well as [the virtuous people we have described] receives praise. For here also one person is called intermediate, and another—the person excessively prone to shame, who is ashamed about everything—is called excessive; the person 35 who is deficient in shame or never feels shame at all is said to have no sense of disgrace; and the intermediate one is called prone to shame. 1108b

§15 Proper indignation is the mean between envy and spite; these conditions are concerned with pleasure and pain at what happens to our neighbors. For the properly indignant person feels pain when someone does well undeservedly; the envious person exceeds him by feeling pain when anyone does well, while the spiteful person is so deficient in feeling pain that he actually enjoys [other people's misfortunes].*

§16 There will also be an opportunity elsewhere to speak of these. We must consider justice after these.* Since it is spoken of in more than one way, we shall distinguish its two types and say how each of them is a mean. Similarly, we must also consider the virtues that belong to reason.

8

[Relations between Mean and Extreme States]

Among these three conditions, then, two are vices—one of excess, one of deficiency—and one, the mean, is virtue. In a way, each of them is opposed to each of the others, since each extreme is contrary both to the intermediate condition and to the other extreme, while the intermediate is contrary to the extremes.

§2 For, just as the equal is greater in comparison to the smaller, and smaller in comparison to the greater, so also the intermediate states are excessive in comparison to the deficiencies and deficient in comparison to the excesses—both in feelings and in actions. For the brave person, for instance, appears rash in comparison to the coward, and cowardly in comparison to the rash person; the temperate person appears intemperate in comparison to the insensible person, and insensible in comparison with the intemperate person; and the generous person appears wasteful in comparison to the ungenerous, and ungenerous in comparison to the wasteful person.* §3 That is why each of the extreme people tries to push the intermediate person to the other extreme, so that the coward, for instance, calls the brave person rash, and the rash person calls him a coward, and similarly in the other cases.

§4 Since these conditions of soul are opposed to each other in these ways, the extremes are more contrary to each other than to the intermediate. For they are further from each other than from the intermediate, just as the large is further from the small, and the small from the large, than either is from the equal.

§5 Further, sometimes one extreme—rashness or wastefulness, for instance—appears somewhat like the intermediate state, bravery or generosity. But the extremes are most unlike one another; and the things that are furthest apart from each other are defined as contraries. And so 35 the things that are further apart are more contrary.

§6 In some cases the deficiency, in others the excess, is more opposed 1109a to the intermediate condition. For instance, cowardice, the deficiency, not rashness, the excess, is more opposed to bravery, whereas intemperance, the excess, not insensibility, the deficiency, is more opposed to temperance. 5

§7 This happens for two reasons: One reason is derived from the object itself. Since sometimes one extreme is closer and more similar to the intermediate condition, we oppose the contrary extreme, more than this closer one, to the intermediate condition.* Since rashness, for instance, seems to be closer and more similar to bravery, and cowardice 10 less similar, we oppose cowardice, more than rashness, to bravery; for what is further from the intermediate condition seems to be more contrary to it. This, then, is one reason, derived from the object itself.

§8 The other reason is derived from ourselves. For when we ourselves have some natural tendency to one extreme more than to the other, this extreme appears more opposed to the intermediate condition. Since, for instance, we have more of a natural tendency to pleasure, we drift more 15 easily toward intemperance than toward orderliness. Hence we say that an extreme is more contrary if we naturally develop more in that direction; and this is why intemperance is more contrary to temperance, since *1109a* it is the excess [of pleasure].

9

[How Can We Reach the Mean?]

We have said enough, then, to show that virtue of character is a mean 20 and what sort of mean it is; that it is a mean between two vices, one of excess and one of deficiency; and that it is a mean because it aims at the intermediate condition in feelings and actions.

§2 That is why it is also hard work to be excellent. For in each case 25 it is hard work to find the intermediate; for instance, not everyone, but only one who knows, finds the midpoint in a circle. So also getting angry, or giving and spending money, is easy and everyone can do it; but doing it to the right person, in the right amount, at the right time, for the right

end, and in the right way is no longer easy, nor can everyone do it. Hence
30 doing these things well is rare, praiseworthy, and fine.

§3 That is why anyone who aims at the intermediate condition must first of all steer clear of the more contrary extreme, following the advice that Calypso also gives: 'Hold the ship outside the spray and surge.'* For one extreme is more in error, the other less. §4 Since, therefore, it is hard to hit the intermediate extremely accurately,* the second-best
35 tack, as they say, is to take the lesser of the evils. We shall succeed best
1109b in this by the method we describe.

We must also examine what we ourselves drift into easily. For different people have different natural tendencies toward different goals, and we
5 shall come to know our own tendencies from the pleasure or pain that arises in us. §5 We must drag ourselves off in the contrary direction; for if we pull far away from error, as they do in straightening bent wood, we shall reach the intermediate condition.

§6 And in everything we must beware above all of pleasure and its sources; for we are already biased in its favor when we come to judge it.
10 Hence we must react to it as the elders reacted to Helen, and on each occasion repeat what they said; for if we do this, and send it off, we shall be less in error.*

§7 In summary, then, if we do these things we shall best be able to reach the intermediate condition. But presumably this is difficult, especially
15 in particular cases, since it is not easy to define the way we should be angry, with whom, about what, for how long. For sometimes, indeed, we ourselves praise deficient people and call them mild, and sometimes praise quarrelsome people and call them manly.

§8 Still, we are not blamed if we deviate a little in excess or deficiency
20 from doing well, but only if we deviate a long way, since then we are easily noticed. But how great and how serious a deviation receives blame is
1109b not easy to define in an account; for nothing else perceptible is easily defined either. Such things* are among particulars,* and the judgment depends on perception.*

§9 This is enough, then, to make it clear that in every case the inter-
25 mediate state is praised, but we must sometimes incline toward the excess, sometimes toward the deficiency; for that is the easiest way to hit the intermediate and good condition.

Book VI

Virtues of Thought

Aristotle

....

1

[The Mean and the Virtues of Thought]

Since we have said previously that we must choose the intermediate condi- *1138b*
tion, not the excess or the deficiency, and that the intermediate condition 20
is as the correct reason says, let us now determine what it says.* For in all
the states of character we have mentioned, as well as in the others, there
is a target that the person who has reason focuses on and so tightens or
relaxes; and there is a definition of the means, which we say are between
excess and deficiency because they accord with the correct reason. 25

§2 To say this is admittedly true, but it is not at all clear.* For in
other pursuits directed by a science, it is equally true that we must labor
and be idle neither too much nor too little, but the intermediate amount
prescribed by correct reason. But knowing only this, we would be none 30
the wiser about, for instance, the medicines to be applied to the body, if
we were told we must apply the ones that medical science prescribes and
in the way that the medical scientist applies them.

§3 That is why our account of the states of the soul, in the same way,
must not only be true as far as it has gone, but we must also determine
what the correct reason is, that is to say,* what its definition is.

§4 After we divided the virtues of the soul, we said that some are virtues 35
of character and some of thought. And so, having finished our discussion *1139a*
of the virtues of character, let us now discuss the others as follows, after
speaking first about the soul.

§5 Previously, then, we said there are two parts of the soul, one that 5
has reason, and one nonrational.* Now we should divide in the same

way the part that has reason. Let us assume there are two parts that have reason: with one we study beings whose principles do not admit of being otherwise than they are, and with the other we study beings whose principles admit of being otherwise.* For when the beings are of different kinds, the parts of the soul naturally suited to each of them are also of different kinds, since the parts possess knowledge by being somehow similar and appropriate [to their objects].

§6 Let us call one of these the scientific part, and the other the rationally calculating part; for deliberating is the same as rationally calculating, and no one deliberates about what cannot be otherwise. Hence the rationally calculating part is one part of the part of the soul that has reason.

§7 Hence we should find the best state* of the scientific part and the best state of the rationally calculating part; for this state is the virtue of each of them. Now a thing's virtue is relative to its own proper function, [and so we must consider the function of each part].*

2

[Thought, Desire, and Decision]

1139a There are three [capacities] in the soul—sense perception, understanding, desire*—that control action and truth. §2 Of these three, sense perception is clearly not the principle of any action, since beasts have perception, but no share in action.*

As assertion and denial are to thought, so pursuit and avoidance are to desire. Now virtue of character is a state that decides; and decision is a deliberative desire. If, then, the decision is excellent, the reason must be true and the desire correct, so that what reason asserts is what desire pursues. This, then, is thought and truth concerned with action. §3 The thought concerned with study, not with action or production, has its good or bad state in being true or false; for truth is the function of whatever thinks. But the function of what thinks about action is truth agreeing with correct desire.*

§4 The principle of an action—the source of motion, not the goal—is decision;* the principle of decision is desire and goal-directed reason.* That is why decision requires understanding and thought, and also a state of character; for acting well* or badly requires both thought and character.

§5 Thought by itself moves nothing; what moves us is goal-directed thought concerned with action.* For this thought is also the principle of productive thought; for every producer in his production aims at some [further] goal,* and the unqualified goal is not the product, which is only the [qualified] goal of some [production], and aims at some [further] goal. [An unqualified goal is] what we achieve in *action*, since acting well is the goal, and desire is for the goal. That is why* decision is either understanding combined with desire or desire combined with thought; and this is the sort of principle that a human being is.

§6 We do not decide to do what is already past; no one decides, for instance, to have sacked Troy. For neither do we deliberate about what is past, but only about what will be and admits of being or not being; and what is past does not admit of not having happened. That is why Agathon is correct to say 'Of this alone even a god is deprived—to make what is all done to have never happened.'*

The function of each of the understanding parts, then, is truth. And so the virtues of each part will be the states that best direct it toward the truth.*

3

[Scientific Knowledge]

Then let us begin again, and discuss these states of the soul.* Let us say, then, that there are five states in which the soul grasps the truth in its affirmation or denials. These are craft, scientific knowledge, prudence, wisdom, and understanding; for belief and supposition admit of being false.

§2 What science is, is evident from the following, if we must speak exactly and not be guided by [mere] similarities.* For we all suppose that what we know scientifically does not even admit of being otherwise; and whenever what admits of being otherwise escapes observation, we do not notice whether it is or is not, [and hence we do not know about it]. Hence what is known scientifically is by necessity. Hence it is everlasting; for the things that are by unqualified necessity are all everlasting, and everlasting things are ingenerable and indestructible.

§3 Further, every science seems to be teachable, and what is scientifically knowable is learnable. But all teaching is from what is already known, as we also say in the *Analytics*;* for some teaching is through induction, some by deduction, [which both require previous knowledge]. Induction [leads to] the principle, i.e., the universal,* whereas deduction proceeds from the universal. Hence deduction has principles from which

5

10

15

1139b

20

25

30

it proceeds and which are not themselves [reached] by deduction. Hence they are [reached] by induction.

§4 Scientific knowledge, then, is a demonstrative state, and has all the other features that in the *Analytics** we add to the definition. For one has scientific knowledge whenever one has the appropriate sort of confidence, and knows the principles; for if one does not know them better than the conclusion, one will have scientific knowledge [only] coincidentally.

So much for a definition of scientific knowledge.

4

[Craft Knowledge]

1140a What admits of being otherwise includes what is produced and what is achieved in action.* §2 Production and action are different; about them we rely also on [our] popular discussions. And so the state involving reason and concerned with action is different from the state involving reason and concerned with production. Nor is one included in the other;* for action is not production, and production is not action.

§3 Now building, for instance, is a craft, and is essentially a certain state involving reason concerned with production; there is no craft that is not a state involving reason concerned with production, and no such state that is not a craft. Hence a craft is the same as a state involving true reason concerned with production.

§4 Every craft is concerned with coming to be, and the exercise of the craft is the study* of how something that admits of being and not being comes to be, something whose principle is in the producer and not in the product. For a craft is not concerned with things that are or come to be by necessity; nor with things that are by nature, since these have their principle in themselves.*

§5 Since production and action are different, craft must be concerned with production, not with action.

In a way craft and fortune are concerned with the same things, as Agathon says: 'Craft was fond of fortune, and fortune of craft.'*

§6 A craft, then, as we have said, is a state involving true reason concerned with production. Lack of craft is the contrary state involving false reason and concerned with production. Both are concerned with what admits of being otherwise.

5

[Prudence]

To grasp what prudence is, we should first study the sort of people we call 25
prudent. It seems proper to a prudent person to be able to deliberate finely*
about things that are good and beneficial for himself, not about some
restricted area*—about what sorts of things promote health or strength, for
instance—but about what sorts of things promote living well in general.*

§2 A sign of this is the fact that we call people prudent about some
[restricted area] whenever they calculate well to promote some excellent 30
end, in an area where there is no craft.* Hence where [living well] as a
whole is concerned, the deliberative person will also be prudent.

§3 Now no one deliberates about things that cannot be otherwise
or about things that cannot be achieved in his action. Hence, if science
involves demonstration, but there is no demonstration of anything whose
principles admit of being otherwise (since every such thing itself admits 35
of being otherwise); and if we cannot deliberate about things that are by 1140b
necessity; it follows that prudence is not science nor yet craft knowledge.
It is not science, because what is achievable in action admits of being
otherwise; and it is not craft knowledge, because action and production
belong to different kinds.

§4 The remaining possibility, then, is that prudence is a state grasping 5
the truth, involving reason, concerned with action about things that are
good or bad for a human being. For production has its end in something
other than itself, but action does not, since its end is acting well itself.*

§5 That is why Pericles and such people are the ones whom we regard
as prudent, because they are able to study what is good for themselves 10
and for human beings; we think that household managers and politicians
are such people.*

This is also how we come to give temperance (*sōphrosunē*) its name,
because we think that it preserves prudence (*sōzousan tēn phronēsin*).* 1140b
§6 It preserves the [right] sort of supposition. For the sort of supposition
that is corrupted and perverted by the pleasant or painful is not every
sort—not, for instance, the supposition that the triangle does or does 15
not have two right angles—but suppositions about what is achievable in
action. For the principles of things achievable in action are their goal,
but if someone is corrupted because of pleasure or pain, no [appropriate]
principle can appear to him, and it cannot appear that this is the right
goal and cause of all his choice and action; for vice corrupts the principle.* 20

And so prudence must be a state grasping the truth, involving reason, and concerned with action about human goods.*

§7 Moreover, there is virtue [or vice in the use] of craft, but not [in the use] of prudence. Further, in a craft, someone who makes errors voluntarily is more choiceworthy; but with prudence, as with the virtues, the reverse is true. Clearly, then, prudence is a virtue, not craft knowledge.*

§8 There are two parts of the soul that have reason. Prudence is a virtue of one of them, of the part that has belief; for belief is concerned, as prudence is, with what admits of being otherwise.

Moreover, it is not only a state involving reason. A sign of this is the fact that such a state can be forgotten, but prudence cannot.*

6

[Understanding]

Scientific knowledge is supposition about universals, things that are by necessity. Further, everything demonstrable and every science have principles, since scientific knowledge involves reason. Hence there can be neither scientific knowledge nor craft knowledge nor prudence about the principles of what is scientifically known. For what is scientifically known is demonstrable, [but the principles are not]; and craft and prudence are about what admits of being otherwise. Nor is wisdom [exclusively] about principles;* for it is proper to the wise person to have a demonstration of some things.

§2 [The states of the soul] by which we always grasp the truth and never make mistakes, about what can or cannot be otherwise, are scientific knowledge, prudence, wisdom, and understanding. But none of the first three—prudence, scientific knowledge, wisdom—is possible about principles. The remaining possibility, then, is that we have understanding about principles.*

7

[Wisdom versus Prudence]

We ascribe wisdom in crafts to the people who have the most exact expertise in the crafts.* For instance, we call Pheidias a wise stoneworker and Polycleitus a wise bronze worker; and by wisdom we signify precisely virtue in a craft. §2 But we also think some people are wise in general,

not wise in some [restricted] area, or in some other [specific] way (as   15
Homer says in the *Margites*: 'The gods did not make him a digger or a
ploughman or wise in anything else').* Clearly, then, wisdom is the most
exact [form] of scientific knowledge.

§3 Hence the wise person must not only know what is derived from
the principles of a science, but also grasp the truth about the principles. Therefore wisdom is understanding plus scientific knowledge; it
is scientific knowledge of the most honorable things that has received
[understanding as] its coping stone.*

For it would be absurd for someone to think that political science or   20
prudence is the most excellent science;* for the best thing in the universe
is not a human being [and the most excellent science must be of the best
things].

§4 Moreover,* if what is good and healthy for human beings and for
fish is not the same, whereas what is white or straight is always the same,
everyone would also say that the content of wisdom is the same in every   25
case, but the content of prudence* is not. For the agent they would call
prudent is the one who studies well each question about his own [good],
and he is the one to whom they would entrust such questions.* That is
why prudence is also ascribed to some of the beasts, the ones that are
evidently capable of forethought about their own life.*

It is also evident that wisdom is not the same as political science.* For   30
if people are to say that science about what is beneficial to themselves [as
human beings] counts as wisdom, there will be many types of wisdom
[corresponding to the different species of animals]. For if there is no one
medical science about all beings, there is no one science about the good
of all animals, but a different science about each specific good. [Hence
there will be many types of wisdom, contrary to our assumption that it has
always the same content.] It does not matter if human beings are the best
among the animals; for there are other beings of a far more divine nature   1141b
than human beings—most evidently, for instance, the beings composing
the universe.

§5 What we have said makes it clear that wisdom is both scientific
knowledge and understanding about the things that are by nature most
honorable. That is why people say that Anaxagoras or Thales* or that sort   5
of person is wise, but not prudent, whenever they see that he is ignorant of
what benefits himself. And so they say that what he knows is extraordinary,
amazing, difficult, and divine, but useless, because it is not human goods
that he looks for.

10 §6 Prudence, by contrast, is about human concerns, about things open to deliberation. For we say that deliberating well is the function of the prudent person more than anyone else; but no one deliberates about

1141b things that cannot be otherwise, or about things lacking any goal that is a good achievable in action.* The unqualifiedly good deliberator is the one whose aim accords with rational calculation in pursuit of the best good for a human being that is achievable in action.*

15 §7 Nor is prudence about universals only. It must also acquire knowledge of particulars, since it is concerned with action and action is about particulars.* That is why in other areas also some people who lack knowledge but have experience are better in action than others who have knowledge. For someone who knows that light meats are digestible and

20 [hence] healthy,* but not which sorts of meats are light, will not produce health; the one who knows that bird meats are light and healthy* will be better at producing health. And since prudence is concerned with action, it must possess both [the universal and the particular knowledge] or the [particular] more [than the universal]. Here too, however, [as in medicine] there is a ruling [science].*

8

[Types of Prudence]

Political science and prudence are the same state, but their being is not the same.*

25 §2 One type of prudence about the city is the ruling part; this is legislative science. The type concerned with particulars [often] monopolizes the name 'political science' that [properly] applies to both types in common.* This type is concerned with action and deliberation, since [it is concerned with decrees and] the decree* is to be acted on as the last thing [reached in deliberation]. Hence these people are the only ones who are said to be politically active; for these are the only ones who put [political science] into practice, as hand-craftsmen put [a craft] into practice.

30 §3 Similarly, prudence concerned with the individual himself seems most of all to be counted as prudence; and this [type of prudence often] monopolizes the name 'prudence' that [properly] applies [to all types] in common. Of the other types, one is household science, another legislative, another political, one type of which is deliberative and another judicial.

§4 In fact knowledge of what is [good] for oneself is one species [of prudence].* But there is much difference [in opinions] about it.* The one who knows about himself, and spends his time on his own concerns, seems to be prudent, while politicians seem to be too active.* Hence Euripides says, 'Surely I cannot be prudent, since I could have been inactive, numbered among all the many in the army, and have had an equal share. ... For those who go too far and are too active....'* For people seek what is good for themselves, and suppose that this [inactivity] is the right action [to achieve their good]. Hence this belief has led to the view that these are the prudent people.* Presumably, however, one's own welfare requires household management and a political system. Further, [another reason for the difference of opinion is that] it is unclear, and should be examined, how one must manage one's own affairs.

§5 A sign of what has been said [about the unclarity of what prudence requires] is the fact that whereas young people become accomplished in geometry and mathematics, and wise within these limits, prudent young people do not seem to be found.* The reason is that prudence is concerned with particulars as well as universals, and particulars become known from experience, but a young person lacks experience, since some length of time is needed to produce it.

§6 Indeed [to understand the difficulty and importance of experience] we might consider why a child can become accomplished in mathematics, but not in wisdom or natural science. Surely it is because mathematical objects are reached through abstraction,* whereas in these other cases the principles* are reached from experience. Young people, then, [lacking experience], have no real conviction in these other sciences, but only say the words,* whereas the nature of mathematical objects is clear to them.

§7 Further, [prudence is difficult because it is deliberative and] deliberation may be in error about either the universal or the particular.* For [we may wrongly suppose] either that all sorts of heavy water are bad or that this water is heavy.

§8 It is apparent that prudence is not scientific knowledge; for, as we said, it concerns the last thing [i.e., the particular], since this is what is achievable in action.* §9 Hence it is opposite to understanding.* For understanding is about the [first] terms,* [those] that have no account of them; but prudence is about the last thing, an object of perception, not of scientific knowledge. This is not the perception of special objects,* but the sort by which we perceive that the last among mathematical objects is a

1142a

1142a

5

10

15

20

25

30 triangle; for it will stop there too.* This is another species [of perception than perception of special objects]; but it is still perception more than prudence is.*

9

[Good Deliberation]

Inquiry and deliberation are different, since deliberation is a type of inquiry. We must also grasp what good deliberation is,* and see whether it is some sort of scientific knowledge, or belief, or good guessing, or some other kind of thing.

1142b   §2 First of all, then, it is not scientific knowledge. For we do not inquire for what we already know; but good deliberation is a type of deliberation, and a deliberator inquires and rationally calculates.

1142b   Moreover, it is not good guessing either. For good guessing involves no reasoning, and is done quickly; but we deliberate a long time, and it is
5   said that we must act quickly on the result of our deliberation, but deliberate slowly.* §3 Further, quick thinking is different from good deliberation, and quick thinking is a kind of good guessing.

Nor is good deliberation just any sort of belief. Rather, since the bad deliberator is in error, and the good deliberator deliberates correctly, good deliberation is clearly some sort of correctness.

10   But it is not correctness in scientific knowledge or in belief. For there is no correctness in scientific knowledge,* since there is no error in it either; and correctness in belief consists in truth, [but correctness in deliberation does not].* Further, everything about which one has belief is already determined, [but what is deliberated about is not yet determined].

However, good deliberation requires reason; hence the remaining possibility is that it belongs to thought. For thought is not yet assertion; [and this is why it is not belief]. For belief is not inquiry, but already an
15   assertion; but in deliberating, either well or badly, we inquire for something and rationally calculate about it.

§4 But good deliberation is a certain sort of correctness in deliberation. That is why we must first inquire what [this correctness] is and what it is [correctness] about.* Since there are several types of correctness, clearly good deliberation will not be every type.* For the incontinent or base person will use rational calculation to reach what he proposes to see, and
20   so will have deliberated correctly [if that is all it takes], but will have got

himself a great evil.* Having deliberated well seems, on the contrary, to be some sort of good; for the sort of correctness in deliberation that makes it good deliberation is the sort that reaches a good.*

§5 However, we can reach a good by a false inference, as well [as by correct deliberation], so that we reach the right thing to do, but by the wrong steps, when the middle term is false.* Hence this type of deliberation, leading us by the wrong steps to the right thing to do, is not enough for good deliberation either.

§6 Further, one person may deliberate a long time before reaching the right thing to do, while another reaches it quickly. Nor, then, is the first condition enough for good deliberation; good deliberation is correctness that accords with what is beneficial, about the right thing, in the right way, and at the right time.

§7 Further, our deliberation may be either good without qualification or good only to the extent that it promotes some [limited] end.* Hence unqualifiedly good deliberation is the sort that correctly promotes the unqualified end [i.e., the highest good], while the [limited] sort is the sort that correctly promotes some [limited] end.* If, then, having deliberated well is proper to a prudent person, good deliberation will be the type of correctness that accords with what is expedient for promoting the end about which prudence is true supposition.*

10

[Comprehension]

Comprehension, i.e. good comprehension, makes people, as we say, comprehend and comprehend well.* It is not the same as scientific knowledge in general. Nor is it the same as belief, since, if it were, everyone would have comprehension. Nor is it any one of the specific sciences [with its own specific area], in the way that medicine is about what is healthy or geometry is about magnitudes. For comprehension is neither about what always is and is unchanging nor about just anything that comes to be. It is about what we might be puzzled about and might deliberate about. That is why it is about the same things as prudence, but not the same as prudence.

§2 For prudence is prescriptive, since its end is what action we must or must not do, whereas comprehension only judges.* (For comprehension and good comprehension are the same; and so are people with

25

30

1143a

5

10

comprehension and with good comprehension.) Comprehension is neither having prudence nor acquiring it.

§3 Rather, it is similar to the way learning is called comprehending when someone applies scientific knowledge. In the same way comprehension consists in the application of belief to judge someone else's remarks on a question that concerns prudence, and moreover it must judge them finely since judging well is the same as judging finely. §4 That is how the name 'comprehension' was attached to the comprehension that makes people have good comprehension. It is derived from the comprehension found in learning; for we often call learning comprehending.*

11

[Practical Thought and Particulars]

The [state] called consideration makes people, as we say, considerate and makes them have consideration; it is the correct judgment of the decent person.* A sign of this is our saying that the decent person more than others is considerate, and that it is decent to be considerate about some things. Considerateness is the correct consideration that judges what is decent; and correct consideration judges what is true.

§2 It is reasonable that all these states tend in the same direction.* For we ascribe consideration, comprehension, prudence, and understanding to the same people, and say that these have consideration, and thereby understanding, and that they are prudent and comprehending. For all these capacities are about the last things, i.e., particulars.* Moreover, someone has comprehension and good consideration, or has considerateness, in being able to judge about the matters that concern the prudent person; for the decent is the common concern of all good people in relations with other people.

§3 [These states are all concerned with particulars because] all the things achievable in action are particular and last things. For the prudent person also must recognize [things achievable in action], while comprehension and consideration are concerned with things achievable in action, and these are last things.

§4 Understanding is also concerned with the last things, and in both directions.* For there is understanding, not a rational account, both about the first terms and about the last.* In demonstrations understanding is about the unchanging terms that are first. In [premises] about action understanding is about the last term, the one that admits of being otherwise, and [hence] about the minor premise.* For these last terms are beginnings of the [end] to be aimed at, since universals are reached from particulars.* 5

§5 We must, therefore, have perception of these particulars, and this perception is understanding.* §6 That is why understanding is both 9, 10 beginning and end; for demonstrations [begin] from these things and are about them.*

§5 That is why these states actually seem to grow naturally,* so that, 6 whereas no one seems to have natural wisdom,* people seem to have natural consideration, comprehension, and judgment. §6 A sign [of their apparent natural character] is our thinking that they also correspond to someone's age, and the fact that understanding and consideration belong to a certain age, as though nature were the cause. And so we must attend to the undemonstrated remarks and beliefs of experienced and older people or of prudent people, no less than to demonstrations. For these people see correctly because experience has given them their eye.

§7 We have said, then, what prudence and wisdom are; what each is 15 about; and that each is the virtue of a different part of the soul.*

12

[Puzzles about Prudence and Wisdom]

One might, however, go through some puzzles about what use they are.* For wisdom is not concerned with any sort of coming into being, and 20 hence will not study any source of human happiness. Admittedly, prudence will study this; but what do we need it for? For knowledge of what 25, 26 is healthy or fit (i.e., of what results from the state of health, not of what produces it) makes us no readier to act appropriately if we are already 27 healthy; for having the science of medicine or gymnastics makes us no 21 readier to act appropriately. Similarly, prudence is the science of what is just and what is fine, and what is good for a human being; but this is how the good man acts; and if we are already good, knowledge of them makes 25 us no readier to act appropriately, since virtues are states [activated in 1143b actions].*

§2 If we concede that prudence is not useful for this, should we say 28 it is useful for becoming good? In that case it will be no use to those who 30 are already excellent.* Nor, however, will it be any use to those who are not. For it will not matter to them* whether they have it themselves or take the advice of others who have it. The advice of others will be quite adequate for us, just as it is with health: we wish to be healthy, but still do not learn medical science.

35 §3 Besides, it would seem absurd for prudence, inferior as it is to wisdom, to control it [as a superior. But this will be the result], since the science that produces also rules and prescribes about its product.*

We must discuss these questions; for so far we have only raised the puzzles about them.

1144a §4 First of all, let us state that both prudence and wisdom must be choiceworthy in themselves, even if neither produces anything at all; for each is the virtue of one of the two [rational] parts [of the soul].*

§5 Secondly, they do produce something. Wisdom produces happiness, 5 not in the way that medical science produces health, but in the way that health produces [health].* For since wisdom is a part of virtue as a whole, it makes us happy because it is a state that we possess and activate.

§6 Further, we fulfill our function* insofar as we have prudence and virtue of character; for virtue makes the goal correct, and prudence makes 10 the things promoting the goal [correct].* The fourth part of the soul, the nutritive part, has no such virtue [related to our function], since no action is up to it to do or not to do.

§7 To answer the claim that prudence will make us no better at achieving fine and just actions,* we must begin from a little further back [in our 15 discussion]. We begin here: we say that some people who do just actions are not yet thereby just, if, for instance, they do the actions prescribed by the laws either unwillingly or because of ignorance or because of some other end, not because of the actions themselves, even though they do the right actions, those that the excellent person ought to do.* Equally, however, it would seem to be possible for someone to do each type of action in 20 the state that makes him a good person, that is to say, because of decision and for the sake of the actions themselves.*

§8 Now virtue makes the decision correct;* but the actions that are naturally to be done to fulfill the decision are the concern not of virtue, but of another capacity.* We must grasp them more perspicuously before continuing our discussion.

25 §9 There is a capacity, called cleverness, which is such as to be able to do the actions that tend to promote whatever goal is assumed* and to attain them.* If, then, the goal is fine, cleverness is praiseworthy, and if

the goal is base, cleverness is unscrupulousness. That is why both prudent and unscrupulous people are called clever.*

§10 Prudence is not cleverness,* though it requires this capacity. *1144a* [Prudence,] this eye of the soul, requires virtue in order to reach its fully 30 developed state,* as we have said and as is clear. For inferences about actions have a principle, 'Since the end and the best good is this sort of thing' (whatever it actually is—let it be any old thing for the sake of argument).* And this [best good] is apparent only to the good person; for 35 vice perverts us and produces false views about the principles of actions. Evidently, then, we cannot be prudent without being good. *1144b*

13

[Prudence and Virtue of Character]

We must, then, also examine virtue over again.* For virtue is similar [in this way] to prudence; as prudence is related to cleverness, not the same but similar, so natural virtue is related to full virtue.* For each of us seems to possess his type of character to some extent by nature; for in fact we 5 are just, brave, prone to temperance, or have another feature, immediately from birth. But still we look for some further condition to be full goodness, and we expect to possess these features in another way. For these natural states belong to children and to beasts as well [as to adults], but without understanding they are evidently harmful.* At any rate, this much would 10 seem to be clear: Just as a heavy body moving around unable to see suffers a heavy fall because it has no sight, so it is with virtue. [A naturally well-endowed person without understanding will harm himself.]

§2 But if someone acquires understanding, he improves in his actions; and the state he now has, though still similar [to the natural one], will be fully virtue. And so, just as there are two sorts of conditions, cleverness and prudence, in the part of the soul that has belief, so also there are two 15 in the part that has character, natural virtue and full virtue. And of these full virtue cannot be acquired without prudence.*

§3 That is why* some say that all the virtues are [instances of] prudence, and why the inquiries Socrates used to undertake* were in one way correct, and in another way in error. For insofar as he thought all the 20 virtues are [instances of] prudence,* he was in error; but insofar as he thought they all require prudence, what he used to say was right.

§4 Here is a sign of this: Whenever people now define virtue, they all say what state it is and what it is related to, and then add that it is the state in accord with the correct reason.* Now the correct reason is the reason in accord with prudence; it would seem, then, that they all in a way intuitively believe that the state in accord with prudence is virtue.

§5 But we must make a slight change. For it is not merely the state in accord with the correct reason, but the state involving the correct reason, that is virtue.* And it is prudence that is the correct reason in this area. Socrates, then, used to think the virtues are [instances of] reason because he thought they are all [instances of] knowledge, whereas we think they involve reason.

§6 What we have said, then, makes it clear that we cannot be fully good without prudence, or prudent without virtue of character. And in this way we can also solve the dialectical argument that someone might use to show that the virtues are separated from one another.* For, [it is argued], since the same person is not naturally best suited for all the virtues, someone will already have one virtue before he gets another. This is indeed possible in the case of the natural virtues. It is not possible, however, in the case of the [full] virtues that someone must have to be called good without qualification; for one has all the virtues if and only if one has prudence, which is a single state.*

§7 And it is clear that, even if prudence were useless in action, we would need it because it is the virtue of this part of the soul,* and because the decision will not be correct without prudence or without virtue*—for [virtue] makes us achieve the end, whereas [prudence] makes us achieve the things that promote the end.*

§8 Moreover, prudence does not control wisdom or the better part of the soul, just as medical science does not control health.* For medical science does not use health, but only aims to bring health into being; hence it prescribes for the sake of health, but does not prescribe to health. Besides, [saying that prudence controls wisdom] would be like saying that political science rules the gods because it prescribes about everything in the city.

The Individual Virtues of Character

Aristotle

....

6

[Bravery; Its Scope]

First let us discuss bravery. We have already made it apparent that there is a mean about feelings of fear and confidence.* §2 What we fear, clearly, is what is frightening,* and such things are, speaking without qualification, bad things; hence people define fear as expectation of something bad.*

§3 Certainly we fear all bad things—for instance, bad reputation, poverty, sickness, friendlessness, death—but they do not all seem to concern the brave person. For fear of some bad things, such as bad reputation, is actually right and fine, and lack of fear is shameful; for if someone fears bad reputation, he is decent and properly prone to shame, and if he has no fear of it, he has no feeling of disgrace. Some, however, call this fearless person brave, by a transference of the name; for he has some similarity to the brave person, since the brave person is also a type of fearless person.

§4 Presumably it is wrong to fear poverty or sickness or, in general, [bad things] that are not the results of vice or caused by ourselves; still, someone who is fearless about these is not thereby brave. He is also called brave by similarity; for some people who are cowardly in the dangers of war are nonetheless generous, and face with confidence the [danger of] losing money.*

§5 Again, if someone is afraid of committing wanton aggression on children or women,* or of being envious or anything of that sort, that does not make him cowardly. And if someone is confident when he is going to be whipped for his crimes, that does not make him brave.

§6 Then what sorts of frightening conditions concern the brave person? Surely the most frightening; for no one stands firmer against terrifying conditions. Now death is most frightening of all, since it is a boundary, and when someone is dead nothing beyond it seems either good

1115a or bad for him any more. §7 Still, not even death in all conditions—on the sea, for instance, or in sickness—seems to be the brave person's concern.

30 §8 In what conditions, then, is death his concern? Surely in the finest conditions. Now such deaths are those in war, since they occur in the greatest and finest danger.* §9 This judgment is endorsed by the honors given in cities and by monarchs. §10 Hence someone is called fully 35 brave if he is intrepid in facing a fine death and the immediate dangers that bring death. And this is above all true of the dangers of war.

1115b §11 Certainly the brave person is also intrepid on the sea and in sickness, but not in the same way as seafarers are. For he has given up hope of safety, and objects to this sort of death [with nothing fine in it], but seafarers' experience makes them hopeful. §12 Moreover, we act like brave men on 5 occasions when we can use our strength, or when it is fine to be killed; and neither of these is true when we perish from shipwreck or sickness.

7

[Bravery; Its Characteristic Outlook]

Now what is frightening is not the same for everyone. We say, however, that some things are too frightening for a human being to resist;* these, then, are frightening for everyone, at least for everyone with any sense. 10 What is frightening, but not irresistible for a human being, varies in its seriousness and degree; and the same is true of what inspires confidence.

§2 The brave person is unperturbed, as far as a human being can be. Hence, though he will fear even the sorts of things that are not irresistible, he will stand firm against them, in the right way, as reason prescribes, for the sake of the fine, since this is the end aimed at by virtue.*

§3 It is possible to be more or less afraid of these frightening things, 15 and also possible to be afraid of what is not frightening as though it were frightening. §4 The cause of error may be fear of the wrong thing, or in the wrong way, or at the wrong time, or something of that sort; and the same is true for things that inspire confidence.

§5 Hence whoever stands firm against the right things and fears the right things, for the right end, in the right way, at the right time, and is correspondingly confident, is the brave person; for the brave person's actions and feelings accord with what something is worth, and follow what reason prescribes.

§6 Every activity aims at actions in accord with the state of character. 20
Now to the brave person bravery is fine; hence the end it aims at is also
fine, since each thing is defined by its end.* The brave person, then, aims
at the fine when he stands firm and acts in accord with bravery.

§7 Among those who go to excess the excessively fearless person has 25
no name—we said earlier that many cases have no names.* He would be
some sort of madman, or incapable of feeling distress, if he feared nothing, *1115b*
neither earthquake nor waves, as they say about the Celts.*

The person who is excessively confident about frightening things is
rash. §8 The rash person also seems to be a boaster, and a pretender 30
to bravery.* At any rate, the attitude to frightening things that the brave
person really has is the attitude that the rash person wants to appear to
have; hence he imitates the brave person where he can. §9 That is why
most of them are rash cowards; for, rash though they are on these [occa-
sions for imitation], they do not stand firm against anything frightening.
§12 Moreover, rash people are impetuous, wishing for dangers before *1116a7*
they arrive, but they shrink from them when they come. Brave people, on 8, 9
the contrary, are eager when in action, but keep quiet until then.*

§10 The person who is excessively afraid is the coward, since he fears *1115b34*
the wrong things, and in the wrong way, and so on. Certainly, he is also 35
deficient in confidence, but his excessive pain distinguishes him more *1116a*
clearly. §11 Hence, since he is afraid of everything, he is a despairing
sort. The brave person, on the contrary, is hopeful, since [he is confident
and] confidence is proper to a hopeful person.

§12 Hence the coward, the rash person, and the brave person are all 5
concerned with the same things, but have different states related to
them; the others are excessive or defective, but the brave person has the 7
intermediate and right state.

§13 As we have said, then, bravery is a mean about what inspires 10
confidence and about what is frightening in the conditions we have
described; it chooses and stands firm because that is fine or because
anything else is shameful. Dying to avoid poverty or erotic passion or something painful is proper to a coward, not to a brave person. For shirking
burdens is softness, and such a person stands firm [in the face of death] to 15
avoid an evil, not because standing firm is fine.*

8

[Conditions That Resemble Bravery]

Bravery, then, is something of this sort. But five other sorts of things are also called bravery.*

The bravery of citizens comes first, since it looks most like bravery. For citizens seem to stand firm against dangers with the aim of avoiding reproaches and legal penalties and of winning honors; that is why the bravest seem to be those who hold cowards in dishonor and do honor to brave people. §2 That is how Homer also describes them when he speaks of Diomede and Hector: 'Polydamas will be the first to heap disgrace on me', and 'For some time Hector speaking among the Trojans will say, "The son of Tydeus fled from me."'* §3 This is most like the [genuine] bravery described above, because it results from a virtue; for it is caused by shame and by desire for something fine, namely honor,* and by aversion from reproach, which is shameful.

§4 In this class we might also place those who are compelled by their superiors. However, they are worse to the extent that they act because of fear, not because of shame, and to avoid pain, not disgrace. For their commanders compel them, as Hector does; 'If I notice anyone shrinking back from the battle, nothing will save him from being eaten by the dogs.'* §5 Commanders who strike any troops who give ground, or who post them in front of ditches and suchlike, do the same thing, since they all compel them.* The brave person, however, must be moved by the fine, not by compulsion.

§6 Experience about a given situation also seems to be bravery; that is why Socrates actually thought that bravery is scientific knowledge.* Different people have this sort [of apparent courage] in different conditions. In wartime professional soldiers have it; for there seem to be many groundless alarms in war, and the professionals are the most familiar with these.* Hence they appear brave, since others do not know that the alarms are groundless. §7 Moreover, their experience makes them most capable in attack and defense, since they are skilled in the use of their weapons, and have the best weapons for attack and defense. §8 The result is that in fighting nonprofessionals they are like armed troops against unarmed, or trained athletes against ordinary people; for in these contests also the best fighters are the strongest and physically fittest, not the bravest.

§9 Professional soldiers, however, turn out to be cowards whenever the danger overstrains them* and they are inferior in numbers and equipment. For they are the first to run, whereas the citizen troops stand firm and get killed; this was what happened at the temple of Hermes.* For the citizens find it shameful to run, and find death more choiceworthy than safety at this cost. But the professionals from the start were facing the danger on the assumption of their superiority; once they learn their mistake, they run, since they are more afraid of being killed than of doing something shameful. That is not the brave person's character. 20

§10 Spirit is also counted as bravery; for those who act on spirit also seem to be brave—as beasts seem to be when they attack those who have wounded them—because brave people are also full of spirit.* For spirit is most eager to run and face dangers; hence Homer's words, 'put strength in his spirit', 'aroused strength and spirit', and 'his blood boiled'.* All these would seem to signify the arousal and the impulse of spirit. 25

30

§11 Now brave people act because of the fine, and their spirit cooperates with them. But beasts act because of pain; for they attack only because they have been wounded or frightened, (since they keep away from us in a forest). They are not brave, then, since distress and spirit drives them in an impulsive rush to meet danger, foreseeing none of the terrifying prospects. For if they were brave, hungry asses would also be brave, since they keep on feeding even if they are beaten;* and adulterers also do many daring actions because of lust. 35

1117a

§12 Human beings as well as beasts find it painful to be angered, and pleasant to exact a penalty. But those who fight for these reasons are not brave, though they are good fighters; for they fight because of their feelings, not because of the fine nor as reason prescribes. Still, they have something similar [to bravery]. The [bravery] caused by spirit would seem to be the most natural sort, and to be [genuine] bravery once it has also acquired decision and the goal.* 5

4

5

§13 Hopeful people are not brave either; for their many victories over many opponents make them confident in dangers. They are somewhat similar to brave people, since both are confident. But whereas brave people are confident for the reason given earlier, the hopeful are confident because they think they are stronger and nothing could happen to them; §14 drunks do the same sort of thing, since they become hopeful. When things turn out differently from how they expected, they run away. The brave person, on the contrary, stands firm against what is and 9, 10

15

appears frightening to a human being; he does this because it is fine to stand firm and shameful to fail.

§15 Indeed, that is why someone who is unafraid and unperturbed in emergencies seems braver than [someone who is unafraid only] when he is warned in advance; for his action proceeds more from his state of character, because it proceeds less from preparation.* For if we are warned in advance, we might decide what to do [not only because of our state of character, but] also by reason and rational calculation; but in emergencies [we must decide] in accord with our state of character.*

§16 Those who act in ignorance also appear brave, and indeed they are close to hopeful people, though inferior to them insofar as they lack the self-esteem of hopeful people. That is why the hopeful stand firm for some time, whereas if ignorant people have been deceived and then realize or suspect that things are different, they run. That was what happened to the Argives when they stumbled on the Spartans and took them for Sicyonians.*

§17 We have described, then, the character of brave people and of those who seem to be brave.

9

[Feelings Proper to Bravery]

Bravery is about feelings of confidence and fear—not, however, about both in the same way, but more about frightening things. For someone is brave if he is undisturbed and in the right state about these, more than if he is in this state about things inspiring confidence.

§2 As we said, then, standing firm against what is painful makes us call people brave; that is why bravery is both painful and justly praised, since it is harder to stand firm against something painful than to refrain from something pleasant. §3 Nonetheless, the end that bravery aims at seems to be pleasant, though obscured by its surroundings. This is what happens in athletic contests. For boxers find that the end they aim at, the crown and the honors, is pleasant, but, being made of flesh and blood, they find it distressing and painful to take the punches and to bear all the hard work; and because there are so many of these painful things, the end, being small, appears to have nothing pleasant in it.

§4 And so, if the same is true for bravery, the brave person will find death and wounds painful, and suffer them unwillingly, but he will endure

them because that is fine or because failure is shameful.* Indeed, the   10
truer it is that he has every virtue and the happier he is, the more pain
he will feel at the prospect of death. For this sort of person, more than
anyone, finds it worthwhile to be alive, and knows he is being deprived of
the greatest goods, and this is painful. But he is no less brave for all
that; presumably, indeed, he is all the braver, because he chooses what is   15
fine in war at the cost of all these goods. §5 It is not true, then, in the
case of every virtue that its active exercise is pleasant; it is pleasant only
insofar as we attain the end.

§6 But presumably it is quite possible for brave people, given the
character we have described, not to be the best soldiers.* Perhaps the best
will be those who are less brave, but possess no other good; for they are
ready to face dangers, and they sell their lives for small gains.   20

§7 So much for bravery. It is easy to grasp what it is, in outline at least,
from what we have said.

10

[Temperance; Its Scope]

Let us discuss temperance next; for bravery and temperance seem to be the
virtues of the nonrational parts. Temperance, then, is a mean concerned   25
with pleasures, as we have already said; for it is concerned less, and in
a different way, with pains. Intemperance appears in this same area too.
Let us, then, now distinguish the specific pleasures that concern them.

§2 First, let us distinguish pleasures of the soul from those of the body.
Love of honor and of learning, for instance, are among the pleasures of
the soul; for though a lover of one of these enjoys it, only his thought, not   30
his body, is at all affected. Those concerned with such pleasures are called
neither temperate nor intemperate. The same applies to those concerned
with any of the other nonbodily pleasures; for lovers of tales, storytellers,   35
those who waste their days on trivialities, are called babblers, but not   *1117b*
intemperate. Nor do we call people intemperate if they feel pain over   1118a
money or friends.

§3 Temperance, then, will be about bodily pleasures, but not even
about all of these. For those who find enjoyment in objects of sight, such
as colors, shapes, a painting, are called neither temperate nor intemperate,   5
even though it would also seem possible to enjoy these either rightly or
excessively and deficiently. §4 The same is true for hearing; no one is

ever called intemperate for excessive enjoyment of songs or playacting, or temperate for the right enjoyment of them.

§5 Nor is this said about someone enjoying smells, except coincidentally.* For someone is called intemperate not for enjoying the smell of apples or roses or incense, but rather for enjoying the smell of perfumes or cooked delicacies. For these are the smells an intemperate person enjoys because they remind him of the objects of his appetite. §6 And we can see that others also enjoy the smells of food if they are hungry.* It is the enjoyment of the things [that he is reminded of by these smells] that is proper to an intemperate person, since these are the objects of his appetite.

§7 Nor do other animals find pleasures from these senses, except coincidentally. What a hound enjoys, for instance, is not the smell of a hare, but eating it; but the hare's smell made the hound perceive it. And what a lion enjoys is not the sound of the ox, but eating it; but since the ox's sound made the lion perceive that it was near, the lion appears to enjoy the sound. Similarly, what pleases him is not the sight of 'a deer or a wild goat',* but the prospect of food.

§8 The pleasures that concern temperance and intemperance are those that are shared with the other animals, and so appear slavish and bestial.* These pleasures are touch and taste.*

§9 However, they seem to deal even with taste very little or not at all. For taste discriminates flavors—the sort of thing that wine tasters and cooks savoring food do; but people, or intemperate people at any rate, do not much enjoy this. Rather, they enjoy the gratification that comes entirely through touch, in eating and drinking and in what are called the pleasures of sex. §10 That is why a glutton actually prayed for his throat to become longer than a crane's, showing that he took pleasure in the touching.* And so the sense that concerns intemperance is the most widely shared, and seems justifiably open to reproach, since we have it insofar as we are animals, not insofar as we are human beings.

§11 To enjoy these things, then, and to like them most of all, is bestial. For indeed the most civilized of the pleasures coming through touch, such as those produced by rubbing and warming in gymnasia, are excluded from intemperance, since the touching that is proper to the intemperate person concerns only some parts of the body, not all of it.

11

[Temperance; Its Outlook]

Some appetites seem to be shared [by everyone], while others seem to   *1119a*
be additions that are distinctive [of different people]. The appetite for   10
nourishment, for instance, is natural, since everyone who lacks nourishment, dry or liquid, has an appetite for it, sometimes for both; and, as
Homer says, the young in their prime [all] have an appetite for sex.* Not
everyone, however, has an appetite for a specific sort of food or drink or
sex, or for the same things. §2 That is why an appetite of this type seems
to be distinctive of [each of] us. Still, this also includes a natural element,
since different sorts of people find different sorts of things more pleasant,
and there are some things that are more pleasant for everyone than things
chosen at random would be.

§3 In natural appetites few people are in error, and only in one direc-   15
tion, toward excess. Eating indiscriminately or drinking until we are too
full is exceeding the quantity that accords with nature; for [the object of]
natural appetite is the filling of a lack. That is why these people are called
'gluttons', showing that they glut their bellies past what is right;* that is   20
how especially slavish people turn out.

§4 With the pleasures that are distinctive of different people, many
make errors and in many ways; for people are called lovers of something
if they enjoy the wrong things, or if they enjoy something in the wrong
way. And in all these ways intemperate people go to excess. For some of   25
the things they enjoy are hateful, and hence wrong; distinctive pleasures
that it is right to enjoy they enjoy more than is right, and more than most
people enjoy them.

§5 Clearly, then, with pleasures excess is intemperance, and is
blameworthy. With pains, however, we are not called temperate, as we are
called brave, for standing firm against them, or intemperate for not   30
standing firm. Rather, someone is intemperate because he feels more
pain than is right at failing to get pleasant things; and even this pain is
produced by the pleasure [he takes in them]. And someone is temperate
because he does not feel pain at the absence of what is pleasant, or at
refraining from it.

§6 The intemperate person, then, has an appetite for all pleasant   *1119a*
things, or rather for the most pleasant of them, and his appetite leads him
to choose these at the cost of the other things. That is why he also feels

pain both when he fails to get something and when he has an appetite for it, since appetite involves pain. It would seem absurd, however, to suffer pain because of pleasure.

§7 People who are deficient in pleasures and enjoy them less than is right are not found very much. For that sort of insensibility is not human; indeed, even the other animals discriminate among foods, enjoying some but not others. If someone finds nothing pleasant, or preferable to anything else, he is far from being human. The reason he has no name is that he is not found much.

§8 The temperate person has an intermediate state in relation to these [bodily pleasures]. For he finds no pleasure in what most pleases the intemperate person, but finds it disagreeable; he finds no pleasure at all in the wrong things. He finds no intense pleasure in any [bodily pleasures], suffers no pain at their absence, and has no appetite for them, or only a moderate appetite, not to the wrong degree or at the wrong time or anything else at all of that sort.* If something is pleasant and conducive to health or fitness, he will desire this moderately and in the right way; and he will desire in the same way anything else that is pleasant, if it is no obstacle to health and fitness, does not deviate from the fine, and does not exceed his means. For the opposite sort of person likes these pleasures more than they are worth; that is not the temperate person's character, but he likes them as correct reason prescribes.

12

[Intemperance]

Intemperance is more like a voluntary condition than cowardice; for it is caused by pleasure, which is choiceworthy, whereas cowardice is caused by pain, which is to be avoided.* §2 Moreover, pain disturbs and ruins the nature of the sufferer, while pleasure does nothing of the sort; intemperance, then, is more voluntary. That is why it is also more open to reproach. For it is also easier to acquire the habit of facing pleasant things, since our life includes many of them and we can acquire the habit with no danger; but with frightening things the reverse is true.

§3 However, cowardice seems to be more voluntary than particular cowardly actions. For cowardice itself involves no pain, but the particular actions disturb us because of the pain [that causes them], so that people actually throw away their weapons and do all the other disgraceful actions. That is why these actions even seem to be forced [and hence involuntary].*

§4 For the intemperate person the reverse is true. The particular actions are the result of his appetite and desire, and so they are voluntary; but the whole condition is less voluntary [than the actions], since no one has an appetite to be intemperate.

§5 We also apply the name of intemperance to the errors of children, since they have some similarity.* Which gets its name from which does not matter for our present purposes, but clearly the posterior is called after the prior.

§6 The name would seem to be quite appropriately transferred. For the things that need to be tempered are those that desire shameful things and tend to grow large. Appetites and children are most like this; for children also live by appetite, and desire for the pleasant is found more in them than in anyone else.

§7 If, then, [the child or the appetitive part] is not obedient and subordinate to its rulers, it will go far astray. For when someone lacks understanding, his desire for the pleasant is insatiable and seeks indiscriminate satisfaction. The [repeated] active exercise of appetite increases the appetite he already had from birth, and if the appetites are large and intense, they actually expel rational calculation. That is why appetites must be moderate and few, and never contrary to reason. §8 This is the condition we call obedient and temperate. And just as the child's life must follow the instructions of his guide, so too the appetitive part must follow reason.*

§9 Hence the temperate person's appetitive part must agree with reason; for both [his appetitive part and his reason] aim at the fine, and the temperate person's appetites are for the right things, in the right ways, at the right times, which is just what reason also prescribes.

So much, then, for temperance.

1119b

5

1119b

10

15

The Justification of Human Rights

David Little[1]

....

T his article is divided into two sections. The first part summarizes arguments regarding the justification of human rights and the relation of human rights to religion developed more extensively elsewhere.[2] The second part provides the intellectual background of the arguments, and is intended to elaborate and elucidate key ideas contained in the summary.

I

The position defended here follows from an effort to recover and rehabilitate the natural rights tradition. The idea of natural rights is taken not to depend on religious belief, though religious belief is certainly to be protected and accommodated. Rather, the idea of natural rights rests on an understanding of human nature as "rational, self-aware, and morally responsible."[3]

This understanding supports a primary notion of subjective rights, which means that all individuals, simply as individuals, possess an entitlement to demand (or have demanded for them) a certain performance or forbearance under threat of sanction for noncompliance. The understanding also entails certain correlative duties and obligations owed by every individual in respect to protecting the rights of others.

Though moral and legal rights may converge, they are distinguishable in regard to the character of the applicable sanction: *legal rights* are physically enforceable within a system of laws whose

---

1 A version of this summary, entitled "The Justification of Human Rights," was delivered at the Twentieth Annual Symposium on International Law and Religion, J. Reuben Clark Law School, Brigham Young University, October 7, 2013.

2 David Little, Essays On Religion And Human Rights: Ground To Stand On (2015).

3 Brian Tierney, The Idea Of Natural Rights: Studies On Natural Rights, Natural Law And Church Law, 1150–1625 (1997). "A 'right' is an entitlement, a due liberty and power to do or not to do certain things; 'natural' means what is neither of human devising (by law or by agreement) nor conferred by a special command of God [or other supernatural warrant]. Natural rights are thus entitlements belonging to human nature as such, in virtue of the superanimal sensibilities and capacities, and therefore to every human being." T.E. Jessop, *Natural Rights, in* Dictionary Of Christian Ethics 225 (1967). As they developed in the Western Christian tradition, natural rights have been considered "minimal" or "vestigial" in that they are "left over" after "the fall," or the willful defection of human beings from the divinely-appointed standards of human fulfillment. As such, they provide imperatives of moral restraint and guidance that are necessary but by no means sufficient for human fulfillment.

officials possess effective authority over a monopoly of legitimate force; *moral rights* are otherwise enforceable, for example, by verbal censure.

The range of subjective rights under consideration is focused especially on the protection of certain requirements for survival taken to be common to every human being. Among other things, natural rights protect against *arbitrary force*, which, minimally, is the infliction of death, physical impairment, severe pain/suffering for entirely self-serving and/or knowingly mistaken reasons. To refer only to self-interest or knowingly to deceive in the act of inflicting death, severe pain, etc., is "morally incomprehensible" because the reasons given are no reasons at all.[4] This is not an observation about what human beings happen to believe or not. It is an observation about what, as rational and moral agents, human beings *are able* to believe or not, *are able* to make sense of or not. It is about the meaning of moral reason as regards the justification of action pertaining to critical aspects of human survival. Thus, the random slaughter of some twenty-six school children and teachers in Newtown, Connecticut in December 2012 is necessarily regarded as an act of "senseless violence."

On this understanding, force (as sanction) may be used in response to arbitrary force so long as it is demonstrably aimed at combating and restraining arbitrary force, and does that consistent with three "rules of reason": necessity, proportionality, and effectiveness.

Accordingly, it is held that human rights language, consisting of rights regarded as both moral and legal, rests on such an understanding. Six points may help clarify this understanding of human rights language.

1. Such language was drafted and codified in direct response to a paradigmatic case of arbitrary force, namely, the record, particularly, of German fascist practices before and during World War II.

2. It enshrines a basic set of rights, referred to in Article 4 of the International Covenant on Civil and Political Rights as "nonderogable" (nonabridgeable) rights, which protect everyone against the worst forms of arbitrary force: extra-judicial killing, torture, "cruel, inhuman, or degrading treatment or punishment," enslavement, denials of certain forms of due process, and violations of freedom of conscience, religion or belief. Protection against discrimination "solely on the ground of race, colour, sex, language, religion or social origin" is also included.[5] We should add to this list what are called "atrocity crimes," as codified in the Statute of Rome, the Charter of the International Criminal Court. Genocide, crimes against humanity, war crimes, and

---

4 A case of "necessity," in which an innocent party is killed in order for someone else to survive, is not an exception to this statement since the reasons excusing the act must also include strong proof that there was no alternative course of action. Such a defense is based *not only* on a reference to the self-interest of the one doing the killing. It therefore does not utterly disregard the interests of the victim, as in a "pure" case of arbitrary force. Still, cases of necessity *are* inescapably perplexing from a moral point of view precisely because of the gravity of the prohibition against hurting others to one's advantage. As an exhibit of the unavoidable perplexity, see, for example, Hugo Grotius's somewhat tortuous discussion of the issue. Hugo Grotius, Rights of War and Peace, Including the Law of Nature and of Nations 92, 92–94 (1979).

5 Articles 6, 7, 8 (paragraphs 1 and 2), 11, 15, 16 and 18, explicitly identified as non-derogable, appear in Article 4, paragraph 2 of the ICCPR. Int'l Covenant on Civil & Political Rights, Dec. 19, 1966, 999 U.N.T.S. 171–78. The prohibition against discrimination is mentioned in Article 4, paragraph 1 may also be assumed to be non-derogable.

aggression, as defined in the Charter,[6] are all egregious examples of arbitrary force. Beyond these provisions, there is no list of nonderogable rights in the International Covenant on Economic, Social, and Cultural Rights (ICESCR), but there are some interesting developments in that direction. In General Comment 14, the Committee on Economic, Social, and Cultural Rights has enumerated a set of "core obligations" requisite for guaranteeing Article 12 of the ICESCR, which guarantees "the right of everyone to the enjoyment of the highest attainable standard of physical and mental health," and it has ruled that "a State party cannot, under any circumstances whatsoever, justify its non-compliance with the core obligations ... which are non-derogable."[7] Failure to enforce these obligations, where feasible, would constitute *arbitrary neglect*, a close relative of arbitrary force.

3. It adds a set of "derogable" rights (abridgeable under only the most extreme circumstances, such as emergencies), like freedom of speech, assembly, and participation in government, that are designed to assure maximum protection against the violation of nonderogable rights.

4. Though human rights language explicitly obligates individuals, it also obligates states,[8] meaning that states exercise force legitimately insofar as they enforce human rights; otherwise, they administer force illegitimately, which is to say, arbitrarily.

5. With the development of the modern state, the technology of repression has outstripped the organs of restraint, making all the more urgent the protection of human rights.

6. Violations of nonderogable rights and prohibitions against atrocity crimes are "wrong in themselves"—"outrages," that is, against the "conscience of humankind," in the updated language of the Preamble to the UDHR, and they are also a severe threat to "peace in the world," as the Preamble also states.

Thus, the moral foundation of human rights language consists of "natural" rather than "extranatural" or "supernatural" assumptions concerning the absolute inviolability of prohibitions against arbitrary force. The idea of natural rights also pertains to the protection of public goods—health, safety, order,

---

6 Articles 5, 6, 7, and 8. Rome Statute of the Int'l Criminal Court, July 17, 1998, 2187 U.N.T.S. 3–9. The crime of aggression is not defined in the Charter, but left to further negotiation and agreement. Still, endeavoring to prohibit aggression is, at the least, an effort to outlaw "wars of conquest" which regularly exemplified self-serving uses of force.

7 The core obligations, which every State party is bound to comply with, are such things as, "ensuring the right to access to health facilities, goods and services on a nondiscriminatory basis, especially for vulnerable or marginalized groups"; "ensuring access to minimum essential food which is nutritionally adequate and safe, and to ensure freedom from hunger for everyone"; "ensuring access to basic shelter, housing, and sanitation, and an adequate supply of safe and potable water"; and "ensuring equitable distribution of all health facilities, goods and services." Comm. on Econ., Soc., & Cultural Rights, *General Comment 14: The Right to the Highest Attainable Standard of Health (Art. 12)*, U.N. Doc. E/C.12/2000/4 (2000), *reprinted* in Compilation of General Comments and General Recommendations Adopted by Human Rights Treaty Bodies, U.N. Doc. HRI/GEN/1/Rev/6 at 85 (2003), *available at* http://www.unhcr.org/refworld/docid/4538838d0.html.

8 Preambles of the ICCPR and the ICESCR: "*Realizing* that the individual, having duties to other individuals and to the community to which [the individual] belongs, is under responsibility to strive for the promotion and observance of the rights recognized in the present Covenant," and "*Considering* the obligations of States under the Charter of the United Nations to promote universal respect for, and observance of, human rights and freedoms[.]" Int'l Covenant on Civil and Political Rights, *supra* note 5, at pmbl.; Int'l Covenant on Econ., Soc., & Cultural Rights, Dec. 16, 1966, 993 U.N.T.S. 3.

and morals[9]—that are assumed to be of common natural concern as vital requirements for human survival. The natural grounding in both cases is "secular" in the sense that it is accessible to and obligatory upon all human beings, regardless of distinctions "such as religion," in the words of Article 2 of the UDHR.

Where, then, does religion come in? A key feature of arbitrary force as practiced by the German fascists was the relentless imposition by force of a specific set of beliefs upon everyone under their control. That meant the systematic persecution of all religious and other forms of dissent. Such actions were a serious violation, according to a natural rights understanding, because coercion is not a justification for believing the truth or rightness of anything. When someone says, "Believe what I tell you or I'll punish you," that is a clear case of arbitrary force—of using force without justification. Expressions of belief can of course be curtailed by coercion, but that just begs the question whether such coercion is justified.

In human rights language, therefore, such reasoning protects "conscience, religion, or belief" against "being subject to coercion which would impair ... freedom to adopt a religion or belief of [one's] choice."[10]

When held up alongside the "natural" justification of human rights language, the special protection of "conscience, religion, or belief" (and the practices associated with them), assured by Art. 18 of the UDHR and ICCPR, introduces what I call, a "two-tiered" system of justification.

The first tier lays down a "natural" (secular) justification that serves to hold people everywhere accountable to the terms of the language, backed by a provision for universally legitimate enforceability (subject to the three "rules of reason"), as well as to provide standards of protection to which everyone may appeal, regardless of religious or other identity.

The second tier permits and secures a wide, highly pluralistic range of "extranatural" justifications for human rights language, and, of course, for much else related to the broad expanse of human social life and experience. Second-tier matters are irreducibly pluralistic because, among other things, they involve intimate, subjective experience in regard to social attachment, loyalty, and identity, as well as ultimate sacred commitments not readily given up. Learning to tolerate and respect without violence these inescapable differences, by upholding the right to freedom of conscience, religion, or belief, appears to be both "right in itself" and critical to achieving peace, as is conclusively shown in the recent book by Grim and Finke on the connection between violence and violations of religious freedom.[11]

Religious and other forms of second-tier justification are undoubtedly indispensable for mobilizing adherents to the cause of human rights. It is also clear that whether it supports or challenges human rights language, sustained attention to that language by different communities of conscience, religious

---

9 *See* Int'l Covenant on Civil and Political Rights, *supra* note 5, at 178 (referring specifically to Article 18, paragraph 3). It is not clear that the term "public morals" has any determined meaning in human rights jurisprudence.

10 *Id.* at 178 (Article 18, para. 2).

11 BRIAN J. GRIM & ROGER FINKE, THE PRICE OF FREEDOM DENIED: RELIGIOUS PERSECUTION AND CONFLICT IN THE TWENTY-FIRST CENTURY (2011).

or not, can help identify lacunae or blind spots in the human rights instruments. Such attention also can assist in finding, where necessary, colloquially acceptable substitutes for human rights language, and can even bring about significant change, for example, in interpreting and applying religious freedom, as has happened as the result of litigation by minority religions in the United States and elsewhere.

Engagement with human rights matters in these ways illustrates the importance of the second tier in the ongoing, often complicated, and sometimes testy negotiations between the two tiers. One additional function of particular significance, performed by the second tier, is the process of appealing for conscientious exemptions from general and neutral laws permitted by human rights jurisprudence.[12] Of special note is the requirement that in imposing restrictions on conscientious belief and practice, the state bears the burden of proof in demonstrating both that there is a compelling state interest at stake, and that the restriction is as unintrusive as possible. In that way tier two serves to limit the reach of tier one, and to remind it of its obligation of special deference to tier two.

At the same time, all these second tier undertakings are themselves constrained by the first tier, in accord with the underlying assumptions of human rights language. Tier-two justifications must yield to the inviolability of the "natural" prohibitions against arbitrary force and arbitrary neglect, as well as of the state's responsibility, "as prescribed by law" and as is "necessary," for protecting the public goods of safety, health, order, and morals, and the "fundamental rights and freedoms of others."[13]

The proposal, in sum, is that human rights language rests on a natural rights understanding that prescribes a two-tiered theory of justification. Accordingly, the first tier protects, encourages, and is limited by the second tier, but it also constrains the second tier in very important ways.

II

I started attending seriously to the subject of human rights in the 1980s, sparked initially by the election of President Ronald Reagan at the beginning of the decade. Reagan's predecessor, Jimmy Carter, together with an active cohort of members of Congress, had given human rights a central place in the conduct of U.S. foreign policy. When Reagan came to office, he made clear his strong opposition to Carter's emphasis, and his determination to reconfigure radically the role of human rights in foreign affairs. At first, it appeared he would ignore human rights altogether. But gradually he turned to enlisting human rights in the fight against Communism, with especially controversial effects in Central America, where Reagan's policies were perceived by critics as being much more attentive to the abuses of the Communists than of their anti-Communist opponents.

The intense and continuing debates between Carter and Reagan supporters at the time piqued my interest in human rights on the level of law and policy, as well as of theory. It was not, it seemed,

---

12 Human Rights Comm., *General Comment No. 22: The Right to Freedom of Thought, Conscience and Religion (Art. 18)*, July 30, 1993, CCPR/C/21/Rev.1/Add.4, *available at* http://www.refworld.org/docid/453883fb22.html.
13 *See* Int'l Covenant on Civil and Political Rights, *supra* note 5, at 178 (Article 18, para. 3).

simply a question of how the state and others might interpret and apply human rights, but also of how, if at all, they could be justified. That is where the idea of natural rights came in. Whatever other influences there are, human rights language is undeniably rooted in the natural rights tradition, associated, as it is, with Western philosophical and theological thought. The problem was that, at the time, controversies over the status of natural rights theory were as acute and seemingly intractable as the controversies over law and policy. The idea of natural rights is not the only conceivable basis for supporting human rights, but to refute it successfully removes human rights' most venerable foundation.

The idea of natural rights—that human beings "are entitled to make certain claims by virtue simply of their common humanity"[14]—has long been under assault, going back to the well-known attacks in the eighteenth and nineteenth centuries by David Hume, Jeremy Bentham, and Karl Marx. Related attacks continued into the twentieth century, gaining momentum around the time of the adoption of the UDHR by the UN General Assembly in December 1948. Anticipating that event, the American Anthropological Association, for example, submitted a widely noted statement on human rights to the UN Human Rights Commission in 1947, denouncing the very idea of universally binding moral claims. Margaret Macdonald's influential essay on natural rights, written that same year, supported this conclusion.[15] Subsequently, similarly skeptical statements appeared up into the eighties, advanced by figures like Alasdair MacIntyre[16] and Richard Rorty.[17]

In the midst of all the controversy, I, however, remained unconvinced by the opposition. In 1986, I published an essay on natural rights and human rights,[18] reexamining the ideas of John Locke (1632–1704) in some detail, and arguing that Locke's natural rights theory did not fit the fashionable Marxist model, according to which rights talk expresses nothing more than bourgeois interests that are essentially egoistic in character. On the contrary, the whole point of natural rights for Locke was to protect everyone everywhere *against* self-serving rule, something that permitted anyone in command to "do to all his subjects whatever he pleases, without the least liberty to anyone to question or control those who execute his pleasure[,] … and … whatsoever he does, whether led by reason, mistake, or passion, must be submitted to." Such an arrangement also allowed individuals to stand as judges in their own case, where "he who was so unjust as to do his brother an injury, will scarce be so just as to condemn himself for it."[19] Nor did Locke exempt economic life from these strictures: Everyone everywhere possesses "a right to the surplusage of [another's] goods … as will [prevent] extreme want, where [there is] no means to subsist otherwise." Moreover, no one may "justly make use of another's necessity, to force him to become his vassal, by withholding that relief God requires him to afford to

---

14 Margaret Macdonald, *Natural Rights, in* Human Rights 40, 40 (1970).

15 *Id.*

16 Alasdair MacIntyre, After Virtue: A Study in Moral Theory (1981).

17 Richard Rorty, The Consequences of Pragmatism (1982).

18 David Little, *Natural Rights and Human Rights: The International Imperative, in* Natural Rights and Natural Law: The Legacy of George Mason 67 (Robert Davidoff ed., 1986).

19 John Locke, Two Treatises of Government, 2d Treatise, ch. II, § 13, at 316–17 (1965).

the wants of his brother, than he that has more strength can seize upon a weaker [person], master him …, and with a dagger at his throat offer him death or slavery."[20]

Having endeavored to set the record straight, I proceeded in my article to mount a constructive case in favor of a natural rights approach. The line of argument was stimulated by a passing comment of Locke's and by some perceptive insights of Gregory Vlastos[21] and Thomas Nagel[22] about the nature of the conditions under which pain may or may not be inflicted or relieved. Commenting on the education of youth, Locke bemoaned the high esteem bestowed on military conquerors "who for the most part are but the great butchers of mankind." Their typical exploits, he says, tend to encourage an "unnatural cruelty," "especially the pleasure [taken] to put anything in pain that is capable of it."[23] The implication, supported by the suggestions of Vlastos and Nagel, is that giving self-serving reasons for inflicting pain or for taking advantage of someone in pain by withholding relief is the essence of cruelty, something morally unthinkable or indisputably "wrong in itself."

In this way the idea of a natural right can, I contended, be justified. The argument provides warrant for the notion of a subjective entitlement possessed by all individuals, simply as individuals, to demand (or have demanded for them) that no one of them shall be subjected to arbitrary force or arbitrary neglect under threat of sanction for noncompliance. Given that a claim of this sort is meant to be respected universally, certain correlative duties and obligations so to respect the right are, by implication, owed by every individual to every other individual.

The right is "natural" because *any* mature, competent human being, "without [that is] distinction of any kind, such as race, colour, sex, language, religion, political or other opinion, national or social origin, property birth or other status,"[24] is expected to recognize the blatant incongruity, and, hence, patent unjustifiability, of inflicting pain or taking advantage of those in pain for self-serving motives, and, consequently, is obligated to refrain from acting in that way. Anyone reliably suspected of so acting is therefore liable to sanction—subject, of course, to the three "rules of reason": necessity, proportionality, and effectiveness. That is true whether, as Locke implies, the motives are disguised by reason, or are the result of a knowing or negligent mistake or simply of passion. Indeed, Locke's whole theory of government, including the design for administering legal sanctions, is grounded in this understanding. "I easily grant," he says, that civil government is the proper remedy for the inconveniences of the state of nature" where "self-love will make men partial to themselves and to their friends, … and that ill-nature, passion, and revenge will carry them too far in punishing others[.]"[25] In short, the ultimate objective of government is that everyone "may be restrained from invading

---

20 *Id.* at 1st Treatise, ch.4, § 42, at 205–06.

21 Gregory Vlastos, *Justice and Equality, in* Social Justice 51 (Richard B. Brandt ed., 1962).

22 Thomas Nagel, *Limits of Objectivity, in* Tanner Lectures on Human Values 108 (Sterling M. McMurrin ed., 1980).

23 James L. Axtell, The Educational Writings of John Locke 226–27 (1968).

24 Universal Declaration of Human Rights, art. 2 (1948).

25 Locke, *supra* note 17, at 316, 2d Treatise, ch. II, § 13.

others' rights and from doing hurt to one another, and [that] the law of nature be observed, which wills the peace and preservation of all mankind."[26]

Around the time the article supporting natural rights appeared, I published a related essay on the Puritan dissident and founder of the Rhode Island colony, Roger Williams (1603–1683), in which I analyzed and promoted his defense of freedom of conscience and separation of church and state.[27] I believed the effort was important not only because Williams's arguments were intrinsically appealing, as well as anticipating some of Locke's ideas, but also because Williams had, for the most part, been so badly misunderstood by those who should know better. In particular, there was (and continues to be) the widespread failure to understand the Calvinist roots of Williams's thinking, a point I introduced in the essay, but went on to develop more extensively in subsequent writings.[28] The key idea is the distinction between the two tables of the Decalogue, or the Ten Commandments. The article focused on the deep and abiding tension in Reformed Christianity, beginning with Calvin himself. Early in his career, Calvin taught that it was not the state's job to enforce the first table—matters of religious belief or conscience, but only the second table—moral and civic matters, whose principle is that "all individuals should preserve their rights" in regard to life, liberty, and property, or what Calvin often called natural rights. This teaching assumed a distinction between the "inward forum" or conscience that should not be coerced, and the "outward forum" or affairs of state that should. Later in his career, Calvin sharply altered his position, authorizing the state to regulate the first as well as the second table.

Williams's position on freedom of conscience and church-state relations was, in large part, simply an elaboration of the early Calvin, whereas his opponents, the authorities of the Massachusetts Bay colony who expelled him, sided with the later Calvin. In defending himself, Williams provided extensive commentary on the two tables of the Decalogue, on the distinction between the jurisdictions of the "inward" and "outward" forums, and, like Calvin and other members of the Reformed tradition, on the importance of constitutional government, including protection of "natural and civil rights and liberties" that make up the "natural freedom of the people." Noteworthy was his ability to advance his views in the Rhode Island colony by successfully excluding any reference to religious privileges in the Charter of 1644 and the Civil Code 1647, and by explicitly codifying an expansive right to freedom of conscience in the Charter of 1663. His mode of discourse, intermixing extensive biblical exposition with "free-standing" appeals to reason, nature, and experience is very much in the Calvinist tradition, starting with Calvin himself.[29]

While for Williams the idea of temporal government is divinely ordained, he leaves no doubt that the "power, might or authority" of particular governments "is not religious, Christian, etc., but

---

26 *Id.* at 312, ch. II, § 7.

27 David Little, *Roger Williams and the Separation of Church and State, in* Religion and State: Essays in Honor of Leo Pfeffer 3 (James E. Wood, Jr. ed., 1985).

28 David Little, *Roger Williams and the Puritan Background of the Establishment Clause, in* T. Jeremy Gunn & John Witte, Jr., No Establishment of Religion: America's Original Contribution to Religious Liberty 100 (2012).

29 *See* David Little, *Calvin and Natural Rights*, 10 Pol. Theology 411 (2009).

natural, humane, and civil."[30] Clearly implied is a notion of "secular" or "public reason," according to which any well-ordered government should be conducted. The notion rests on "natural" rather than "extranatural" or "supernatural" assumptions concerning the protection of public goods, like health, safety, and order, taken to be of universal concern as vital requirements of human survival.

It also rests on the idea that any attempt by an earthly government to regulate coercively matters of conscience or belief, beside those that incite to a violation of public safety or order, constitutes an act of arbitrary or unjustified force—of "soul rape," as Williams repeatedly calls it. "The binding and rebinding of conscience [by force], contrary [to] or without its own persuasion, so weakens and defiles it that it ... loseth its strength and the very nature of a common honest conscience."[31] The essence of conscience is inward consent based on a conviction of truth and right. Physical force, in and of itself, cannot produce that. Belief depends on reasons consisting of argument and evidence, and the threat of force, as in a case of robbery or rape, is not a reason in the proper sense because it lacks justification. Thus, the only "weapons" suitably employed in the inward forum are "spiritual," namely appeals and arguments subject to rational standards, whose object is consensual or heartfelt agreement. Accordingly, "forcing the conscience of any person" is action that deforms conscience by inducing hypocrisy, narrow-mindedness, or self-betrayal.

Consequently, Williams favored a broadly pluralistic society including all manner of Protestants, Catholics,[32] Jews, "Mohammedans," and "pagans" or Native Americans, and even those "who turn atheistical and irreligious." By no means did he support protection only for those groups manifesting a "hyperindividualistic," strongly "protestant" religious outlook, as has been alleged. On the contrary, Williams advocated accommodating as diverse a range as possible in matters of religion and conscience, urging only that the rights and duties, the benefits and burdens, of citizenship be kept scrupulously separate from such considerations. As with Locke, the overriding objective of such an arrangement is "keeping the peace." "Among those that profess the same God and Christ as Papists and Protestants, or the same Muhammed as the Turks and Persians, ... civil peace would [not] be broken (notwithstanding their differences in religion) were it not for the bloody doctrine of persecution, which alone breaks the bonds of civil peace, and makes spiritual causes the causes of their bloody dissensions ...."[33]

It is true that throughout his lifetime, and well into the eighteenth century, Williams's ideas had little impact outside Rhode Island. However, as I argued in the article, that all changed around the time of the American Revolution and the founding of the Republic by way of Williams's influence

---

30 3 THE COMPLETE WRITINGS OF ROGER WILLIAMS 398 (1963).

31 4 THE COMPLETE WRITINGS OF ROGER WILLIAMS 209 (1963).

32 Williams does flirt at one point with the acceptability of requiring the display of special insignia on members of religious groups like the Catholics in protecting national security, though he does that in the context of a discussion of reasons for trusting and respecting Catholics, and, in fact, for considering some extremist Protestant sectarians as a greater threat to national security than Catholics. *Id.* at 313–15.

33 Roger Williams, *Bloody Tenent Yet More Bloody*, *in* ON RELIGIOUS LIBERTY: SELECTIONS FROM THE WORKS OF ROGER WILLIAMS 183 (James Calvin Davis ed., 2008).

on Locke and Isaac Backus (1724–1806), the intrepid lobbyist for religious liberty at the time of the Constitutional convention. Williams's impact on Backus is indisputable, since Backus wrote what amounted to an early biography of Williams, and regularly cited him, even though he was not as radical as Williams. Backus sought to remove established religion such as existed in many of the colonies at the time, but he still advocated support for a form of civil religion requiring a religious test for public office. Williams's influence on Locke is a more uncertain matter, though there is significant scholarly support for it,[34] and the similarities of argument in regard to natural rights, freedom of conscience, and the separation of church and state are striking. Nevertheless, whatever Williams's impact on Locke, Locke, like Backus, was not as liberal as Williams, arguing that atheists, Catholics, and Muslims should not be accorded freedom of conscience.

Since I wrote those two essays in the 1980s, the literature on natural rights, including the connection to freedom of conscience, has grown substantially, often in appreciation of certain lines of argument in the tradition. Brian Tierney's book, *The Idea of Natural Rights*,[35] published in 1997, revolutionized study of the topic by refuting the popular belief that natural rights represent a "deformed version of Christian ideas." Tierney also rejected the assertions that natural rights glorify egoistic individualism (as Marx claimed), and emphasize an anti-religious bias derived from the Enlightenment (as many still claim). Rather, the natural rights are to be understood as the product of a "great age of creative jurisprudence" in twelfth- and thirteenth-century medieval Europe at the hands of inventive canon lawyers and monastic theologians whose moral and legal theories "may still prove of value in our political discourse."[36] Of special importance in anticipating Locke's arguments against arbitrary force is Tierney's description of the right of self-defense—considered in the tradition as "the greatest of rights"—namely, "a natural inalienable right [inhering] in individuals and communities ... that could be exercised by subjects against a tyrannical ruler."[37]

Judith Shklar's influential essay, "The Liberalism of Fear," appearing in 1989,[38] strongly reinforced the approach I was developing. She claimed that the critical feature of a liberal theory of government is the prevention of "arbitrary, unexpected, unnecessary, and unlicensed acts of force [including] habitual and pervasive acts of cruelty and torture performed by military, paramilitary, and police agents in any regime."[39] She eloquently rephrased and updated Locke's view, which I had highlighted in my 1986 essay. She also contended that the liberalism of fear "certainly does begin with a *summum*

---

34 *See* MARTHA C. NUSSBAUM, LIBERTY OF CONSCIENCE: IN DEFENSE OF AMERICA'S TRADITION OF RELIGIOUS EQUALITY, 371 n.18 (2008) (noting that Quentin Skinner confirmed that "Williams [was] a prominent part of the literature ... with which Locke was certainly familiar"); *cf.* EDWIN S. GAUSTAD, LIBERTY OF CONSCIENCE: ROGER WILLIAMS IN AMERICA 196 (1991), AND WILLIAM LEE MILLER, THE FIRST LIBERTY: AMERICA'S FOUNDATION IN RELIGIOUS LIBERTY 176 (2003).

35 TIERNEY, *supra* note 3.

36 *Id.* at 27, 42

37 *Id.* at 314.

38 Judith Shklar, *The Liberalism of Fear, in* LIBERALISM AND THE MORAL LIFE 21, 21–38 (Nancy L. Rosenblum, ed., 1989).

39 *Id.* at 29.

malum, which all of us know and would avoid if only we could"—namely, the deliberate infliction of physical and emotional pain on the weak in order to satisfy the interests of the strong.[40]

Shklar did caution against too readily drawing moral conclusions from the fact that "the fear of systematic cruelty is so universal," since stating facts about beliefs does not prove they are morally right or wrong.[41] However, that difficulty is avoided, as it seemed to me, since the implication of Locke's theory is not, finally, about what human beings do believe, but about what they are capable of believing; not about reporting facts, but about what makes sense, about what can be believed, in taking a position on right and wrong.

The Realm of Rights by Judith Jarvis Thomson, published in 1990,[42] gave new energy to the philosophical defense of natural rights, arguing in a way consistent with the tradition that "there is no possible world in which an act's being an instance of 'causes a person pain' is irrelevant to the question whether it is wrongful."[43] Going further, she advances a proposition very close to the conclusion drawn earlier about Locke: That non-trivial necessary moral truths exist such as, "[o]ne ought not torture babies to death for fun."[44]

As to Locke scholarship, John Simmons's volume, *The Lockean Theory of Rights*,[45] appearing in 1992, goes a long way toward showing both that Locke had "a developed and consistent theory of rights," which deserves to be taken seriously, and that his theory serves not only "as a viable foundation for *his* political philosophy," but also "may serve as a viable foundation for *ours*."[46]

John Witte's book, *The Reformation of Rights: Law, Religion, and Human Rights in Early Modern Calvinism* (2007), illuminates the way the Calvinist tradition carried forward the natural rights narrative, more or less picking up where Tierney left off. Unlike Tierney, Witte also shows the relevance of the natural rights tradition to questions of freedom of conscience and religious pluralism. This tradition is both the more restrictive approach of the later Calvin, Theodore Beza, and Johannes Althusius, as well as the more inclusive approach of John Milton, a friend and ally, personally and intellectually, of Roger Williams.

Martha Nussbaum's impressive study, *Liberty of Conscience: In Defense of America's Tradition of Religious Equality* (2008), compellingly commends Williams for his distinctive contribution to guaranteeing equal freedom of conscience in the American experience. To her credit, she correctly emphasizes Williams's appeals to natural or "secular" reason, which are certainly there. Unfortunately, she ignores the importance of his supplementary appeals to scripture and doctrine, as well as the central place in his thought of natural rights thinking, impressed upon him by the Calvinist tradition in which he stood. Her failure to appreciate the role of natural rights is especially surprising since she

---

40 *Id.*

41 *Id.* at 30.

42 Judith Jarvis Thomson, The Realm of Rights (1990).

43 *Id.* at 15.

44 *Id.* at 18–19.

45 A. John Simmons, The Lockean Theory of Rights (1992).

46 *Id.* at 354.

highlighted it in an earlier book,[47] and has proceeded, revisionistically, to be sure, to appropriate it in developing her "capabilities" approach to social reform and development.

But most important in the effort to bring natural rights and human rights together—my overall objective in the 1986 article—was a book published in 1999 by Johannes Morsink, *The Universal Declaration of Human Rights: Origins, Drafting, and Intent.*[48] Morsink indicates that at the very start of the process of drafting the UDHR, one delegation proposed to begin the document with the following words, "Recognizing that the United Nations has been established for the specific purpose of enthroning the natural rights of man ...."[49]

Although the words were not adopted, Morsink thinks they support the presumption that there is "some kind of connection" between "natural rights philosophies," which Morsink identifies with the Enlightenment, and the language adopted in the UDHR.[50] It is not that the drafters self-consciously and intentionally attempted to enshrine natural rights theory. For the most part, they were not interested in philosophical questions and wanted to minimize, as much as possible, what they took to be loaded terms.[51] Rather, they shared, usually unreflectively, certain moral assumptions with the natural rights tradition. One assumption was that "by nature" everyone everywhere possesses an "inalienable" set of moral rights that are independent of, and prior to, any legal rights temporal governments may bestow, thereby constituting a standard for judging the conduct of government, and especially the administration of force.[52]

Another assumption was the expectation of standard moral reactions to events of a certain kind. Drafters did not object to the language of the Preamble, "Whereas disregard and contempt for human rights have resulted in barbarous acts which have outraged the conscience of mankind," because they all shared the view that any other way of assessing the practices of the Nazis before and during World War II was unthinkable.[53] More than anything else, it was their common "outrage," prompted by the "horrors of the war," and dramatized, particularly, by the Holocaust, that energized and guided the drafting of the UDHR.[54] In his careful analysis of some of the articles of the UDHR, Morsink shows how the final wording was consciously and specifically formulated in reaction to what were considered egregious violations in regard to taking life, inflicting pain and suffering, enslaving, and so on.[55] Morsink states that one reason the drafters did not draw on "Enlightenment precedents" is

---

47 Martha C. Nussbaum, Frontiers of Justice: Disability, Nationality, Species Membership 9–92 (2006).

48 Johannes Morsink, The Universal Declaration of Human Rights: Origins, Drafting, and Intent (1999).

49 *Id.* at 282.

50 *Id.*

51 *Id.* at 294.

52 *Id.* at 290–295.

53 *Id.* at 90–91.

54 *Id.* at 27, 91, 300.

55 *Id.* at 36–58.

that they "had no need for examples from the Enlightenment . ... The horrors of World War II gave them all ... they needed to be justified" in producing the UDHR.[56]

Part of the underlying expectation in face of the "outrages" under consideration was an assumption concerning the two-fold foundation of rights language. In the first place, "the drafters surely thought that proclaiming [the] Declaration would serve the cause of world peace," a sentiment strictly in line with the thinking of Williams and Locke.[57] However, Morsink continues, "[T]hey did not think of the human rights they proclaimed as only or merely a means to that end."[58] They also thought "these rights have an independent grounding [for] the members of the human family to whom they belong and who possess them as birthrights. If this were not so, a government could torture people (or violate any other right) as long as it was thought ... to serve the cause of ... peace."[59]

Morsink does not call attention to a third assumption concerning a connection between natural rights and human rights over the question of freedom of conscience, but a connection would be hard to miss in light of what he says about the understanding underlying the provisions in the UDHR. "There is no presumption in the Declaration that the morality of human rights requires any kind of religious foundation. ... [T]he drafters went out of their way to avoid having the Declaration make a reference to God or to man's divine origin. ... [It] gives everyone total freedom of religion, including the right not to have one."[60]

As indispensable as Morsink's discussion is for connecting natural rights and human rights, it is seriously deficient in that he unduly limits the natural rights tradition to the Enlightenment. Thanks to Tierney, we now know how mistaken that view is, as are beliefs that natural rights are to be understood as invariably egoistic and anti-religious.

Morsink also causes confusion when he states that the drafters paid no heed to natural rights thinking since all they needed was their impression of "the horrors of World War II" to feel justified in producing the UDHR. The point is that the drafters' reaction to the horrors of World War II was a prime example of natural rights thinking. The practices designed and implemented by Hitler and the German Nazi regime exemplified paradigmatically "disregard and contempt" for the fundamental moral prohibitions aimed at punishing and preventing arbitrary force (and its relative, arbitrary neglect). Those prohibitions underlie all three of the common assumptions just laid out between natural rights and human rights: Priority of moral rights over legal rights; the expectation of standard moral reactions to events of a certain kind, including convictions concerning the two-fold justification of basic rights—promoting world peace, and considering the violation of basic rights "wrong in itself"; and the "natural" (secular) grounding of basic rights.

---

56 *Id*. at 320.

57 *Id*.

58 *Id*.

59 *Id*.

60 *Id*. at 263.

In keeping with our summary of a proposed way of justifying human rights and the relation of human rights to religion, we have argued that a common theme of great importance brings the natural rights tradition and human rights language together. That is a fundamental commitment to a set of moral and legal rights designed to combat and restrain arbitrary force (and arbitrary neglect), whether manifested as inflicting death, suffering, or pain; or failing to prevent or relieve them for purely self-serving reasons; or coercively regulating expressions of conscience, religion; or belief that pose no threat to public order, safety or health. In regard to the subject of religion and human rights, we hope, in a word, to have provided some "ground to stand on."

Letter From The Birmingham City Jail

(First Version)

Martin Luther King, Jr.

....

Martin Luther King, Jr.
Birmingham City Jail
April 16, 1963

My dear Fellow Clergymen,

While confined here in the Birmingham City Jail, I came across your recent statement calling our present activities "unwise and untimely." Seldom, if ever, do I pause to answer criticism of my work and ideas. If I sought to answer all the criticisms that cross my desk, my secretaries would be engaged in little else in the course of the day and I would have no time for constructive work. But since I feel that you are men of genuine goodwill and your criticisms are sincerely set forth, I would like to answer your statement in what I hope will be patient and reasonable terms.

I think I should give the reason for my being in Birmingham, since you have been influenced by the argument of "outsiders coming in." I have the honor of serving as president of the Southern Christian Leadership Conference, an organization operating in every Southern state with headquarters in Atlanta, Georgia. We have some eighty-five affiliate organizations all across the South—one being the Alabama Christian Movement for Human Rights. Whenever necessary and possible we share staff, educational, and financial resources with our affiliates. Several months ago our local affiliate here in Birmingham invited us to be on call to engage in a nonviolent direct action program if such were deemed necessary. We readily consented and when the hour came we lived up to our promises. So I am here, along with several members of my staff, because we were invited here. I am here because I have basic organizational ties here. Beyond this, I am in Birmingham because injustice is here. Just as the eighth century prophets left their little villages and carried their "thus saith the Lord" far beyond the boundaries of their home town, and just as the Apostle Paul left his little village of Tarsus and carried the gospel of Jesus Christ to practically every hamlet and city of the Graeco-Roman world, I too am compelled to carry the gospel of freedom beyond my particular home town. Like Paul, I must constantly respond to the Macedonian call for aid.

Moreover, I am cognizant of the interrelatedness of all communities and states. I cannot sit idly by in Atlanta and not be concerned about what happens in Birmingham. Injustice anywhere is a threat to justice everywhere. We are caught in an inescapable network of mutuality tied in a single garment of destiny. Whatever affects one directly affects all indirectly. Never again can we afford to live with the narrow, provincial "outside agitator" idea. Anyone who lives inside the United States can never be considered an outsider anywhere in this country.

You deplore the demonstrations that are presently taking place in Birmingham. But I am sorry that your statement did not express a similar concern for the conditions that brought the demonstrations into being. I am sure that each of you would want to go beyond the superficial social analyst who looks merely at effects, and does not grapple with underlying causes. I would not hesitate to say that it is unfortunate that so-called demonstrations are taking place in Birmingham at this time, but I would say in more emphatic terms that it is even more unfortunate that the white power structure of this city left the Negro community with no other alternative.

In any nonviolent campaign there are four basic steps: (1) Collection of the facts to determine whether injustices are alive; (2) Negotiation; (3) Self-purification; and (4) Direct action. We have gone through all of these steps in Birmingham. There can be no gainsaying of the fact that racial injustice engulfs this community. Birmingham is probably the most thoroughly segregated city in the United States. Its ugly record of police brutality is known in every section of this country. Its unjust treatment of Negroes in the courts is a notorious reality. There have been more unsolved bombings of Negro homes and churches in Birmingham than any city in this nation. These are the hard, brutal, and unbelievable facts. On the basis of these conditions Negro leaders sought to negotiate with the city fathers. But the political leaders consistently refused to engage in good faith negotiation.

Then came the opportunity last September to talk with some of the leaders of the economic community. In these negotiating sessions certain promises were made by the merchants—such as the promise to remove the humiliating racial signs from the stores. On the basis of these promises Rev. Shuttlesworth and the leaders of the Alabama Christian Movement for Human Rights agreed to call a moratorium on any type of demonstrations. As the weeks and months unfolded we realized that we were the victims of a broken promise. The signs remained. As in so many experiences of the past we were confronted with blasted hopes, and the dark shadow of a deep disappointment settled upon us. So we had no alternative except that of preparing for direct action, whereby we would present our very bodies as a means of laying our case before the conscience of the local and national community. We were not unmindful of the difficulties involved. So we decided to go through a process of self-purification. We started having workshops on nonviolence and repeatedly asked ourselves the questions, "Are you able to accept blows without retaliating?" "Are you able to endure the ordeals of jail?"

We decided to set our direct-action program around the Easter season, realizing that with the exception of Christmas, this was the largest shopping period of the year. Knowing that a strong economic withdrawal program would be the by-product of direct action, we felt that this was the best time to bring pressure on the merchants for the needed changes. Then it occurred to us that the

March election was ahead, and so we speedily decided to postpone action until after election day. When we discovered that Mr. Connor was in the run-off, we decided again to postpone action so that the demonstrations could not be used to cloud the issues. At this time we agreed to begin our nonviolent witness the day after the run-off.

This reveals that we did not move irresponsibly into direct action. We too wanted to see Mr. Connor defeated; so we went through postponement after postponement to aid in this community need. After this we felt that direct action could be delayed no longer.

You may well ask, "Why direct action? Why sit-ins, marches, etc.? Isn't negotiation a better path?" You are exactly right in your call for negotiation. Indeed, this is the purpose of direct action. Nonviolent direct action seeks to create such a crisis and establish such creative tension that a community that has constantly refused to negotiate is forced to confront the issue. It seeks so to dramatize the issue that it can no longer be ignored. I just referred to the creation of tension as a part of the work of the nonviolent resister. This may sound rather shocking. But I must confess that I am not afraid of the word tension. I have earnestly worked and preached against violent tension, but there is a type of constructive nonviolent tension that is necessary for growth. Just as Socrates felt that it was necessary to create a tension in the mind so that individuals could rise from the bondage of myths and half-truths to the unfettered realm of creative analysis and objective appraisal, we must see the need of having nonviolent gadflies to create the kind of tension in society that will help men rise from the dark depths of prejudice and racism to the majestic heights of understanding and brotherhood. So the purpose of the direct action is to create a situation so crisis-packed that it will inevitably open the door to negotiation. We, therefore, concur with you in your call for negotiation. Too long has our beloved Southland been bogged down in the tragic attempt to live in monologue rather than dialogue.

One of the basic points in your statement is that our acts are untimely. Some have asked, "Why didn't you give the new administration time to act?" The only answer that I can give to this inquiry is that the new administration must be prodded about as much as the outgoing one before it acts. We will be sadly mistaken if we feel that the election of Mr. Boutwell will bring the millennium to Birmingham. While Mr. Boutwell is much more articulate and gentle than Mr. Connor, they are both segregationists dedicated to the task of maintaining the status quo. The hope I see in Mr. Boutwell is that he will be reasonable enough to see the futility of massive resistance to desegregation. But he will not see this without pressure from the devotees of civil rights. My friends, I must say to you that we have not made a single gain in civil rights without determined legal and nonviolent pressure. History is the long and tragic story of the fact that privileged groups seldom give up their privileges voluntarily. Individuals may see the moral light and voluntarily give up their unjust posture; but as Reinhold Niebuhr has reminded us, groups are more immoral than individuals.

We know through painful experience that freedom is never voluntarily given by the oppressor; it must be demanded by the oppressed. Frankly I have never yet engaged in a direct action movement that was "well timed," according to the timetable of those who have not suffered unduly from the disease of segregation. For years now I have heard the word "Wait!" It rings in the ear of every Negro with a piercing familiarity. This "wait" has almost always meant "never." It has been a tranquilizing thalidomide, relieving the emotional stress for a moment, only to give birth to an ill-formed infant of frustration. We must come to see with the distinguished jurist of yesterday that "justice too long delayed is justice denied." We have waited for more than three hundred and forty years for our constitutional and God-given rights. The nations of Asia and Africa are moving with jet-like speed toward the goal of political independence, and we still creep at horse and buggy pace toward the gaining of a cup of coffee at a lunch counter.

I guess it is easy for those who have never felt the stinging darts of segregation to say wait. But when you have seen vicious mobs lynch your mothers and fathers at will and drown your sisters and brothers at whim; when you have seen hate filled policemen curse, kick, brutalize, and even kill your black brothers and sisters with impunity; when you see the vast majority of your twenty million Negro brothers smothering in an air-tight cage of poverty in the midst of an affluent society; when you suddenly find your tongue twisted and your speech stammering as you seek to explain to your six-year-old daughter why she can't go to the public amusement park that has just been advertised on television, and see tears welling up in her little eyes when she is told that Funtown is closed to colored children, and see the depressing clouds of inferiority begin to form in her little mental sky, and see her begin to distort her little personality by unconsciously developing a bitterness toward white people; when you have to concoct an answer for a five-year-old son asking in agonizing pathos: "Daddy, why do white people treat colored people so mean?"; when you take a cross-country drive and find it necessary to sleep night after night in the uncomfortable corners of your automobile because no motel will accept you; when you are humiliated day in and day out by nagging signs reading "white" men and "colored"; when your first name becomes "nigger" and your middle name becomes "boy" (however old you are) and your last name becomes "John," and when your wife and mother are never given the respected title "Mrs."; when you are harried by day and haunted by night by the fact that you are a Negro, living constantly at tip-toe stance never quite knowing what to expect next, and plagued with inner fears and outer resentments; when you are forever fighting a degenerating sense of "nobodiness"—then you will understand why we find it difficult to wait. There comes a time when the cup of endurance runs over, and men are no longer willing to be plunged into an abyss of injustice where they experience the bleakness of corroding despair. I hope, sirs, you can understand our legitimate and unavoidable impatience.

You express a great deal of anxiety over our willingness to break laws. This is certainly a legitimate concern. Since we so diligently urge people to obey the Supreme Court's decision of 1954 outlawing segregation in the public schools, it is rather strange and paradoxical to find us consciously breaking laws. One may well ask: "How can you advocate breaking some laws and obeying others?" The answer is found in the fact that there are two types of laws: There are just laws and there are unjust laws. I would be the first to advocate obeying just laws. One has not only a legal but moral responsibility to obey just laws. Conversely, one has a moral responsibility to disobey unjust laws. I would agree with Saint Augustine that "An unjust law is no law at all."

Now what is the difference between the two? How does one determine when a law is just or unjust? A just law is a man-made code that squares with the moral law or the law of God. An unjust law is a code that is out of harmony with the moral law. To put it in the terms of Saint Thomas Aquinas, an unjust law is a human law that is not rooted in eternal and natural law. Any law that uplifts human personality is just. Any law that degrades human personality is unjust. All segregation statutes are unjust because segregation distorts the soul and damages the personality. It gives the segregator a false sense of superiority and the segregated a false sense of inferiority. To use the words of Martin Buber, the great Jewish philosopher, segregation substitutes an "I-it" relationship for an "I-thou" relationship, and ends up relegating persons to the status of things. So segregation is not only politically, economically, and sociologically unsound, but it is morally wrong and sinful. Paul Tillich has said that sin is separation. Isn't segregation an existential expression of man's tragic separation, an expression of his awful estrangement, his terrible sinfulness? So I can urge men to obey the 1954 decision of the Supreme Court because it is morally right, and I can urge them to disobey segregation ordinances because they are morally wrong.

Let us turn to a more concrete example of just and unjust laws. An unjust law is a code that a majority inflicts on a minority that is not binding on itself. This is difference made legal. On the other hand a just law is a code that a majority compels a minority to follow that it is willing to follow itself. This is sameness made legal.

Let me give another explanation. An unjust law is a code inflicted upon a minority which that minority had no part in enacting or creating because they did not have the unhampered right to vote. Who can say that the legislature of Alabama which set up the segregation laws was democratically elected? Throughout the state of Alabama all types of conniving methods are used to prevent Negroes from becoming registered voters and there are some counties without a single Negro registered to vote despite the fact that the Negro constitutes a majority of the population. Can any law set up in such a state be considered democratically structured?

These are just a few examples of unjust and just laws. There are some instances when a law is just on its face but unjust in its application. For instance, I was arrested Friday on a charge of parading without a permit. Now there is nothing wrong with an ordinance which requires a permit for a parade, but when the ordinance is used to preserve segregation and to deny citizens the First Amendment privilege of peaceful assembly and peaceful protest, then it becomes unjust.

I hope you can see the distinction I am trying to point out. In no sense do I advocate evading or defying the law as the rabid segregationist would do. This would lead to anarchy. One who breaks an unjust law must do it openly, lovingly (not hatefully as the white mothers did in New Orleans when they were seen on television screaming "nigger, nigger, nigger") and with a willingness to accept the penalty. I submit that an individual who breaks a law that conscience tells him is unjust, and willingly accepts the penalty by staying in jail to arouse the conscience of the community over its injustice, is in reality expressing the very highest respect for law.

Of course there is nothing new about this kind of civil disobedience. It was seen sublimely in the refusal of Shadrach, Meshach, and Abednego to obey the laws of Nebuchadnezzar because a higher moral law was involved. It was practiced superbly by the early Christians who were willing to face hungry lions and the excruciating pain of chopping blocks, before submitting to certain unjust laws of the Roman Empire. To a degree academic freedom is a reality today because Socrates practiced civil disobedience.

We can never forget that everything Hitler did in Germany was "legal" and everything the Hungarian freedom fighters did in Hungary was "illegal." It was "illegal" to aid and comfort a Jew in Hitler's Germany. But I am sure that, if I had lived in Germany during that time, I would have aided and comforted my Jewish brothers even though it was illegal. If I lived in a communist country today where certain principles dear to the Christian faith are suppressed, I believe I would openly advocate disobeying these anti-religious laws.

I must make two honest confessions to you, my Christian and Jewish brothers. First, I must confess that over the last few years I have been gravely disappointed with the white moderate. I have almost reached the regrettable conclusion that the Negroes' great stumbling block in the stride toward freedom is not the White Citizen's "Counciler" or the Ku Klux Klanner, but the white moderate who is more devoted to "order" than to justice; who prefers a negative peace which is the absence of tension to a positive peace which is the presence of justice; who constantly says "I agree with you in the goal you seek, but I can't agree with your methods of direct action"; who paternalistically feels that he can set the timetable for another man's freedom; who lives by the myth of time and who constantly advises the Negro to wait until a "more convenient season." Shallow understanding from people of good will is more frustrating than absolute misunderstanding from people of ill will. Lukewarm acceptance is much more bewildering than outright rejection.

I had hoped that the white moderate would understand that law and order exist for the purpose of establishing justice, and that when they fail to do this they become dangerously structured dams that block the flow of social progress. I had hoped that the white moderate would understand that the present tension in the South is merely a necessary phase of the transition from an obnoxious negative peace, where the Negro passively accepted his unjust plight, to a substance-filled positive peace, where all men will respect the dignity and worth of human personality. Actually, we who engage in nonviolent direct action are not the creators of tension. We merely bring to the surface the hidden tension that is already alive. We bring it out in the open where it can be seen and dealt with. Like a boil that can never be cured as long as it is covered up but must be opened with all its pus-flowing ugliness to the natural medicines of air and light, injustice must likewise be exposed, with all of the tension its exposing creates, to the light of human conscience and the air of national opinion before it can be cured.

In your statement you asserted that our actions, even though peaceful, must be condemned because they precipitate violence. But can this assertion be logically made? Isn't this like condemning the robbed man because his possession of money precipitated the evil act of robbery? Isn't this like condemning Socrates because his unswerving commitment to truth and his philosophical delvings precipitated the misguided popular mind to make him drink the hemlock? Isn't this like condemning

Jesus because His unique God consciousness and never-ceasing devotion to His will precipitated the evil act of crucifixion? We must come to see, as federal courts have consistently affirmed, that it is immoral to urge an individual to withdraw his efforts to gain his basic constitutional rights because the quest precipitates violence. Society must protect the robbed and punish the robber.

I had also hoped that the white moderate would reject the myth of time. I received a letter this morning from a white brother in Texas which said: "All Christians know that the colored people will receive equal rights eventually, but is it possible that you are in too great of a religious hurry? It has taken Christianity almost 2,000 years to accomplish what it has. The teachings of Christ take time to come to earth." All that is said here grows out of a tragic misconception of time. It is the strangely irrational notion that there is something in the very flow of time that will inevitably cure all ills. Actually time is neutral. It can be used either destructively or constructively. I am coming to feel that the people of ill will have used time much more effectively than the people of good will. We will have to repent in this generation not merely for the vitriolic words and actions of the bad people, but for the appalling silence of the good people. We must come to see that human progress never rolls in on wheels of inevitability. It comes through the tireless efforts and persistent work of men willing to be co-workers with God, and without this hard work time itself becomes an ally of the forces of social stagnation.

We must use time creatively, and forever realize that the time is always ripe to do right. Now is the time to make real the promise of democracy, and transform our pending national elegy into a creative psalm of brotherhood. Now is the time to lift our national policy from the quicksand of racial injustice to the solid rock of human dignity.

You spoke of our activity in Birmingham as extreme. At first I was rather disappointed that fellow clergymen would see my nonviolent efforts as those of the extremist. I started thinking about the fact that I stand in the middle of two opposing forces in the Negro community. One is a force of complacency made up of Negroes who, as a result of long years of oppression, have been so completely drained of self-respect and a sense of "somebodiness" that they have adjusted to segregation, and of a few Negroes in the middle class who, because of a degree of academic and economic security, and because at points they profit by segregation, have unconsciously become insensitive to the problems of the masses. The other force is one of bitterness and hatred and comes perilously close to advocating violence. It is expressed in the various black nationalist groups that are springing up over the nation, the largest and best known being Elijah Muhammad's Muslim movement. This movement is nourished by the contemporary frustration over the continued existence of racial discrimination. It is made up of people who have lost faith in America, who have absolutely repudiated Christianity, and who have concluded that the white man is an incurable "devil." I have tried to stand between these two forces saying that we need not follow the "do-nothingism" of the complacent or the hatred and despair of the black nationalist. There is the more excellent way of love and nonviolent protest. I'm grateful to God that, through the Negro church, the dimension of nonviolence entered our struggle. If this philosophy had not emerged I am convinced that by now many streets of the South would be flowing with floods of blood. And I am further convinced that if our white brothers dismiss us as "rabble rousers" and "outside agitators"—those of us who are working through the channels of nonviolent direct action—and refuse to support our nonviolent efforts, millions of Negroes, out of frustration and despair, will seek solace and security in black-nationalist ideologies, a development that will lead inevitably to a frightening racial nightmare.

Oppressed people cannot remain oppressed forever. The urge for freedom will eventually come. This is what has happened to the American Negro. Something within has reminded him of his birthright of freedom; something without has reminded him that he can gain it. Consciously and unconsciously, he has been swept in by what the Germans call the Zeitgeist, and with his black brothers of Africa, and his brown and yellow brothers of Asia, South America, and the Caribbean, he is moving with a sense of cosmic urgency toward the promised land of racial justice. Recognizing this vital urge that has engulfed the Negro community, one should readily understand public demonstrations. The Negro has many pent-up resentments and latent frustrations. He has to get them out. So let him march sometime; let him have his prayer pilgrimages to the city hall; understand why he must have sit-ins and freedom rides. If his repressed emotions do not come out in these nonviolent ways, they will come out in ominous expressions of violence. This is not a threat; it is a fact of history. So I have not said to my people, "Get rid of your discontent." But I have tried to say that this normal and healthy discontent can be channeled through the creative outlet of nonviolent direct action. Now this approach is being dismissed as extremist. I must admit that I was initially disappointed in being so categorized.

But as I continued to think about the matter I gradually gained a bit of satisfaction from being considered an extremist. Was not Jesus an extremist in love? "Love your enemies, bless them that curse you, pray for them that despitefully use you." Was not Amos an extremist for justice—"Let justice roll down like waters and righteousness like a mighty stream." Was not Paul an extremist for the gospel of Jesus Christ—"I bear in my body the marks of the Lord Jesus." Was not Martin Luther an extremist—"Here I stand; I can do none other so help me God." Was not John Bunyan an extremist—"I will stay in jail to the end of my days before I make a butchery of my conscience." Was not Abraham Lincoln an extremist—"This nation cannot survive half slave and half free." Was not Thomas Jefferson an extremist—"We hold these truths to be self-evident, that all men are created equal." So the question is not whether we will be extremist but what kind of extremist will we be. Will we be extremists for hate or will we be extremists for love? Will we be extremists for the preservation of injustice—or will we be extremists for the cause of justice? In that dramatic scene on Calvary's hill three men were crucified. We must never forget that all three were crucified for the same crime—the crime of extremism. Two were extremists for immorality, and thus fell below their environment. The other, Jesus Christ, was an extremist for love, truth, and goodness, and thereby rose above His environment. So, after all, maybe the South, the nation, and the world are in dire need of creative extremists.

I had hoped that the white moderate would see this. Maybe I was too optimistic. Maybe I expected too much. I guess I should have realized that few members of a race that has oppressed another race can understand or appreciate the deep groans and passionate yearnings of those that have been oppressed, and still fewer have the vision to see that injustice must be rooted out by strong, persistent, and determined action. I am thankful, however, that some of our white brothers have grasped the meaning of this social revolution and committed themselves to it. They are still all too small in quantity, but they are big in quality. Some like Ralph McGill, Lillian Smith, Harry Golden, and James Dabbs have written about our struggle in eloquent, prophetic, and understanding terms. Others have marched with us down nameless streets of the South. They have languished in filthy, roach-infested jails, suffering the abuse and brutality of angry policemen who see them as "dirty nigger lovers." They, unlike so many of their moderate brothers and sisters, have recognized the urgency of the moment and sensed the need for powerful "action" antidotes to combat the disease of segregation.

Let me rush on to mention my other disappointment. I have been so greatly disappointed with the white Church and its leadership. Of course there are some notable exceptions. I am not unmindful of the fact that each of you has taken some significant stands on this issue. I commend you, Rev. Stallings, for your Christian stand on this past Sunday, in welcoming Negroes to your worship service on a non-segregated basis. I commend the Catholic leaders of this state for integrating Spring Hill College several years ago.

But despite these notable exceptions I must honestly reiterate that I have been disappointed with the Church. I do not say that as one of those negative critics who can always find something wrong with the Church. I say it as a minister of the gospel, who loves the Church; who was nurtured in its bosom; who has been sustained by its spiritual blessings and who will remain true to it as long as the cord of life shall lengthen.

I had the strange feeling when I was suddenly catapulted into the leadership of the bus protest in Montgomery several years ago that we would have the support of the white Church. I felt that the white ministers, priests, and rabbis of the South would be some of our strongest allies. Instead, some have been outright opponents, refusing to understand the freedom movement and misrepresenting its leaders; all too many others have been more cautious than courageous and have remained silent behind the anesthetizing security of the stained glass windows.

In spite of my shattered dreams of the past, I came to Birmingham with the hope that the white religious leadership of this community would see the justice of our cause and with deep moral concern, serve as the channel through which our just grievances could get to the power structure. I had hoped that each of you would understand. But again I have been disappointed.

I have heard numerous religious leaders of the South call upon their worshippers to comply with a desegregation decision because it is the law, but I have longed to hear white ministers say follow this decree because integration is morally right and the Negro is your brother. In the midst of blatant injustices inflicted upon the Negro, I have watched white churches stand on the sideline and merely mouth pious irrelevancies and sanctimonious trivialities. In the midst of a mighty struggle to rid our nation of racial and economic injustice, I have heard so many ministers say, "Those are social issues with which the gospel has no real concern," and I have watched so many churches commit themselves to a completely other-worldly religion which made a strange distinction between body and soul, the sacred and the secular.

So here we are moving toward the exit of the twentieth century with a religious community largely adjusted to the status quo, standing as a tail-light behind other community agencies rather than a headlight leading men to higher levels of justice.

I have travelled the length and breadth of Alabama, Mississippi and all the other southern states. On sweltering summer days and crisp autumn mornings I have looked at her beautiful churches with their spires pointing heavenward. I have beheld the impressive outlay of her massive religious education buildings. Over and over again I have found myself asking: "Who worships here? Who is their God? Where were their voices when the lips of Governor Barnett dripped with words of interposition and nullification? Where were they when Governor Wallace gave the clarion call for defiance and hatred? Where were their voices of support when tired, bruised, and weary Negro men and women decided to rise from the dark dungeons of complacency to the bright hills of creative protest?"

Yes, these questions are still in my mind. In deep disappointment, I have wept over the laxity of the Church. But be assured that my tears have been tears of love. There can be no deep disappointment where there is not deep love. Yes, I love the Church; I love her sacred walls. How could I do otherwise? I am in the rather unique position of being the son, the grandson, and the great-grandson of preachers. Yes, I see the Church as the body of Christ. But, oh! How we have blemished and scarred that body through social neglect and fear of being nonconformist.

There was a time when the Church was very powerful. It was during that period when the early Christians rejoiced when they were deemed worthy to suffer for what they believed. In those days the Church was not merely a thermometer that recorded the ideas and principles of popular opinion; it was a thermostat that transformed the mores of society. Wherever the early Christians entered a town the power structure got disturbed and immediately sought to convict them for being "disturbers of the peace" and "outside agitators." But they went on with the conviction that they were "a colony of heaven" and had to obey God rather than man. They were small in number but big in commitment. They were too God-intoxicated to be "astronomically intimidated." They brought an end to such ancient evils as infanticide and gladiatorial contest.

Things are different now. The contemporary Church is so often a weak, ineffectual voice with an uncertain sound. It is so often the arch-supporter of the status quo. Far from being disturbed by the presence of the Church, the power structure of the average community is consoled by the Church's silent and often vocal sanction of things as they are.

But the judgment of God is upon the Church as never before. If the Church of today does not recapture the sacrificial spirit of the early Church, it will lose its authentic ring, forfeit the loyalty of millions, and be dismissed as an irrelevant social club with no meaning for the twentieth century. I am meeting young people every day whose disappointment with the Church has risen to outright disgust.

Maybe again I have been too optimistic. Is organized religion too inextricably bound to the status quo to save our nation and the world? Maybe I must turn my faith to the inner spiritual Church, the church within the Church, as the true ecclesia and the hope of the world. But again I am thankful to God that some noble souls from the ranks of organized religion have broken loose from the paralyzing chains of conformity and joined us as active partners in the struggle for freedom. They have left their secure congregations and walked the streets of Albany, Georgia, with us. They have gone through the highways of the South on torturous rides for freedom. Yes, they have gone to jail with us. Some have been kicked out of their churches and lost the support of their bishops and fellow ministers. But they have gone with the faith that right defeated is stronger than evil triumphant. These men have been the leaven in the lump of the race. Their witness has been the spiritual salt that has preserved the true meaning of the Gospel in these troubled times. They have carved a tunnel of hope through the dark mountain of disappointment.

I hope the Church as a whole will meet the challenge of this decisive hour. But even if the Church does not come to the aid of justice, I have no despair about the future. I have no fear about the outcome of our struggle in Birmingham, even if our motives are presently misunderstood. We will reach the goal of freedom in Birmingham and all over the nation, because the goal of America is freedom. Abused and scorned though we may be, our destiny is tied up with the destiny of America. Before the pilgrims landed at Plymouth, we were here. Before the pen of Jefferson etched across the pages of history the majestic words of the Declaration of Independence, we were here. For more than two centuries our foreparents labored in this country without wages; they made cotton "king"; and they built the homes of their masters in the midst of brutal injustice and shameful humiliation—and yet out of a bottomless vitality they continued to thrive and develop. If the inexpressible cruelties of slavery could not stop us, the opposition we now face will surely fail. We will win our freedom because the sacred heritage of our nation and the eternal will of God are embodied in our echoing demands.

I must close now. But before closing I am impelled to mention one other point in your statement that troubled me profoundly. You warmly commend the Birmingham police force for keeping "order" and "preventing violence." I don't believe you would have so warmly commended the police force if you had seen its angry violent dogs literally biting six unarmed, nonviolent Negroes. I don't believe you would so quickly commend the policemen if you would observe their ugly and inhuman treatment of Negroes here in the city jail; if you would watch them push and curse old Negro women and young Negro girls; if you would see them slap and kick old Negro men and young Negro boys; if you will observe them, as they did on two occasions, refuse to give us food because we wanted to sing our grace together. I'm sorry that I can't join you in your praise for the police department.

It is true that they have been rather disciplined in their public handling of the demonstrators. In this sense they have been rather publicly "nonviolent." But for what purpose? To preserve the evil system of segregation. Over the last few years I have consistently preached that nonviolence demands the means we use must be as pure as the ends we seek. So I have tried to make it clear that it is wrong to use immoral means to attain moral ends. But now I must affirm that it is just as wrong or even more so to use moral means to preserve immoral ends. Maybe Mr. Connor and his policemen have been rather publicly nonviolent, as Chief Pritchett was in Albany, Georgia, but they have used the moral means of nonviolence to maintain the immoral end of flagrant injustice. T. S. Eliot has said that there is no greater treason than to do the right deed for the wrong reason.

I wish you had commended the Negro sit-inners and demonstrators of Birmingham for their sublime courage, their willingness to suffer, and their amazing discipline in the midst of the most inhuman provocation. One day the South will recognize its real heroes. They will be the James Merediths, courageously and with a majestic sense of purpose, facing jeering and hostile mobs and the agonizing loneliness that characterizes the life of the pioneer. They will be old, oppressed, battered Negro women, symbolized in a seventy-two year old woman of Montgomery, Alabama, who rose up with a sense of dignity and with her people decided not to ride the segregated buses, and responded to one who inquired about her tiredness with ungrammatical profundity: "My feets is tired, but my soul is rested." They will be the young high school and college students, young ministers of the gospel and a host of their elders courageously and nonviolently sitting-in at lunch counters and willingly going to jail for conscience sake. One day the South will know that when these disinherited children of God sat down at lunch counters they were in reality standing up for the best in the American dream and the most sacred values in our Judaeo-Christian heritage, and thus carrying our whole nation back to great wells of democracy which were dug deep by the founding fathers in the formulation of the Constitution and the Declaration of Independence.

Never before have I written a letter this long (or should I say a book?). I'm afraid it is much too long to take your precious time. I can assure you that it would have been much shorter if I had been writing from a comfortable desk, but what else is there to do when you are alone for days in the dull monotony of a narrow jail cell other than write long letters, think strange thoughts, and pray long prayers?

If I have said anything in this letter that is an overstatement of the truth and is indicative of an unreasonable impatience, I beg you to forgive me. If I have said anything in this letter that is an understatement of the truth and is indicative of my having a patience that makes me patient with anything less than brotherhood, I beg God to forgive me.

I hope this letter finds you strong in the faith. I also hope that circumstances will soon make it possible for me to meet each of you, not as an integrationist or a civil rights leader, but as a fellow clergyman and a Christian brother. Let us all hope that the dark clouds of racial prejudice will soon pass away and the deep fog of misunderstanding will be lifted from our fear-drenched communities and in some not too distant tomorrow the radiant stars of love and brotherhood will shine over our great nation with all their scintillating beauty.

Yours for the cause of
Peace and Brotherhood,

Martin Luther King, Jr.

The Concept of Race as Applied to Social Culture

Leonard Harris

T he foundation for this article was "Race Contacts and Inter-Racial Relations: A Study in the Theory and Practice of Race," Syllabus, 1915–1916, prepared under the auspices of the Howard Social Science Club and the NAACP. It was the basis for a new course that the university rejected.

Locke attacks a host of social evolutionists, including Tylor, Morgan, and Spencer. His thesis is that race and culture are two distinct variables, often correlated, but not causally connected. Nor do they form an organic unity. "Race" is not an unchanging biological category but an anthropological tool and a social myth with significant explanatory value and problematics. Cultural idioms, styles, and temperaments are also variables subject to historical change. Contrary to R. H. Lowie's view, however, Locke holds that there are important relationships between social race and culture.

The Concept of Race as Applied to Social Culture

In dealing with race and culture we undoubtedly confront two of the most inevitable but at the same time most unsatisfactory concepts involved in the broad-scale consideration of man and society. There is the general presumption and feeling that they have some quite vital and relevant connection, but as to the nature of this or even as to the scientific meaning of the individual concepts there is the greatest diversity of scientific opinion and theory. An analytic study of their highly variable meanings, confining this even to the more or less strictly scientific versions, would constitute two important and highly desirable treatises. But what we are here attempting is something quite more immediate and practical from the point of view of the use of these terms in the social sciences, and quite capable perhaps, if the analysis be successful, of settling some of these complexly controversial differences as to meaning by a process of elimination, namely an examination into their supposed relationship one to the other. For it seems that in the erroneous assumption of fixed relationships between the two, most of the serious difficulties and confusions lie. It will be our contention that far from being constants, these important aspects of human society are variables, and in the majority of instances not even paired variables, and that though they have at all times significant and definite relationships,

Alain Locke, "The Concept of Race as Applied to Social Culture," *Howard Review*, vol. 1, pp. 290–299, 1924.

they nevertheless are in no determinate way organically or causally connected. And if this should be so, whole masses of elaborately constructed social theory and cultural philosophizing fall with the destruction of a common basic assumption, that has been taken as a common foundation for otherwise highly divergent and even antagonistic theorizing. This position, differing from that of the school of interpretation which denies all significant connection between racial and cultural factors,[1] does not deny that race stands for significant social characters and culture-traits or represents in given historical contexts characteristic differentiations of culture-type. However, it does insist against the assumption of any such constancy, historical or intrinsic, as would make it possible to posit an organic connection between them and to argue on such grounds the determination of one by the other.

But the unwarranted assumption of race as a determinant of culture is still very current, and contemporary discussion, especially in ethnology, is still primarily concerned with the destructive criticism of this inveterate and chronic notion. We would by no means minimize the success and scientific service of such criticism as that of Boas in the field of anthropology and "race psychology," of Flinders-Petrie in archeology, of Finot, Babington, Hertz, and von Zollschan in social and political theory, and of Lowie and Wissler in ethnology,[2] in saying that as yet, however, we seem to be only at a transitional stage in the scientific consideration of the relationship of race to culture. In some revised and reconstructed form, we may anticipate the continued even if restricted use of these terms as more or less necessary and basic concepts that cannot be eliminated altogether, but that must nevertheless be so safe-guarded in this continued use as not to give further currency to the invalidated assumptions concerning them. It is too early to assume that there is no significant connection between race and culture because of the manifestly false and arbitrary linkage which has previously been asserted.

In the interval between these two stages of the discussion, as one might normally expect, there is considerable tendency to continue the corollaries of the older view even where the main position and hypothesis has been abandoned. Goldenweiser[3] is therefore quite justified in his insistence upon linking up these corollaries with the position of classical social evolutionism which gave them such vogue and standing, and disestablishing both by the same line of argument. For although this notion of race as a prime determining factor in culture was historically established by the theory and influence of de Gobineau,[4] its scientific justification has been associated with the doctrines of the strictly evolutionary interpretation of culture, especially with the influence of the social evolutionism of Spencer. The primary scientific use of this fixed linkage between race and culture was to justify the classical evolutionary scheme of a series of stepped stages in an historical progression of cultural development. In this connection it has been the analogue in the theory of society of the heredity factor in the biological field, and its stock notions of *race capacity* and *racial heredity* have had approximately the same phases of acceptance, repudiation, and revision. In their "classical" form they are now equally discredited by several lines of detailed evidence where the historical succession of stages does not coincide with those posited as the ground basis of the supposedly universal process of development,[5] and by the more intensive and objective study of primitive cultures which has shown how insidiously their consideration in the light of such evolutionary schemes has distorted their concrete facts and values. There is considerable warrant therefore for the position that wishes to exclude all further misinterpretation by a complete disassociation of the concept of race from the concept of culture.

This is the position of Lowie[6] who concludes after a brilliant and rigorous examination as to the inter connection between culture and race that not only are cultural changes "manifestly independent of the racial factor," but that no race has permanent or even uniform alignment with reference to culture-type or cultural stages. His position, though one of the closest reasoned of any, is the most iconoclastic with respect to the assumption of any significant relation between race and culture, as may be estimated from the following passage:

> With great confidence we can say that since the same race at different times or in different subdivisions at the same time represents vastly different cultural stages, there is obviously no direct proportional between culture and race and if great changes of culture can occur without any change of race whatsoever, we are justified in considering it probable that a relatively minute change of hereditary ability might produce enormous differences.

But the extreme cultural relativism of Lowie leaves an open question as to the association of certain ethnic groups with definite culture-traits and culture types under circumstances where there is evidently a greater persistence of certain strains and characteristics in their culture than of other factors. The stability of such factors and their resistance to direct historical modification marks out the province of that aspect of the problem of race which is distinctly ethnological and which the revised notion of ethnic race must cover. It seems quite clear that no adequate explanation can be expected from the factors and principles of anthropological race distinctions. In the light of the most recent and accepted investigations any attempt to explain one in terms of the other must be regarded as pseudoscientific. Nevertheless though there is lacking for the present any demonstrable explanation, there are certain ethnic traits the peculiarly stable and stock character of which must be interpreted as ethnically characteristic. They are in no sense absolutely permanent, the best psychological evidence as yet gives us no reason for construing them as inherent, yet they are factors not without an integral relationship one to the other not satisfactorily explained as mere historical combinations. Indeed it seems difficult and in some cases impossible to discover common historical factors to account for their relative constancy. Few challenge the specific factuality of these peculiarly resistant combinations of group traits.

As Sapir[7] aptly says,

> Here, as so often, the precise knowledge of the scientist lags somewhat behind the more naive but more powerful insights of non-professional experience and impression. To deny to the genius of a people an ultimate psychological significance and to refer it to the specific historical development of that people

is not, after all is said and done, to analyze it out of existence. It remains true that large groups of people everywhere tend to think and to act in accordance with established and all but instinctive forms, which are in a large measure peculiar to it.

The point that seems to be important to note and stress is that we do not need to deny the existence of these characteristic racial molds in denying that they are rooted in "inherent hereditary traits either of a biological or a psychological nature."

If, instead of the anthropological, the ethnic characters had been more in the focus of scientific attention, there probably would have resulted a much more scientific and tenable doctrine of the relationship of race to culture. Race would have been regarded as primarily a matter of social heredity, and its distinctions due to the selective psychological "set" of established cultural reactions. There is a social determination involved in this which quite more rationally interprets and explains the relative stability or so-called permanency that the old theorists were trying to account for on the basis of fixed anthropological characters and factors. To quote again from Sapir:[8]

> The current assumption that the so-called 'genius' of a people is ultimately reducible to certain inherent heredity traits of a biological and psychological nature does not, for the most part, bear very serious examination. Frequently enough, what is assumed to be an innate racial characteristic turns out on closer study to be the resultant of purely historical causes. A mode of thinking, a distinctive type of reaction, gets itself established in the course of a complex historical development as typical, as normal; it serves then as a model for the working over of new elements of civilization.

The best consensus of opinion then seems to be that race is a fact in the social or ethnic sense, that it has been very erroneously associated with race in the physical sense and is therefore not scientifically commensurate with factors or conditions which explain or have produced physical race characters and differentiation, that it has a vital and significant relation to social culture, and that it must be explained in terms of social and historical causes such as have caused similar differentiations of culture-type as pertain in lesser degree between nations, tribes, classes, and even family strains. Most authorities are now reconciled to two things,—first, the necessity of a thorough-going redefinition of the nature of race, and second, the independent definition of race in the ethnic or social sense together with the independent investigation of its differences and their causes apart from the investigation of the factors and differentiae of physical race. Of course eventually there may be some interesting correlation possible at the conclusion of these two lines of investigation, but up to the present they seem only to have needlessly handicapped and complicated one another and to have brought comparative ethnology and comparative anthropology both to a deadlock of confusion because of their incompatible points of view and incommensurable values. It is undoubtedly this necessity of a new start that Wissler[9] has in mind when he says, "So it is obvious that the relation between culture and race is a subject of more than passing interest, and though as yet not seriously investigated, the time is near at hand when its solution must be sought, if life is to be understood rationally and socially." Similarly we find Flinders-Petrie[10] in his address before the British Association saying, "The definition of the nature of race is the most requisite element for any clear ideas about man," and then veering over to the strictly social definition of race by adding, "The only meaning a race can have is a group of persons whose type has become unified by their rate of assimilation and affection by their conditions exceeding the rate of change produced by foreign elements." Evidently the thought here is that blood intermixture is only one of the conducive conditions to cultural assimilation and absorption and that therefore *culture-type* or *social race* is the important fact and concept. Race in the vital and basic sense is simply and primarily the culture-heredity, and that in its blendings and differentiations is properly analyzed on the basis of conformity to or variance from culture-type.

Gault,[11] discussing Stevenson's study, *Socio-Anthropometry: An Inter-racial Critique,* and several studies of Indian cross-breeds, all of which draw conclusions that differences are due to blood-race factors, says:

> There is always the possibility that the Indian of mixed blood owes a degree of his superiority (we should say 'difference') to the *social* stimuli of one or the other parent from earliest infancy: stimuli that from the beginning have induced a level of reactions that otherwise would have been lacking, and have built up personality complexes that are next to original nature as respects substantiality.

Thus even in instances where physical assimilation is the condition responsible for cultural assimilation, the latter takes place in terms of social factors. Divorced then by every line of objectively considered evidence from the anthropological notion and criteria of race with which its distinctions rarely if ever coincide, ethnic race or what Gault calls "sociologic type" becomes the most scientifically tenable and useful concept.

Instead therefore of regarding culture as expressive of race, race by this interpretation is regarded as itself a culture product. Goldenweiser[12] puts the matter this way; he says:

> Enough has been said to show that the view generally held of the relation between race and culture may well be reversed. According to the prevailing view, man is many and civilization one, meaning by this that the races differ significantly in potential ability and that only one, the white race, could have and has achieved civilization. The reverse view, forced upon the ethnologist and the historian by a more critical and open-minded survey of the facts, reads thus: *man is one, civilizations are many,* meaning by this that the races do not differ significantly

in psychological endowment, that the variety of possible civilizations is great and of actual ones, considerable, and that many civilizations other than ours have achieved things of genuine and unique worth.

Perhaps the revolutionary significance of this can only be realized when we see it applied to specific descriptive analysis as in the case of Rivers'[13] use of the term race solely in a sense which means the people who had such and such culture-traits, whose customs dominated this or that period and set the pattern upon which a certain culture-type was developed.

Nothing seems more likely than that there will gradually develop out of this new and more objective analysis of culture a series of relatively divergent and basic culture-types, for each of which perhaps some more or less organic principle of development or evolution can be worked out, so that we may eventually get a standard of value for relative culture grading. Meanwhile we must grant the logic of the position of Lowie which is that the most objective study at present gives no warrant for the relative scientific grading of cultures. Meanwhile each culture must be treated as specific and as highly composite, and each ethnic group as the peculiar resultant of its own social history. This is what we mean then by this reversal of emphasis, that instead of the race explaining the cultural condition, the cultural conditions must explain the race traits, and that instead of artificially extracted units representing race types, the newer scientific approach demands that we deal with concrete culture-types which as often as not are composite racially speaking, and have only an artificial ethnic unity of historical derivation and manufacture.

Confident that this is the correct scientific conception of culture and its most warrantable scientific basis of approach and study, we return to the consideration of whether or not by such interpretation the concept of race is not entirely relegated from serious consideration in connection with it. So considerable is the shift of emphasis and meaning that at times it does seem that the best procedure would be to substitute for the term *race* the term *culture-group*. But what has become absolutely disqualified for the explanation of culture groups taken as totalities becomes in a much more scientific and verifiable way a main factor of explanation of its various cultural components. Race accounts for a great many of the specific elements of the cultural heredity, and the sense of race may itself be regarded as one of the operative factors in culture since it determines the stressed values which become the conscious symbols and tradition of the culture. Such stressed values are themselves factors in the process of culture making, and account primarily for the persistence and resistance of culture-traits. For these determine what is the dominant pattern in any given culture, and it is toward these dominants as social norms that social conformation converges and according to which it eventually establishes the type. It is with respect to such principles of determination that the newer psychology of race must be worked out instead of with reference to assumed innate traits and capacities. The type itself may have been established by accident or fortuitous combinations of historical circumstances, but re-enforced by the sense of race as perhaps the most intense of the feelings of commonality, it becomes an accepted, preferred and highly resistant culture complex that seems to be and often is self-perpetuating.

Race operates as tradition, as preferred traits and values, and when these things change culturally speaking ethnic remoulding is taking place. Race then, so far as the ethnologist is concerned, seems to lie in that peculiar selective preference for certain culture-traits and resistance to certain others which is characteristic of all types and levels of social organization. And instead of decreasing as a result of contacts this sense and its accumulative results seems on the whole to increase, so that we get accumulative effect. It intensifies therefore with contacts and increases with the increasing complexity of the culture elements in any particular area. A diversity of cultural types temporarily at least accentuates the racial stresses involved, so that even when a fusion eventuates it takes place under the conditions determined by the resistance developed and the relative strength of the several cultural components.

Indeed, the evidence shows most cultures to be highly composite. Sometimes there seems to be a race relatively pure physically with a considerably mixed culture, sometimes, perhaps more frequently, a highly mixed race with a relatively fused culture. But in the large majority of cases the culture is only to be explained as the resultant of the meeting and reciprocal influence of several culture strains, several ethnic contributions. Such facts nullify two of the most prevalent popular and scientific fallacies, the ascription of a total culture to any one ethnic strain, and the interpretation of culture in terms of the intrinsic rather than the fusion values of its various constituent elements. Especially does this newer view insist upon the disassociation of the claims of political dominance and cultural productivity, and combat the traditional view that all or even the best elements of a culture are the contribution of the ethnic group which in a mixed culture has political dominance and is in dynastic control. Already a number of such politically proprietary claims have been disallowed and disestablished by the more intensive and objectively comparative study of culture-traits. Such procedure promises to redeem the fields of discussion which till recently have been so vitiated by racial and national bias that some ethnologists have been led to conclude the impossibility of the scientific evaluation of cultures. After all, the failure to maintain objective standards, relevant values, and parity of values ought not be taken as evidence that this is not possible. So great is the tendency to lapse back into the former positions of bias, that the rigid maintenance of objective description as the sole aim of the ethnologist may, however, be fully warranted for the time being.

But races may, and must eventually be compared with respect to their relative and characteristic abilities and tendencies with respect to cultural origins, cultural assimilation, cultural survival, and their concrete institutional contributions. But in every case absolute objective parity of condition and values must be maintained. An instance in point is Lowie's[14] own illustration in a discussion of the relative rating of cultures on the basis of cultural originality and assimilation. He says: "If the Japanese deserve no credit for having appropriated our culture, we must also carefully eliminate from that culture all elements not demonstrably due to the creative genius of our race before laying claim to the residue as our distinctive product." This seems simple enough to be axiomatic, yet as a principle of comparison one can find in treatise after treatise a score of breaches for every single observance of what ought to be a fundamental procedure. Irrelevant evaluation and invidious comparisons that do not even make the pretense of establishing either parity or equivalence of values abound, yet it is not to be corrected by excluding values, but rather through insistence upon the only properly scientific criteria—intrinsic values for the interpretation of any culture, and strictly commensurate or equivalent values as a basis of comparisons between them.

The chief source of error in the evaluation of cultures can be traced as the same source already described as responsible for the prevalent errors in the description of cultures. It is incumbent upon us to see clearly why the evolutionary formula has led in both these instances to such unsoundness of interpretation. It would seem that by putting all types and varieties into the same series, and this is the crux of the straight evolutionary point of view, the error of assuming basic common factors and commensurate values has almost irretrievably been made. Not that such factors may not exist, but that they are not to be discovered except from the point of view of a more objective and detailed comparison than has in most cases been attempted. Since the days of the Indo-Germanic myth, and its twin fancy the Aryan hypothesis, the desire and suppressed objective in many investigations has been to build a social pyramid of straight line progressive stages, and subtle variations of this point of view have been introducing error upon error into the interpretation of cultures, especially primitive and alien cultures which have naturally borne the brunt of the scheme through having been distorted and pinched into alignment with the pre-conceived formula.[15] We have a clear and succinct statement of the responsibility in this regard in the following passage:[16]

> The earlier anthropologists and sociologists, swayed by the biological theories of evolution, posited parallel development in every people, following upon innate psychological tendencies. Complete systems, with stages of development culminating in our own particular type of civilization, were posited by such early writers as Morgan, Spencer, Tylor and others. However, it has been found that the other cultural mechanism, that of diffusion, constituted a grave stumbling block to this a priori scheme of stage development, and it is now known that independent origins of inventions are infinitely more rare than was believed, and that they are conditioned not by innate psychological tendencies, but by the cultural milieu in which they occur.

Gradually it has become apparent that the procedure of using primitive cultures as the stock arguments and illustrations for societal evolution has disorganized the organic unity of these cultures, and merely used certain aspects of them as illustrating a comparative series which even if it were correct for the institution in question from which the accentuated culture-elements were taken, would not place correctly in scale as totalities the cultures respectively in question.

It follows then that the work of correction will have to begin at the very point where originally the errors and distortions have been introduced, namely, the more carefully objective study and organic interpretation of primitive cultures. This would be necessary from the purely corrective point of view, even if it were not also true as Wissler[17] says that "our clearest insight into the mechanisms of culture is attained when we examine the more primitive marginal cultures of the world." After the application of the reconstructed notion of race as social in manifestation and derivation, this would seem to be the most important and promising revision of idea and method in the entire field of our discussion. As a straight methodological question then we get the following as the only correct and acceptable procedure in the study of any given culture—first, its analytic and complete description in terms of its own culture-elements, second, its organic interpretation in terms of its own intrinsic values as a vital mode of living, combined if possible with an historical account of its development and derivation, and then finally and not till then its assignment to culture-type and interpretation as a stage of culture. Almost any culture so treated will be found to be radically different both in description and evaluation from that account which would have been given it if immediately submitted on first analysis to the general scale and to universal comparison. Let us call this the *principle of organic interpretation* and the other the *principle of cultural relativity,* and conclude that in combination with the dynamic and social interpretation of race, the three are the methodological foundation and platform of the newer science of social culture. Especially in connection with the concept of race are all of the biased and partisan points of view and scales of evaluation obviated by such procedure so that it becomes possible to continue the term scientifically and usefully in the context of discussion to which it is most relevant, but into which until recently it has introduced primarily serious errors both of fact and of value.

Notes

1. R. H. Lowie, *Culture and Ethnology,* Chap. II, 1923.
2. Franz Boas, *The Mind of Primitive Man,* (1911); W. M. Flinders-Petrie, *Race and Civilization* (Proc. Brit. Assoc., 1895); Jean Finot, *Race Prejudice* (Trans. 1907); W. D. Babington, *Fallacies of Race Theories*; Hertz, *Moderne Rassentheorien;* I. von Zollschan, *Das Rassenproblem* (Vienna, 1912).
3. A. Goldenweiser, *Early Civilization,* Chap. 1. pp. 14–15.
4. de Gobineau, *Essai sur l'inegalite des races humains* (Paris, 1854).
5. [The reference is probably to R. H. Lowie, *Culture and Ethnology.*]
6. R. H. Lowie, *Culture and Ethnology,* p. 41.
7. E. Sapir, "Culture, Genuine and Spurious." *American Journal of Sociology* 29, p. 406.
8. *Ibid.,* pp. 405–406.
9. Wissler, C., *Man and Culture* (1923).
10. Flinders-Petrie, *Race and Civilization* (Proc. Brit. Assoc., 1895).
11. Gault, R. H., *Social Psychology* (New York, 1923), p. 104.
12. Goldenweiser, *Early Civilization,* p. 14.

13. Compare Rivers, W. H., *Psychology and Ethnology* (London, 1926).

14. Lowie, *Culture and Ethnology,* pp. 32–33.

15. Compare Goldenweiser, Chap. 1 and p. 125.

16. Herskovits and Willey, "The Cultural Approach to Sociology," *American Journal of Sociology* 29, p. 195.

17. Wissler, *Man and Culture,* p. 286.

What Mr. Creosote Knows about Laughter

Noël Carroll

And by his side rode loathsome Gluttony,

Deformed creature, on a filthie swyne:

His belly was up-blown with luxury,

And eke with fatnesse swollen were his eyne,

And like a Crane his necke was long and fyne,

With which he swallowed up excessive feast,

For want whereof poore people oft did pyne;

And all the way, most like a brutish bear,

He spued up his gorge, that all did him deteast.

…

In shape and life more like a monster, than a man.

—Edmund Spenser, *The Faerie Queene*

Part VI: "The Autumn Years" of *Monty Python's The Meaning of Life* begins with a song about the glories of having a penis which is appreciated by all the audience in the cabaret, including the talking fish in an aquarium in the vicinity of the piano. The fish have the human faces of the Monty Python crew superimposed over their bodies and they call to mind something of the unsettling hybrid creatures found on hellish landscapes by Hieronymus Bosch, the fifteenth- and sixteenth-century Dutch artist. Their enjoyment of the ditty, however, quickly vanishes when they catch sight of the entrance of Mr. Creosote into the restaurant. "Oh shit!" cries one of them as they whiz off-screen.

Mr. Creosote, a gargantuan figure, lumbers into the dining room. The music that accompanies his entry recalls the giant shark's in *Jaws*, and his belly is so ponderous it nearly scrapes the floor. His face, framed by muttonchops, is swollen to the point of swinishness. He is dressed in a tuxedo but his body is mis-shaped, more like a pyramid of wobbling flesh than a human form. As Creosote ambles to his table, he commands a flurry of attention from the sycophantic maitre d'. This is obviously a very, very good customer, one who could eat whole families under the exceedingly expensive tables of this lavish eatery.

Creosote is also a very churlish customer. He is consistently curt to the point of rudeness. When asked how he is faring, he says "Better" and pauses before completing his thought—"Better get a bucket." In other words, he never responds civilly, but only commands imperiously. When the aforesaid bucket is brought to him, he proceeds to vomit into it with the force of a fire hose in complete obliviousness to his surroundings and to the sensibilities of his fellow diners. He doesn't do this once but several times and then repeats the spectacle on the back of the cleaning woman who is trying to clean up the mess he is making. He shows no concern for anyone else; his inclinations are the only lights by which he steers. In every way, Creosote is crude, gruff, and utterly selfish.

Thus, his vomiting elicits no sympathy. He treats it as his privilege; he's paying for it; so he'll do whatever he wants. Creosote clearly, as a matter of course, stuffs himself to the point that his body cannot absorb the mass he ingests. He retches in order to gorge himself again. He is gluttony personified.

The maitre d' hands him a menu; he disgorges himself all over it. The servant has to wipe it off so that he can read it. Moreover, it should be added, this vomit looks pretty convincing. Even the most ardent Python fan is apt to feel a twinge of nausea coming on.

Hearing the specials, all delicacies of a diversity befitting the original Gargantua, Creosote orders the lot, mixed into a bucket with eggs on top, along with a double portion of *pâté*, six bottles of wine, two magnums of champagne and perhaps some ale. Pope Gregory the Great defined gluttony as eating too soon, too delicately, too expensively, too greedily, and too much. Creosote's nausea indicates he is not ready for his next meal; it is too soon. He eats expensive delicacies as if they were potato chips. And he eats too much; he eats the entire menu. It is no wonder that Michael Palin called this routine a "Gothic Extravaganza."[1] It is like an illustration of one of the Deadly Sins.

Creosote, reminding one of an image out of James Ensor, the nineteenth–twentieth-century Belgian expressionist, continues to vomit as he eats. Other customers are disgusted and start leaving to the visible chagrin of the maitre d'; some are heaving themselves. The maitre d' accidentally steps into Creosote's pail of vomit and Creosote erupts upon his leg, to the evident great annoyance of the maitre d'. The maitre d' is reaching the end of his tether. Finally, Creosote is finished, but the maitre d' willfully tempts him, even prods him, to take one more bite, just a bit of a thin wafer of mint, despite the fact that Creosote protests that he is absolutely full.

Almost immediately, that slice of mint does its vengeful work. Creosote literally explodes, issuing forth a tidal wave of vomit that splashes every corner of the dining room. In the center of this dripping mess, then, sits Creosote, his belly blown open so that one can see his rib cage; but his red, fist-like heart relentlessly continues pumping as it dangles under his chin. His eyes are open, his face still carrying

---

1 The Pythons with Bob McCabe, *The Pythons: Autobiography by the Pythons* (New York: St. Martin's Press, 2003), p. 326.

that mask of impassive brutishness he has worn throughout the scene. The maitre d', overjoyed and very self-satisfied by the success of his revenge plot, gives Creosote the check.

To Laugh, or To Scream?

This scene, involving non-stop nausea and a graphically exploded body, sounds more horrific than comic. It, like so much of the humor of Monty Python, is on the dark side. The scene has few peers in the annals of motion picture comedy, save perhaps the pie-eating sequence in *Stand By Me*. But even that seems tame next to the spectacle of Mr. Creosote's extravasation. The philosophical question it raises is: how is it possible to laugh at humor as black as this? Though it may seem paradoxical that mirth could issue from depicting a situation so gruesome and disgusting, perhaps this will not strike us as so strange when we recall how much humor—such as bathroom humor—revels in the repulsive. And yet there is nevertheless something perplexing about this scene. How can the gag function as a source of comic amusement for so many, rather than leaving them trembling in horror? Why is the sequence comic rather than horrific? This seems paradoxical. Since negotiating paradoxes is one of the charges of philosophy, answering that question is the aim of this chapter. And in the process, we wish to learn what Mr. Creosote can teach us about laughter.

Let us agree from the outset that many people laugh at this scene; they find it comically amusing. This is not to deny that some also find it disgusting, and even unwatchable. And even those who enjoy the routine may experience moments during it when their stomach feels on the verge of revolting. Nevertheless, there are a significant number of people who find the scene on balance risible, and even continuously so—that is, they laugh all the way through. Our question is, How can they do so? How can anyone find the explosion of a human body to be comically amusing? If anything, the prospect is horrifying.

One way to make some headway with this problem is to think about what makes for horror, especially in mass culture.[2] In popular fictions, including literature and motion pictures, horror is typically focused upon a particular sort of object, namely, a monster—that is, a creature whose existence is unacknowledged by science and who, in addition, is dangerous and disgusting. For example, the Frankenstein monster is a scientific impossibility—electrifying dead flesh will fry it, not animate it—and the monster is disgusting, an impure being constructed of rotting, dismembered body parts. And perhaps most obviously, the monster is dangerous: it kidnaps, maims, and kills people.

Maybe we are tempted to think of the restaurant vomiting scene as horror rather than comedy because Creosote, it would appear, shares many of the attributes that characterize horror. For example,

---

2   The ensuing account of horror derives from Noël Carroll, *The Philosophy of Horror* (New York: Routledge, 1990), especially the first chapter. For further background on comic amusement, see my article, "Humour," in *The Oxford Handbook of Aesthetics*, edited by Jerrold Levinson (Oxford: Oxford University Press, 2003), pp. 344–365.

I expect that he is a physiological impossibility; even supposing that someone could reach his girth, it is unlikely that he would be able to move on his own power. Creosote is of a scale of obesity where the patient usually has to be moved by handlers. But Creosote is also beyond the ken of science, both in the manner of his explosion and, then, of his survival. People don't burst like that, balloons do; and if they did, they would not live to tell the tale. But one suspects that Creosote will have himself sewn up again in order to eat another day.

Moreover, Creosote, like Frankenstein's monster, is certainly disgusting. In the first instance, his behavior is disgusting. His constant vomiting presents a challenge to the strongest stomach. I think that were it not the case that film is odorless—that, thankfully, smell-o-rama has not yet been perfected—many viewers would be unable to hold onto their own dinners throughout this episode. Indeed, Creosote's name suggests a foul odor, inasmuch as it labels a colorless liquid, a pungent burning agent, that smells of smoked meat and tar. Creosote's incontinence, furthermore, functions metonymically in the same way in which the rats, spiders, and other vermin that inhabit the vampire's lair function—namely, as disgusting things designed to accentuate the abominableness of the thing to which they are attached or which they surround.

But it is not only what is connected to Creosote that is disgusting. Creosote himself is loathsome, an abomination. Undoubtedly, he is the sort of thing we call monstrous in ordinary language. Like the Frankenstein monster or the creatures in the *Alien* and *Predator* series, Creosote is physically repulsive. The thought of being hugged by Creosote is probably enough to make most of us squirm; and imagine what visualizing a kiss on the lips from him might do to your digestion. Once again, like the Frank-enstein monster, the Alien, and the Predator, there is something viscerally revolting, unclean, and impure about Creosote.

It's the impurity of the monster in horror fictions that elicits the response of disgust from audiences. This impurity, in turn, is rooted in the ontology, or being, of horrific creatures. Such creatures are violations or problematizations of our standing cultural categories. For that reason they are abominations possessing a combination or collection of properties that our culture trains us to revile on contact. For instance, the Frankenstein monster violates the categorical distinction between life and death. It is both. It is a walking contradiction, as is Chucky, the puppet that kills, from the film *Child's Play*. The Predator, a category violation if there ever was one, is part crab and part primate. The Blob defies our categories by not fitting into any of them; it is stuff out of control. The Amazing Colossal Man is horrifically repulsive because he is too colossal; he violates the criteria of what it is to be human in virtue of his scale. Creosote likewise is monstrous just because his figure seems to go beyond not only what is normal but even beyond what is humanly possible. He is a travesty of the human form; he is an affront to our norms of the human form. He strikes us as inhuman or nonhuman. But as a result of effectively claiming membership in that category—that is, in our species—he triggers an aversive response on our part.

Who's Afraid of Mr. Creosote?

Creosote is a monster and he incurs our disgust. So far the horror formula is realized. But two points need to be made. First, disgust, including disgust elicited by the violation of our standing norms and categories, does not belong solely to the domain of the genre of horror. It is, as noted earlier, also a natural ingredient of comedy. This, of course, should be extremely evident. Think of how much humor, especially juvenile humor, hinges on celebrating disgusting things—farts, feces, and slime. Insofar as mention of these things, which are themselves categorically interstitial (ambiguously both part of me and outside of me), is also a violation of the norms of propriety, they are staples of humor. Disgust, that is, belongs as much to comedy as to horror. But in order for a categorical violation to turn into an occasion for horror, something else must be added, namely, fear. So the second point to be addressed is whether the fear-condition for the elicitation of horror has been met in the Creosote sequence. For if it has not been, then we can start to explain why the Creosote scene is comic rather than horrific.

In horror fictions, the monster is fearsome and disgusting because it is dangerous and impure. Standardly, the monster in a horror fiction is not threatening to the audience. They know that they are encountering a fiction and that they can suffer no harm from the creatures that rule the page and the screen. Rather they feel fear for the humans in the fiction who are being stalked or otherwise imperiled by the monsters. Insofar as we feel concern for the plight of those fictional characters—that is, insofar as we anticipate that harm will befall them at the hands, talons, or other instruments of the monsters—the fear condition of the horror formula is activated.

However, when we turn to the scene with Mr. Creosote, there is no fear factor. We do not fear for the other customers in the restaurant. They are in no great danger from Mr. Creosote. They are unquestionably offended by him. This may garner some sympathy for them (or, it may not, if you regard them as insufferable swells deserving of being taken down a peg). But it will not elicit fear in their behalf, since they are in no grievous danger, bodily or otherwise.

But perhaps Creosote is the human who should elicit our concern. After all, he's a person (ain't he got some rights?), and he does explode. And he is harmed by the machinations of the maitre d'. However, here Creosote shows us something about how comedy works. Creosote is not quite human. Not only is he too outsized. But he is utterly impervious to his repeated bouts of nausea—what human can take fits of retching in his stride the way Creosote does?—and he, of course, survives the massive explosion of his belly. In this, Creosote not only resembles the monster of horror fictions. He also resembles that staple of slapstick comedy, the clown.

The clown is not exactly human. With respect of our norms for the average human, the clown is either too fat or too tall, too thin or too short. His mouth is painted to appear exaggeratedly large and his eyes and head are often too small. He is a misproportioned human. Nor are his cognitive skills near the norm; generally he is too stupid. And his body can also take abuse that no actual person could. He can be hit on the head with a sledge hammer and suffer no more than a dizzy swoon where the rest of us would be hospitalized with a concussion. He takes falls with abandon and always pops up for another slam. It is as if his bones were made of rubber. Instead of breaking, they snap back into place.

It's because the clown is marked as so ontologically different from us—especially in terms of his imperviousness to bodily harm—that we have no fear for his life and limb. We can laugh at the way in which his body with its incongruities taunts our concept of the human, because the mayhem the clown engages is nonthreatening. We need not fear for the clown; nor, in the standard case, need we fear clowns. They are, for the most part, benign. Thus, though monstrous, clowns and the other denizens of slapstick incur no horror, since no genuine harm will result in or from their shenanigans.

Mr. Creosote belongs to the same fantastic species as the clown. He is not precisely human, so we do not fear for him as we do for the characters in horror fictions. He is able to suffer through things that would incapacitate or destroy ordinary mortals, because he is marked as of a different ontological order. Because Creosote can neither harm nor can he be harmed, his monstrosity becomes an occasion for comic amusement rather than horror. This is one thing that Mr. Creosote shows us about laughter.

It has been established experimentally that children will laugh when confronted with something incongruous—like a "funny face"—if the face is offered by someone with whom they are familiar, but they will cringe if it is presented by a stranger. This suggests that our responses to incongruities, anomalies, unexpected deviations from norms and standing categories will vary in terms of certain conditions. If the incongruity occurs in a context where it is threatening, it will dispose us toward a fearful response. This is perhaps the origin of the horror genre. On the other hand, if the context is one that is marked as non-threatening—where the prospect of harm and danger has been subtracted—the circumstances are ripe for comedy. The Mr. Creosote scene illustrates this principle dramatically by getting as perilously close to the conditions that satisfy the horrific, but remaining on the side of amusement. In this it exemplifies a principle that makes much cruel humor possible: we need not fear for the victims of all the violence and malevolence done in darker shades of comedy, including slapstick, because they are not completely human. Punch and Judy can be beaten mercilessly but they will never come within an inch of their lives. Mr. Creosote never suffers or dies. He is not precisely our kind of creature. Thus, we may laugh at him.

Just Desserts

But this is not all that Mr. Creosote tells us about laughter. It's true that in order to find a routine like his comically amusing we must not fear for him. And we do not, since he is not subject to human vulnerability. Instead we focus on his monstrous incongruity, his absurdity. But it's not just that we do not feel concern about Creosote because we know he cannot be harmed. We also are encouraged to form a positive animus against Creosote. We do not just laugh at the ontological incongruity of Creosote and what befalls him. Part of our laughter, even if it is not pure comic laughter, originates in our sense that Creosote gets what he deserves. Part of our laughter is vindictive or, at least, retributive. What has happened to Creosote, or so we are invited to suppose, is just. Though Creosote is not completely human, he is human enough to engender our scorn morally and to merit punishment. Moreover, we cannot help but think that his punishment fits his crime ever so appropriately. Think of how often we describe the aftermath of our own gluttonous escapades in terms of a feeling that we are about to explode. Creosote gets his just desserts, one might say. On the one hand, Creosote is a despicable character. He treats others with contempt, presumably because he thinks his evident wealth entitles him to do so. He spits up on servants with no sense of shame; they are beneath his selfish concern. He has no inkling of decorum and is insensitive to the existence of other people and their rightful claims. He is an egoist of stupendous proportions. And, of course, he has abused himself immensely. His vast bulk appears to be his own fault. It is the height of self-indulgence to eat so far past the point of satiation that one continues to press on while one is still egesting the surplus of one's last meal. Creosote has sown what he reaps. He has asked for what he has gotten. His own greedy appetite has backfired, so to speak. His explosion is poetic justice. The maitre d's retribution was warranted. To repeat, Creosote's predicament almost literally amounts to nothing more or less than his just desserts. The pun is intended by me, as it was also probably intended by the Pythons.

We laugh, but it is not precisely the laughter of comic amusement. It is the laughter that accompanies the apprehension that someone has "gotten what's coming to them." Thus, there should be no surprise that people laugh at the scene instead of being horrified by it. We are not repelled by the violence Creosote undergoes, in part because we believe that he has brought it upon himself; he invited it. Ours is the laughter of justice—the laughter that obtains when we perceive that the punishment suits the crime ever so neatly.

As already suggested, there is something medieval about the Creosote episode; indeed, a medieval theme runs throughout the film, including dungeons and the Grim Reaper (perhaps this is a result of taking up, and then dismissing, Roman Catholicism as a source of the meaning of life). In many ways, the scene is the modern equivalent of a morality play, an allegory of gluttony and its consequences. If you eat to the point where you feel like exploding, you will. The scene culminates in a visual pun or verbal image—that is, it literalizes the way we describe ourselves when we've overindulged at the table gluttonously. Creosote's *sentence* is the sentence "I've eaten so much that I'd burst if took another morsel." He does and he does. It is a punishment befitting Dante's *Inferno* or Kafka's "The Penal Colony" in its diabolical ingenuity and appropriateness. Indeed, it provokes laughter for being *so* appropriate, so well-deserved.

The laughter engendered by Creosote's predicament is, then, over-determined. Part of it is rooted in incongruity—the absurdities of the scene presented in a context bereft of any perceived danger to human life and limb. But there is also another route to laughter here: the sense that justice is served, that the punishment matches the crime perfectly. Moreover, with respect to this second source of joy, Mr. Creosote, I think, gives us additional insight into the springs of laughter. Much comedy, especially satire and even much of what is called black comedy, induces laughter because we feel that the objects of the indignities and violence suffered by its objects is deserved.[3] It is a different kind of laughter than the laughter prompted by an innocent pun. And it is our sense of justice that makes such comic genres possible. This too is something that Mr. Creosote shows us about laughter.

Perhaps one thing that is so artistically effective about the Creosote episode is that it is able to weld these two sources of laughter so exquisitely. I suspect that it achieves this by the way in which the visual pun it articulates both comically amuses us with its absurdity—its violation of biological norms—while simultaneously satisfying our sense of justice in the most devilish manner. Like many medieval visions of hell, such as the punishments meted out in Dante's *Inferno*, the travails of Creosote mix horror and humor in a way that seems natural. Whether the scene has the same pedagogical intent is doubtful. But it is not a parody of such extravaganzas. Rather it taps into the same emotional well by being an updated version of them. Horrific imagery and humor are often interlaced. Mr. Creosote shows us how these two ostensibly opposed elements can co-exist. They belong together because they both specialize in the incongruous and the impure—in violations of our standing cultural categories and norms. But the overall effect of these subversions of our cultural categories will not dispose us toward horror, unless they occur in the context of some clear and present danger. Where there is no danger to anything we would call human, there is no cause for horror, and there is an opening for laughter. That is Creosote. Moreover, Creosote is not just comically amusing for being a biological absurdity. He is also worthy of our derision for his sins (in his case, perhaps he is the sin itself personified). And this helps us to see that underlying the vitriol of humor is often a perception of justice.

---

3 It may seem that this does not apply to a great deal of black comedy. In many instances the cruelties dealt in black humor do not appear to be directed at objects that morally deserve such punishment. Think of such genres of dark humor as dead baby jokes. However, in cases like this, the cruel humorist is encouraging us to direct our moral rancor not at the babies in the jokes, but at sentimental attitudes that usually accompany discourse about infants. It is that complacent sentimentality that the dark humorist thinks deserves a moral whack.

Similarly, the recurring mentally-challenged "Gumby" characters in *Monty Python's Flying Circus* (see, for example, "Gumby Crooner" in Episode 9, "The Ant: An Introduction") seem to be basically an assault, by his own hand, on excessive sentimentality. It is not that Gumby deserves to be hit on the head with a brick, as he is; rather, the ethical energy underwriting the harsh laughter here is aimed at the sentimentalization of the mentally ill. The butt of the laughter lives off-screen, in a manner of speaking. It resides wherever pompous types congratulate themselves for caring for their "inferiors."

What Utilitarianism Is

John Stuart Mill

A passing remark is all that needs be given to the ignorant blunder of supposing that those who stand up for utility as the test of right and wrong, use the term in that restricted and merely colloquial sense in which utility is opposed to pleasure. An apology is due to the philosophical opponents of utilitarianism, for even the momentary appearance of confounding them with any one capable of so absurd a misconception; which is the more extraordinary, inasmuch as the contrary accusation, of referring everything to pleasure, and that too in its grossest form, is another of the common charges against utilitarianism: and, as has been pointedly remarked by an able writer, the same sort of persons, and often the very same persons, denounce the theory "as impracticably dry when the word utility precedes the word pleasure, and as too practically voluptuous when the word pleasure precedes the word utility." Those who know anything about the matter are aware that every writer, from Epicurus to Bentham, who maintained the theory of utility, meant by it, not something to be contradistinguished from pleasure, but pleasure itself, together with exemption from pain; and instead of opposing the useful to the agreeable or the ornamental, have always declared that the useful means these, among other things. Yet the common herd, including the herd of writers, not only in newspapers and periodicals, but in books of weight and pretension, are perpetually falling into this shallow mistake. Having caught up the word utilitarian, while knowing nothing whatever about it but its sound, they habitually express by it the rejection, or the neglect, of pleasure in some of its forms; of beauty, of ornament, or of amusement. Nor is the term thus ignorantly misapplied solely in disparagement, but occasionally in compliment; as though it implied superiority to frivolity and the mere pleasures of the moment. And this perverted use is the only one in which the word is popularly known, and the one from which the new generation are acquiring their sole notion of its meaning. Those who introduced the word, but who had for many years discontinued it as a distinctive appellation, may well feel themselves called upon to resume it, if by doing so they can hope to contribute anything towards rescuing it from this utter degradation.[A]

The creed which accepts as the foundation of morals, Utility, or the Greatest Happiness Principle, holds that actions are right in proportion as they tend to promote happiness, wrong as they tend to produce the reverse of happiness. By happiness is intended pleasure, and the absence of pain; by unhappiness, pain, and the privation of pleasure. To give a clear view of the moral standard set up

John Stuart Mill, "What Utilitarianism Is," *Utilitarianism*, pp. 4–17, 1861.

by the theory, much more requires to be said; in particular, what things it includes in the ideas of pain and pleasure; and to what extent this is left an open question. But these supplementary explanations do not affect the theory of life on which this theory of morality is grounded—namely, that pleasure, and freedom from pain, are the only things desirable as ends; and that all desirable things (which are as numerous in the utilitarian as in any other scheme) are desirable either for the pleasure inherent in themselves, or as means to the promotion of pleasure and the prevention of pain.

Now, such a theory of life excites in many minds, and among them in some of the most estimable in feeling and purpose, inveterate dislike. To suppose that life has (as they express it) no higher end than pleasure—no better and nobler object of desire and pursuit—they designate as utterly mean and grovelling; as a doctrine worthy only of swine, to whom the followers of Epicurus were, at a very early period, contemptuously likened; and modern holders of the doctrine are occasionally made the subject of equally polite comparisons by its German, French, and English assailants.

When thus attacked, the Epicureans have always answered, that it is not they, but their accusers, who represent human nature in a degrading light; since the accusation supposes human beings to be capable of no pleasures except those of which swine are capable. If this supposition were true, the charge could not be gainsaid, but would then be no longer an imputation; for if the sources of pleasure were precisely the same to human beings and to swine, the rule of life which is good enough for the one would be good enough for the other. The comparison of the Epicurean life to that of beasts is felt as degrading, precisely because a beast's pleasures do not satisfy a human being's conceptions of happiness. Human beings have faculties more elevated than the animal appetites, and when once made conscious of them, do not regard anything as happiness which does not include their gratification. I do not, indeed, consider the Epicureans to have been by any means faultless in drawing out their scheme of consequences from the utilitarian principle. To do this in any sufficient manner, many Stoic, as well as Christian elements require to be included. But there is no known Epicurean theory of life which does not assign to the pleasures of the intellect; of the feelings and imagination, and of the moral sentiments, a much higher value as pleasures than to those of mere sensation. It must be admitted, however, that utilitarian writers in general have placed the superiority of mental over bodily pleasures chiefly in the greater permanency, safety, uncostliness, &c., of the former—that is, in their circumstantial advantages rather than in their intrinsic nature. And on all these points utilitarians have fully proved their case; but they might have taken the other, and, as it may be called, higher ground, with entire consistency. It is quite compatible with the principle of utility to recognise the fact, that some *kinds* of pleasure are more desirable and more valuable than others. It would be absurd that while, in estimating all other things, quality is considered as well as quantity, the estimation of pleasures should be supposed to depend on quantity alone.

If I am asked, what I mean by difference of quality in pleasures, or what makes one pleasure more valuable than another, merely as a pleasure, except its being greater in amount, there is but one possible answer. Of two pleasures, if there be one to which all or almost all who have experience of both give a decided preference, irrespective of any feeling of moral obligation to prefer it, that is the more desirable pleasure. If one of the two is, by those who are competently acquainted with both, placed so far above the other that they prefer it, even though knowing it to be attended with a greater amount of discontent, and would not resign it for any quantity of the other pleasure which their nature is capable of, we are justified in ascribing to the preferred enjoyment a superiority in quality, so far outweighing quantity as to render it, in comparison, of small account.

Now it is an unquestionable fact that those who are equally acquainted with, and equally capable of appreciating and enjoying, both, do give a most marked preference to the manner of existence which employs their higher faculties. Few human creatures would consent to be changed into any of the lower animals, for a promise of the fullest allowance of a beast's pleasures; no intelligent human being would consent to be a fool, no instructed person would be an ignoramus, no person of feeling and conscience would be selfish and base, even though they should be persuaded that the fool, the dunce, or the rascal is better satisfied with his lot than they are with theirs. They would not resign what they possess more than he, for the most complete satisfaction of all the desires which they have in common with him. If they ever fancy they would, it is only in cases of unhappiness so extreme, that to escape from it they would exchange their lot for almost any other, however undesirable in their own eyes. A being of higher faculties requires more to make him happy, is capable probably of more acute suffering, and is certainly accessible to it at more points, than one of an inferior type; but in spite of these liabilities, he can never really wish to sink into what he feels to be a lower grade of existence. We may give what explanation we please of this unwillingness; we may attribute it to pride, a name which is given indiscriminately to some of the most and to some of the least estimable feelings of which mankind are capable; we may refer it to the love of liberty and personal independence, an appeal to which was with the Stoics one of the most effective means for the inculcation of it; to the love of power, or to the love of excitement, both of which do really enter into and contribute to it: but its most appropriate appellation is a sense of dignity, which all human beings possess in one form or other, and in some, though by no means in exact, proportion to their higher faculties, and which is so essential a part of the happiness of those in whom it is strong, that nothing which conflicts with it could be, otherwise than momentarily, an object of desire to them. Whoever supposes that this preference takes place at a sacrifice of happiness—that the superior being, in anything like equal circumstances, is not happier than the inferior—confounds the two very different ideas, of happiness, and content. It is indisputable that the being whose capacities of enjoyment are low, has the greatest chance of having them fully satisfied; and a highly-endowed being will always feel that any happiness which he can look for, as the world is constituted, is imperfect. But he can learn to bear its imperfections, if they are at all bearable; and they will not make him envy the being who is indeed unconscious of the imperfections, but only because he feels not at all the good which those imperfections qualify. It is better to be a human being dissatisfied than a pig satisfied; better to be Socrates dissatisfied than a fool satisfied. And if the fool, or the pig, is of a different opinion, it is because they only know their own side of the question. The other party to the comparison knows both sides.

It may be objected, that many who are capable of the higher pleasures, occasionally, under the influence of temptation, postpone them to the lower. But this is quite compatible with a full appreciation of the intrinsic superiority of the higher. Men often, from infirmity of character, make their election for the nearer good, though they know it to be the less valuable; and this no less when the choice is between two bodily pleasures, than when it is between bodily and mental. They pursue sensual indulgences to the injury of health, though perfectly aware that health is the greater good. It may be further objected, that many who begin with youthful enthusiasm for everything noble, as they advance in years sink into indolence and selfishness. But I do not believe that those who undergo this very common change, voluntarily choose the lower description of pleasures in preference to the higher. I believe that before they devote themselves exclusively to the one, they have already become incapable of the other. Capacity for the nobler feelings is in most natures a very tender plant, easily killed, not only by hostile influences, but by mere want of sustenance; and in the majority of young persons it speedily dies away if the occupations to which their position in life has devoted them, and the society into which it has thrown them, are not favourable to keeping that higher capacity in exercise. Men lose their high aspirations as they lose their intellectual tastes, because they have not time or opportunity for indulging them; and they addict themselves to inferior pleasures, not because they deliberately prefer them, but because they are either the only ones to which they have access, or the only ones which they are any longer capable of enjoying. It may be questioned whether any one who has remained equally susceptible to both classes of pleasures, ever knowingly and calmly preferred the lower; though many, in all ages, have broken down in an ineffectual attempt to combine both.

From this verdict of the only competent judges, I apprehend there can be no appeal. On a question which is the best worth having of two pleasures, or which of two modes of existence is the most grateful to the feelings, apart from its moral attributes and from its consequences, the judgment of those who are qualified by knowledge of both, or, if they differ, that of the majority among them, must be admitted as final. And there needs be the less hesitation to accept this judgment respecting the quality of pleasures, since there is no other tribunal to be referred to even on the question of quantity. What means are there of determining which is the acutest of two pains, or the intensest of two pleasurable sensations, except the general suffrage of those who are familiar with both? Neither pains nor pleasures are homogeneous, and pain is always heterogeneous with pleasure. What is there to decide whether a particular pleasure is worth purchasing at the cost of a particular pain, except the feelings and judgment of the experienced? When, therefore, those feelings and judgment declare the pleasures derived from the higher faculties to be preferable *in kind*, apart from the question of intensity, to those of which the animal nature, disjoined from the higher faculties, is susceptible, they are entitled on this subject to the same regard.

I have dwelt on this point, as being a necessary part of a perfectly just conception of Utility or Happiness, considered as the directive rule of human conduct. But it is by no means an indispensable condition to the acceptance of the utilitarian standard; for that standard is not the agent's own greatest happiness, but the greatest amount of happiness altogether; and if it may possibly be doubted whether a noble character is always the happier for its nobleness, there can be no doubt that it makes other people happier, and that the world in general is immensely a gainer by it. Utilitarianism, therefore, could only attain its end by the general cultivation of nobleness of character, even if each individual were only benefited by the nobleness of others, and his own, so far as happiness is concerned, were a sheer deduction from the benefit. But the bare enunciation of such an absurdity as this last, renders refutation superfluous.

According to the Greatest Happiness Principle, as above explained, the ultimate end, with reference to and for the sake of which all other things are desirable (whether we are considering our own good or that of other people), is an existence exempt as far as possible from pain, and as rich as possible in enjoyments, both in point of quantity and quality; the test of quality, and the rule for measuring it against quantity, being the preference felt by those who, in their opportunities of experience, to which must be added their habits of self-consciousness and self-observation, are best furnished with the means of comparison. This, being, according to the utilitarian opinion, the end of human action, is necessarily also the standard of morality; which may accordingly be defined, the rules and precepts for human conduct, by the observance of which an existence such as has been described might be, to the greatest extent possible, secured to all mankind; and not to them only, but, so far as the nature of things admits, to the whole sentient creation.

Against this doctrine, however, arises another class of objectors, who say that happiness, in any form, cannot be the rational purpose of human life and action; because, in the first place, it is unattainable: and they contemptuously ask, What right hast thou to be happy? a question which Mr. Carlyle clenches by the addition, What right, a short time ago, hadst thou even *to be*? Next, they say, that men can do *without* happiness; that all noble human beings have felt this, and could not have become noble but by learning the lesson of Entsagen, or renunciation; which lesson, thoroughly learnt and submitted to, they affirm to be the beginning and necessary condition of all virtue.

The first of these objections would go to the root of the matter were it well founded; for if no happiness is to be had at all by human beings, the attainment of it cannot be the end of morality, or of any rational conduct. Though, even in that case, something might still be said for the utilitarian theory; since utility includes not solely the pursuit of happiness, but the prevention or mitigation of unhappiness; and if the former aim be chimerical, there will be all the greater scope and more imperative need for the latter, so long at least as mankind think fit to live, and do not take refuge in the simultaneous act of suicide recommended under certain conditions by Novalis. When, however, it is thus positively asserted to be impossible that human life should be happy, the assertion, if not something like a verbal quibble, is at least an exaggeration. If by happiness be meant a continuity of highly pleasurable excitement, it is evident enough that this is impossible. A state of exalted pleasure lasts only moments, or in some cases, and with some intermissions, hours or days, and is the occasional brilliant flash of enjoyment, not its permanent and steady flame. Of this the philosophers who have taught that happiness is the end of life were as fully aware as those who taunt them. The happiness which they meant was not a life of rapture, but moments of such, in an existence made up of few and transitory pains, many and various pleasures, with a decided predominance of the active over the passive, and having as the foundation of the whole, not to expect more from life than it is capable of bestowing. A life thus composed, to those who have been fortunate enough to obtain it, has always appeared worthy of the name of happiness. And such an existence is even now the lot of many, during some considerable portion of their lives. The present wretched education, and wretched social arrangements, are the only real hindrance to its being attainable by almost all.

The objectors perhaps may doubt whether human beings, if taught to consider happiness as the end of life, would be satisfied with such a moderate share of it. But great numbers of mankind have been satisfied with much less. The main constituents of a satisfied life appear to be two, either of which by itself is often found sufficient for the purpose: tranquillity, and excitement. With much tranquillity, many find that they can be content with very little pleasure: with much excitement, many can reconcile themselves to a considerable quantity of pain. There is assuredly no inherent impossibility in enabling even the mass of mankind to unite both; since the two are so far from being incompatible that they are in natural alliance, the prolongation of either being a preparation for, and exciting a wish for, the other. It is only those in whom indolence amounts to a vice, that do not desire excitement after an interval of repose; it is only those in whom the need of excitement is a disease, that feel the tranquillity which follows excitement dull and insipid, instead of pleasurable in direct proportion to the excitement which preceded it. When people who are tolerably fortunate in their outward lot do not find in life sufficient enjoyment to make it valuable to them, the cause generally is, caring for nobody but themselves. To those who have neither public nor private affections, the excitements of life are much curtailed, and in any case dwindle in value as the time approaches when all selfish interests must be terminated by death: while those who leave after them objects of personal affection, and especially those who have also cultivated a fellow-feeling with the collective interests of mankind, retain as lively an interest in life on the eve of death as in the vigour of youth and health. Next to selfishness, the principal cause which makes life unsatisfactory, is want of mental cultivation. A cultivated mind—I do not mean that of a philosopher, but any mind to which the fountains of knowledge have been opened, and which has been taught, in any tolerable degree, to exercise its faculties—finds sources of inexhaustible interest in all that surrounds it; in the objects of nature, the achievements of art, the imaginations of poetry, the incidents of history, the ways of mankind past and present, and their prospects in the future. It is possible, indeed, to become indifferent to all this, and that too without having exhausted a thousandth part of it; but only when one has had from the beginning no moral or human interest in these things, and has sought in them only the gratification of curiosity.

Now there is absolutely no reason in the nature of things why an amount of mental culture sufficient to give an intelligent interest in these objects of contemplation, should not be the inheritance of every one born in a civilized country. As little is there an inherent necessity that any human being should be a selfish egotist, devoid of every feeling or care but those which centre in his own miserable individuality. Something far superior to this is sufficiently common even now, to give ample earnest of what the human species may be made. Genuine private affections, and a sincere interest in the public good, are possible, though in unequal degrees, to every rightly brought-up human being. In a world in which there is so much to interest, so much to enjoy, and so much also to correct and improve, every one who has this moderate amount of moral and intellectual requisites is capable of an existence which may be called enviable; and unless such a person, through bad laws, or subjection to the will of others, is denied the liberty to use the sources of happiness within his reach, he will not fail to find this enviable existence, if he escape the positive evils of life, the great sources of physical and mental suffering—such as indigence, disease, and the unkindness, worthlessness, or premature loss of objects of affection. The main stress of the problem lies, therefore, in the contest with these calamities, from which it is a rare good fortune entirely to escape; which, as things now are, cannot be obviated, and often cannot be in any material degree mitigated. Yet no one whose opinion deserves a moment's consideration can doubt that most of the great positive evils of the world are in themselves removable, and will, if human affairs continue to improve, be in the end reduced within narrow limits. Poverty, in any sense implying suffering, may be completely extinguished by the wisdom of society, combined with the good sense and providence of individuals. Even that most intractable of enemies, disease, may be indefinitely reduced in dimensions by good physical and moral education, and proper control of noxious influences; while the progress of science holds out a promise for the future of still more direct conquests over this detestable foe. And every advance in that direction relieves us from some, not only of the chances which cut short our own lives, but, what concerns us still more, which deprive us of those in whom our happiness is wrapt up. As for vicissitudes of fortune, and other disappointments connected with worldly circumstances, these are principally the effect either of gross imprudence, of ill-regulated desires, or of bad or imperfect social institutions. All the grand sources, in short, of human suffering are in a great degree, many of them almost entirely, conquerable by human care and effort; and though their removal is grievously slow—though a long succession of generations will perish in the breach before the conquest is completed, and this world becomes all that, if will and knowledge were not wanting, it might easily be made—yet every mind sufficiently intelligent and generous to bear a part, however small and unconspicuous, in the endeavour, will draw a noble enjoyment from the contest itself, which he would not for any bribe in the form of selfish indulgence consent to be without.

And this leads to the true estimation of what is said by the objectors concerning the possibility, and the obligation, of learning to do without happiness. Unquestionably it is possible to do without happiness; it is done involuntarily by nineteen-twentieths of mankind, even in those parts of our present world which are least deep in barbarism; and it often has to be done voluntarily by the hero or the martyr, for the sake of something which he prizes more than his individual happiness. But this something, what is it, unless the happiness of others, or some of the requisites of happiness? It is noble to be capable of resigning entirely one's own portion of happiness, or chances of it: but, after all, this self-sacrifice must be for some end; it is not its own end; and if we are told that its end is not happiness, but virtue, which is better than happiness, I ask, would the sacrifice be made if the hero or martyr did not believe that it would earn for others immunity from similar sacrifices? Would it be made, if he thought that his renunciation of happiness for himself would produce no fruit for any of his fellow creatures, but to make their lot like his, and place them also in the condition of persons who have renounced happiness? All honour to those who can abnegate for themselves the personal enjoyment of life, when by such renunciation they contribute worthily to increase the amount of happiness in the world; but he who does it, or professes to do it, for any other purpose, is no more deserving of admiration than the ascetic mounted on his pillar. He may be an inspiriting proof of what men *can* do, but assuredly not an example of what they *should*.

Though it is only in a very imperfect state of the world's arrangements that any one can best serve the happiness of others by the absolute sacrifice of his own, yet so long as the world is in that imperfect state, I fully acknowledge that the readiness to make such a sacrifice is the highest virtue which can be found in man. I will add, that in this condition of the world, paradoxical as the assertion may be, the conscious ability to do without happiness gives the best prospect of realizing such happiness as is attainable. For nothing except that consciousness can raise a person above the chances of life, by making him feel that, let fate and fortune do their worst, they have not power to subdue him: which, once felt, frees him from excess of anxiety concerning the evils of life, and enables him, like many a Stoic in the worst times of the Roman Empire, to cultivate in tranquillity the sources of satisfaction accessible to him, without concerning himself about the uncertainty of their duration, any more than about their inevitable end.

Meanwhile, let utilitarians never cease to claim the morality of self-devotion as a possession which belongs by as good a right to them, as either to the Stoic or to the Transcendentalist. The utilitarian morality does recognise in human beings the power of sacrificing their own greatest good for the good of others. It only refuses to admit that the sacrifice is itself a good. A sacrifice which does not increase, or tend to increase, the sum total of happiness, it considers as wasted. The only self-renunciation which it applauds, is devotion to the happiness, or to some of the means of happiness, of others; either of mankind collectively, or of individuals within the limits imposed by the collective interests of mankind.

I must again repeat, what the assailants of utilitarianism seldom have the justice to acknowledge, that the happiness which forms the utilitarian standard of what is right in conduct, is not the agent's own happiness, but that of all concerned. As between his own happiness and that of others, utilitarianism requires him to be as strictly impartial as a disinterested and benevolent spectator. In the golden rule of Jesus of Nazareth, we read the complete spirit of the ethics of utility. To do as one would be done by, and to love one's neighbour as oneself, constitute the ideal perfection of utilitarian morality. As the means of making the nearest approach to this ideal, utility would enjoin, first, that laws and social arrangements should place the happiness, or (as speaking practically it may be called) the interest, of every individual, as nearly as possible in harmony with the interest of the whole; and secondly, that education and opinion, which have so vast a power over human character, should so use that power as to establish in the mind of every individual an indissoluble association between his own happiness and the good of the whole; especially between his own happiness and the practice of such modes of conduct, negative and positive, as regard for the universal happiness prescribes: so that not only he may be unable to conceive the possibility of happiness to himself, consistently with conduct opposed to the general good, but also that a direct impulse to promote the general good may be in every individual one of the habitual motives of action, and the sentiments connected therewith may fill a large and prominent place in every human being's sentient existence. If the impugners of the utilitarian morality represented it to their own minds in this its true character, I know not what recommendation possessed by any other morality they could possibly affirm to be wanting to it: what more beautiful or more exalted developments of human nature any other ethical system can be supposed to foster, or what springs of action, not accessible to the utilitarian, such systems rely on for giving effect to their mandates.

The objectors to utilitarianism cannot always be charged with representing it in a discreditable light. On the contrary, those among them who entertain anything like a just idea of its disinterested character, sometimes find fault with its standard as being too high for humanity. They say it is exacting too much to require that people shall always act from the inducement of promoting the general interests of society. But this is to mistake the very meaning of a standard of morals, and to confound the rule of action with the motive of it. It is the business of ethics to tell us what are our duties, or by what test we may know them; but no system of ethics requires that the sole motive of all we do shall be a feeling of duty; on the contrary, ninety-nine hundredths of all our actions are done from other motives, and rightly so done, if the rule of duty does not condemn them. It is the more unjust to utilitarianism that this particular misapprehension should be made a ground of objection to it, inasmuch as utilitarian moralists have gone beyond almost all others in affirming that the motive has nothing to do with the morality of the action, though much with the worth of the agent. He who saves a fellow creature from drowning does what is morally right, whether his motive be duty, or the hope of being paid for his trouble: he who betrays the friend that trusts him, is guilty of a crime, even if his object be to serve another friend to whom he is under greater obligations.[B] But to speak only of actions done from the motive of duty, and in direct obedience to principle: it is a misapprehension of the utilitarian mode of thought, to conceive it as implying that people should fix their minds upon so wide a generality as the world, or society at large. The great majority of good actions are intended, not for the benefit of the world, but for that of individuals, of which the good of the world is made up; and the thoughts of the most virtuous man need not on these occasions travel beyond the particular persons concerned, except so far as is necessary to assure himself that in benefiting them he is not violating the rights—that is, the legitimate and authorized expectations—of any one else. The multiplication of happiness is, according to the utilitarian ethics, the object of virtue: the occasions on which any person (except one in a thousand) has it in his power to do this on an extended scale, in other words, to be a public benefactor, are but exceptional; and on these occasions alone is he called on to consider public utility; in every other case, private utility, the interest or happiness of some few persons, is all he has to attend to. Those alone the influence of whose actions extends to society in general, need concern themselves habitually about so large an object. In the case of abstinences indeed—of things which people forbear to do, from moral considerations, though the consequences in the particular case might be beneficial—it would be unworthy of an intelligent agent not to be consciously aware that the action is of a class which, if practised generally, would be generally injurious, and that this is the ground of the obligation to abstain from it. The amount of regard for the public interest implied in this recognition, is no greater than is demanded by every system of morals; for they all enjoin to abstain from whatever is manifestly pernicious to society.

The same considerations dispose of another reproach against the doctrine of utility, founded on a still grosser misconception of the purpose of a standard of morality, and of the very meaning of the words right and wrong. It is often affirmed that utilitarianism renders men cold and unsympathizing; that it chills their moral feelings towards individuals; that it makes them regard only the dry and hard consideration of the consequences of actions, not taking into their moral estimate the qualities from which those actions emanate. If the assertion means that they do not allow their judgment respecting the rightness or wrongness of an action to be influenced by their opinion of the qualities of the person who does it, this is a complaint not against utilitarianism, but against having any standard of morality at all; for certainly no known ethical standard decides an action to be good or bad because it is done by a good or a bad man, still less because done by an amiable, a brave, or a benevolent man or the contrary. These considerations are relevant, not to the estimation of actions, but of persons; and there is nothing in the utilitarian theory inconsistent with the fact that there are other things which interest us in persons besides the rightness and wrongness of their actions. The Stoics, indeed, with the paradoxical misuse of language which was part of their system, and by which they strove to raise themselves above all concern about anything but virtue, were fond of saying that he who has that has everything; that he, and only he, is rich, is beautiful, is a king. But no claim of this description is made for the virtuous man by the utilitarian doctrine. Utilitarians are quite aware that there are other desirable possessions and qualities besides virtue, and are perfectly willing to allow to all of them their full worth. They are also aware that a right action does not necessarily indicate a virtuous character, and that actions which are blameable often proceed from qualities entitled to praise. When this is apparent in any particular case, it modifies their estimation, not certainly of the act, but of the agent. I grant that they are, notwithstanding, of opinion, that in the long run the best proof of a good character is good actions; and resolutely refuse to consider any mental disposition as good, of which the predominant tendency is to produce bad conduct. This makes them unpopular with many people; but it is an unpopularity which they must share with every one who regards the distinction between right and wrong in a serious light; and the reproach is not one which a conscientious utilitarian need be anxious to repel.

If no more be meant by the objection than that many utilitarians look on the morality of actions, as measured by the utilitarian standard, with too exclusive a regard, and do not lay sufficient stress upon the other beauties of character which go towards making a human being loveable or admirable, this may be admitted. Utilitarians who have cultivated their moral feelings, but not their sympathies nor their artistic perceptions, do fall into this mistake; and so do all other moralists under the same conditions. What can be said in excuse for other moralists is equally available for them, namely, that if there is to be any error, it is better that it should be on that side. As a matter of fact, we may affirm that among utilitarians as among adherents of other systems, there is every imaginable degree of rigidity and of laxity in the application of their standard: some are even puritanically rigorous, while others are as indulgent as can possibly be desired by sinner or by sentimentalist. But on the whole, a doctrine which brings prominently forward the interest that mankind have in the repression and prevention of conduct which violates the moral law, is likely to be inferior to no other in turning the sanctions of opinion against such violations. It is true, the question, What does violate the moral law? is one on which those who recognise different standards of morality are likely now and then to differ. But difference of opinion on moral questions was not first introduced into the world by utilitarianism, while that doctrine does supply, if not always an easy, at all events a tangible and intelligible mode of deciding such differences.

* * * * *

It may not be superfluous to notice a few more of the common misapprehensions of utilitarian ethics, even those which are so obvious and gross that it might appear impossible for any person of candour and intelligence to fall into them: since persons, even of considerable mental endowments, often give themselves so little trouble to understand the bearings of any opinion against which they entertain a prejudice, and men are in general so little conscious of this voluntary ignorance as a defect, that the vulgarest misunderstandings of ethical doctrines are continually met with in the deliberate writings of persons of the greatest pretensions both to high principle and to philosophy. We not uncommonly hear the doctrine of utility inveighed against as a *godless* doctrine. If it be necessary to say anything at all against so mere an assumption, we may say that the question depends upon what idea we have formed of the moral character of the Deity. If it be a true belief that God desires, above all things, the happiness of his creatures, and that this was his purpose in their creation, utility is not only not a godless doctrine, but more profoundly religious than any other. If it be meant that utilitarianism does not recognise the revealed will of God as the supreme law of morals, I answer, that an utilitarian who believes in the perfect goodness and wisdom of God, necessarily believes that whatever God has thought fit to reveal on the subject of morals, must fulfil the requirements of utility in a supreme degree. But others besides utilitarians have been of opinion that the Christian revelation was intended, and is fitted, to inform the hearts and minds of mankind with a spirit which should enable them to find for themselves what is right, and incline them to do it when found, rather than to tell them, except in a very general way, what it is: and that we need a doctrine of ethics, carefully followed out, to *interpret* to us the will of God. Whether this opinion is correct or not, it is superfluous here to discuss; since whatever aid religion, either natural or revealed, can afford to ethical investigation, is as open to the utilitarian moralist as to any other. He can use it as the testimony of God to the usefulness or hurtfulness of any given course of action, by as good a right as others can use it for the indication of a transcendental law, having no connexion with usefulness or with happiness.

Again, Utility is often summarily stigmatized as an immoral doctrine by giving it the name of Expediency, and taking advantage of the popular use of that term to contrast it with Principle. But the Expedient, in the sense in which it is opposed to the Right, generally means that which is expedient for the particular interest of the agent himself: as when a minister sacrifices the interest of his country to keep himself in place. When it means anything better than this, it means that which is expedient for some immediate object, some temporary purpose, but which violates a rule whose observance is expedient in a much higher degree. The Expedient, in this sense, instead of being the same thing with the useful, is a branch of the hurtful. Thus, it would often be expedient, for the purpose of getting over some momentary embarrassment, or attaining some object immediately useful to ourselves or others, to tell a lie. But inasmuch as the cultivation in ourselves of a sensitive feeling on the subject of veracity, is one of the most useful, and the enfeeblement of that feeling one of the most hurtful, things to which our conduct can be instrumental; and inasmuch as any, even unintentional, deviation from truth, does that much towards weakening the trustworthiness of human assertion, which is not only the principal support of all present social well-being, but the insufficiency of which does more than any one thing that can be named to keep back civilisation, virtue, everything on which human happiness on the largest scale depends; we feel that the violation, for a present advantage, of a rule of such transcendent expediency, is not expedient, and that he who, for the sake of a convenience to himself or to some other individual, does what depends on him to deprive mankind of the good, and inflict upon them the evil, involved in the greater or less reliance which they can place in each other's word, acts the part of one of their worst enemies. Yet that even this rule, sacred as it is, admits of possible exceptions, is acknowledged by all moralists; the chief of which is when the withholding of some fact (as of information from a male-factor, or of bad news from a person dangerously ill) would preserve some one (especially a person other than oneself) from great and unmerited evil, and when the withholding can only be effected by denial. But in order that the exception may not extend itself beyond the need, and may have the least possible effect in weakening reliance on veracity, it ought to be recognized, and, if possible, its limits defined; and if the principle of utility is good for anything, it must be good for weighing these conflicting utilities against one another, and marking out the region within which one or the other preponderates.

Again, defenders of utility often find themselves called upon to reply to such objections as this—that there is not time, previous to action, for calculating and weighing the effects of any line of conduct on the general happiness. This is exactly as if any one were to say that it is impossible to guide our conduct by Christianity, because there is not time, on every occasion on which anything has to be done, to read through the Old and New Testaments. The answer to the objection is, that there has been ample time, namely, the whole past duration of the human species. During all that time mankind have been learning by experience the tendencies of actions; on which experience all the prudence, as well as all the morality of life, is dependent. People talk as if the commencement of this course of experience had hitherto been put off, and as if, at the moment when some man feels tempted to meddle with the property or life of another, he had to begin considering for the first time whether murder and theft are injurious to human happiness. Even then I do not think that he would find the question very puzzling; but, at all events, the matter is now done to his hand. It is truly a whimsical supposition, that if mankind were agreed in considering utility to be the test of morality, they would remain without any agreement as to what is useful, and would take no measures for having their notions on the subject taught to the young, and enforced by law and opinion. There is no difficulty in proving any ethical standard whatever to work ill, if we suppose universal idiocy to be conjoined with it, but on any hypothesis short of that, mankind must by this time have acquired positive beliefs as to the effects of some actions on their happiness; and the beliefs which have thus come down are the rules of morality for the multitude, and for the philosopher until he has succeeded in finding better. That philosophers might easily do this, even now, on many subjects; that the received code of ethics is by no means of divine right; and that mankind have still much to learn as to the effects of actions on the general happiness, I admit, or rather, earnestly maintain. The corollaries from the principle of utility, like the precepts of every practical art, admit of indefinite improvement, and, in a progressive state of the human mind, their improvement is perpetually going on. But to consider the rules of morality as improvable, is one thing; to pass over the intermediate generalizations entirely, and endeavour to test each individual action directly by the first principle, is another. It is a strange notion that the acknowledgment of a first principle is inconsistent with the admission of secondary ones. To inform a traveller respecting the place of his ultimate destination, is not to forbid the use of landmarks and direction-posts on the way. The proposition that happiness is the end and aim of morality, does not mean that no road ought to be laid down to that goal, or that persons going thither should not be advised to take one direction rather than another. Men really ought to leave off talking a kind of nonsense on this subject, which they would neither talk nor listen to on other matters of practical concernment. Nobody argues that the art of navigation is not founded on astronomy, because sailors cannot wait to calculate the Nautical Almanack. Being rational creatures, they go to sea with it ready calculated; and all rational creatures go out upon the sea of life with their minds made up on the common questions of right and wrong, as well as on many of the far more difficult questions of wise and foolish. And this, as long as foresight is a human quality, it is to be presumed they will continue to do. Whatever we adopt as the fundamental principle of morality, we require subordinate principles to apply it by: the impossibility of doing without them, being common to all systems, can afford no argument against any one in particular: but gravely to argue as if no such secondary principles could be had, and as if mankind had remained till now, and always must remain, without drawing any general conclusions from the experience of human life, is as high a pitch, I think, as absurdity has ever reached in philosophical controversy.

The remainder of the stock arguments against utilitarianism mostly consist in laying to its charge the common infirmities of human nature, and the general difficulties which embarrass conscientious persons in shaping their course through life. We are told that an utilitarian will be apt to make his own particular case an exception to moral rules, and, when under temptation, will see an utility in the breach of a rule, greater than he will see in its observance. But is utility the only creed which is able to furnish us with excuses for evil doing, and means of cheating our own conscience? They are afforded in abundance by all doctrines which recognise as a fact in morals the existence of conflicting considerations; which all doctrines do, that have been believed by sane persons. It is not the fault of any creed, but of the complicated nature of human affairs, that rules of conduct cannot be so framed as to require no exceptions, and that hardly any kind of action can safely be laid down as either always obligatory or always condemnable. There is no ethical creed which does not temper the rigidity of its laws, by giving a certain latitude, under the moral responsibility of the agent, for accommodation to peculiarities of circumstances; and under every creed, at the opening thus made, self-deception and dishonest casuistry get in. There exists no moral system under which there do not arise unequivocal cases of conflicting obligation. These are the real difficulties, the knotty points both in the theory of ethics, and in the conscientious guidance of personal conduct. They are overcome practically with greater or with less success according to the intellect and virtue of the individual; but it can hardly be pretended that any one will be the less qualified for dealing with them, from possessing an ultimate standard to which conflicting rights and duties can be referred. If utility is the ultimate source of moral obligations, utility may be invoked to decide between them when their demands are incompatible. Though the application of the standard may be difficult, it is better than none at all: while in other systems, the moral laws all claiming independent authority, there is no common umpire entitled to interfere between them; their claims to precedence one over another rest on little better than sophistry, and unless determined, as they generally are, by the unacknowledged influence of considerations of utility, afford a free scope for the action of personal desires and partialities. We must remember that only in these cases of conflict between secondary principles is it requisite that first principles should be appealed to. There is no case of moral obligation in which some secondary principle is not involved; and if only one, there can seldom be any real doubt which one it is, in the mind of any person by whom the principle itself is recognized.

Footnotes

[Footnote A: The author of this essay has reason for believing himself to be the first person who brought the word utilitarian into use. He did not invent it, but adopted it from a passing expression in Mr. Galt's *Annals of the Parish*. After using it as a designation for several years, he and others abandoned it from a growing dislike to anything resembling a badge or watchword of sectarian distinction. But as a name for one single opinion, not a set of opinions—to denote the recognition of utility as a standard, not any particular way of applying it—the term supplies a want in the language, and offers, in many cases, a convenient mode of avoiding tiresome circumlocution.]

[Footnote B: An opponent, whose intellectual and moral fairness it is a pleasure to acknowledge (the Rev. J. Llewellyn Davis), has objected to this passage, saying, "Surely the rightness or wrongness of saving a man from drowning does depend very much upon the motive with which it is done. Suppose that a tyrant, when his enemy jumped into the sea to escape from him, saved him from drowning simply in order that he might inflict upon him more exquisite tortures, would it tend to clearness to speak of that rescue as 'a morally right action?' Or suppose again, according to one of the stock illustrations of ethical inquiries, that a man betrayed a trust received from a friend, because the discharge of it would fatally injure that friend himself or some one belonging to him, would utilitarianism compel one to call the betrayal 'a crime' as much as if it had been done from the meanest motive?"

I submit, that he who saves another from drowning in order to kill him by torture afterwards, does not differ only in motive from him who does the same thing from duty or benevolence; the act itself is different. The rescue of the man is, in the case supposed, only the necessary first step of an act far more atrocious than leaving him to drown would have been. Had Mr. Davis said, "The rightness or wrongness of saving a man from drowning does depend very much"—not upon the motive, but—"upon the *intention*" no utilitarian would have differed from him. Mr. Davis, by an oversight too common not to be quite venial, has in this case confounded the very different ideas of Motive and Intention. There is no point which utilitarian thinkers (and Bentham preeminently) have taken more pains to illustrate than this. The morality of the action depends entirely upon the intention—that is, upon what the agent *wills to do*. But the motive, that is, the feeling which makes him will so to do, when it makes no difference in the act, makes none in the morality: though it makes a great difference in our moral estimation of the agent, especially if it indicates a good or a bad habitual *disposition*—a bent of character from which useful, or from which hurtful actions are likely to arise.]

Selected Fallacies

David R. Morrow

....

AD Hominem (Against the Person)

Criticizing the person who makes a claim or argument rather than criticizing the claim or argument itself.

PERSON 1: The federal government shouldn't raise the minimum wage because that would lead to a lot of poor people losing their jobs.

PERSON 2: You don't really care about poor people! You're just a selfish, rich jerk who is worried that goods and services will become more expensive for you personally if the minimum wage goes up.

Anecdotal Fallacy

Using personal anecdotes or vivid examples, rather than adequate data, to support a broad generalization.

My great-grandmother smoked four packs a day for seventy years, and she never got lung cancer. Therefore, cigarettes don't really cause lung cancer.

Appeal to Authority

Illegitimately arguing that a statement is true because an authority figure said so, especially when the statement is outside the authority figure's area of expertise.

Philosophy is useless. The astrophysicist Neil DeGrasse Tyson said so.

Appeal to Ignorance (*AD Ignoratium*)

Arguing that something is true because it can't be proven false.

PERSON 1: Airplanes are secretly spraying chemicals to control our minds!

PERSON 2: That's a nonsense conspiracy theory.

PERSON 1: Can you prove that it's not happening?

Appeal to Nature

Arguing that something is good because it's natural or that it's bad because it's unnatural or artificial.

It's much better to treat illness using natural herbs than with pharmaceuticals. Pharmaceuticals are full of artificial chemicals!

Appeal to Popularity (*AD Populum*)

Arguing that something is true because everyone believes it or that something is good because everyone likes it.

Most Americans agree that the death penalty deters crime. Therefore, the death penalty does deter crime.

Circular Reasoning (Begging the Question)

Including or assuming your conclusion as one of your premises—often as a hidden premise.

PERSON 1: This salesman is trustworthy; he's not going to try to sell me something I don't need just to get the commission.

PERSON 2: How do you know?

PERSON 1: He told me that all he wants is to help me find the best deal.

Composition

Illegitimately arguing that because something is true of each part of something, it's also true of the whole; or that because something is true of each member of a group, it's true of the group as a whole.

My greenhouse gas emissions don't make any difference to the climate. Nor does my neighbor's, or my friend's, or any other individual's emissions. Therefore, humanity's greenhouse gas emissions don't make any difference to the climate.

Division

Illegitimately arguing that because something is true of a group or thing as a whole, it's also true of each part.

The United States is rich. Therefore, all Americans are rich.

Equivocation

Using the same word or phrase in two different ways to make it seem like an argument works when it really doesn't.

This school is a drug-free zone. Caffeine is a drug, and coffee has caffeine in it. Therefore, coffee isn't allowed in this school.

False Dichotomy (False Dilemma)

Falsely assuming that there are only two options in order to argue *for* one of them simply by arguing *against* the other.

The Egyptians built the Great Pyramid to align with magnetic north. Since they didn't have compasses, that's either a complete coincidence or aliens helped them build it. There's no way the Great Pyramid's alignment is just a coincidence. Thus, aliens helped the Egyptians build the Great Pyramid.

Genetic Fallacy

Arguing that a statement is false or an argument is weak because of the source (i.e., the genesis) of that statement or argument

PERSON 1: Your uncle told me that I should start saving for retirement in my twenties because then my retirement investments will have much more time to grow, and I'll end up with a lot more money when I retire.

PERSON 2: What!? Don't listen to my uncle! He gives terrible advice!

Hasty Generalization

Arguing for a sweeping generalization on the basis of too few examples or examples that aren't representative of the group as a whole.

Only one of my friends was enthusiastic about Hillary Clinton for president. Therefore, very few Americans were enthusiastic about Hillary Clinton for president.

Post HOC Fallacy (Post HOC, ERGO Propter HOC)

Illegitimately arguing that because one event happened after another event, the earlier event caused the later event. From a Latin phrase meaning "after this, therefore because of this."

I got a flu shot, and the next day I came down with the flu. The flu shot must have given me the flu.

Slippery Slope

Arguing that something shouldn't be done because it would inevitably lead to some unacceptable outcome, without giving adequate reasons to think that the first thing really would lead to an unacceptable outcome.

It's not that there's anything wrong with adults using marijuana recreationally. But if we legalize marijuana, then before long, we'll have middle schoolers snorting cocaine and shooting heroin.

Strawman

Arguing against a distorted, weaker version of someone's statement or argument rather than against the real statement or argument.

PERSON 1: This country should implement stricter gun control laws because they'd reduce the number of gun deaths.

PERSON 2: Nonsense! Universal background checks wouldn't eliminate gun deaths, so there's no point in imposing them on law-abiding citizens.

Kantianism

Gordon Graham

....

U p to this point we have been thinking of the idea of the good life as the life it would be most desirable for a human being to lead. But it is time now to consider an important distinction that may be made between two senses of the expression 'the good life'. In one sense 'the good life' means the most desirable or happiest life. In another it means the worthiest or most virtuous human life.

Virtue and Happiness: 'Faring Well' and 'Doing Right'

This is a distinction that plays no significant part in Greek philosophical thinking. It came to real prominence first in eighteenth-century Europe. Although it is only then that we can see the distinction self-consciously drawn, it is arguable that its origin is to be found much earlier with the emergence of Christianity. For one of the innovations of the Christian religion is the idea that the poor and the meek can be blessed, and, conversely (in the words of St Mark's Gospel), that even gaining possession of the whole world is not really profitable if we lose our souls in the process. [...] these Christian ideas if they are to be discussed properly have to be examined within the larger context of religious conceptions of the good life. But there can be little doubt that they have had a large part to play in the formation of common moral ideas and in particular the widespread acceptance of the distinction that provides the focal point of this chapter.

This distinction may be marked in a number of ways. One way is to contrast 'faring well' with 'doing right'. It is a commonplace that even the most unprincipled men and women who never do right can fare well enough. Indeed, since at least the days of the Hebrew Psalmists people have been perplexed by the fact that it is often the wicked who prosper. Moral wrongdoing, it seems, is no bar to material success. Conversely, it is proverbial that the good (often) die young, so that doing right is no guarantee of faring well. In short the two senses of a good life easily and frequently part company.

Now the ancient Greek thinkers, though they did not formulate this distinction expressly, were aware of these familiar facts about happiness and virtue. In much of the philosophical writing that survives from that period, we can see attempts to accommodate such facts. Aristotle, it is true, is quite uncompromising in his belief that to be deprived of the social and material benefits of this life is to be deprived of a good life. But Plato sometimes advances the idea that such benefits are not the benefits that matter. In fact we can see this idea at work in some of the arguments we have considered already. When Socrates argues with Thrasymachus and Callicles, he several times suggests that those who get their own way and triumph over others only *seem* to get the best of it. In reality, he claims, they do almost irreparable damage to their own most fundamental interests—the good of their own souls. Accordingly, Socrates argues that, faced with a choice between doing and suffering evil, those most interested in their own true welfare will choose to suffer rather than to commit evil.

The contrast between material profitability and spiritual loss is made explicitly in the New Testament. 'What shall it profit a man,' Jesus asks, 'if he gain the whole world and lose his own soul?' (Mark 8:36). Often this utterance is used by Christians for purely rhetorical purposes. It is offered not as a challenging thesis so much as a reminder of something we all know, namely that 'Man does not live by bread alone', to use another biblical saying (Deuteronomy 8:6 and Matthew 4:4). But we lose the force of what Jesus is saying if we regard it merely as a pious sentiment which everyone in their less worldly moments will agree with. What we need to ask is just what contrast is at work in the question and just what is meant by 'the soul' here.

This is specially important because for many people (even if it is not always thought nice to admit it) the answer to the New Testament question is obvious: 'His profit is the whole world, and how much more could he want?'. It is this response and its implications which are explored in the famous story of Dr Faustus, the man who gave his soul to Satan in return for unlimited material wealth and power.

The story of Dr Faustus is based, probably, on a real sixteenth-century German magician, Johannes Faust. However, the legend which grew up about this man is much more important than the man himself. According to the legend, Faust entered into a pact with the devil who promised, in return for his soul at death, to give him knowledge and magical power far surpassing that which human beings can normally attain and by which he might accomplish all his worldly desires. To ensure that both parts of the bargain were kept Satan sends one of his more devious servants, Mephistopheles. He it is who conveys the knowledge and power and is the instrument of Faust's death.

The original legend of Faust received much more sophisticated treatment at the hands of the English dramatist Christopher Marlowe in his famous play *The Tragical Life and Death of Dr Faustus*, and in the German poet Goethe's poem *Faust*. What is important about this story in all its versions is the distinction it forces us to make between the two senses of 'the good life'. If we are to find convincing reasons by which to persuade ourselves and others that Faustus has the worst of the bargain, we cannot appeal to his failure to achieve the good things that life has to offer. That is precisely what Satan guaranteed to supply. So the good that he loses out on, and the evil he brings upon himself, must be of a quite different order. There must be a difference in kind and not merely degree between the sorts of good and evil that are brought into question by the case of Faustus. This means that we must elaborate a distinction between senses of the expression 'a good life'.

In doing this we might appeal to the rewards and punishments of an afterlife, as generations of human beings have done. Indeed the story itself encourages us to do this. Such an appeal raises two distinct questions. First, is there an afterlife? And secondly, if there is, do its rewards outweigh everything in this life? [...] though here we might observe that it is the second question which is the more important for a philosophy of the good life. For the moment, if we stick to this world, and if we construe Faustus's loss as contemporaneous rather than in the future, we need to show, first that the *materially* best life (which he undoubtedly enjoys) is not the *morally* best life, and secondly that there is more to commend morality.

In other words, any adequate reply to the challenge represented by the story of Faustus which aims to show that he makes a mistake must draw upon the distinction between material and moral goodness, between how we fare and how we behave, between a *having* good life and *leading* a good life. We should notice, however, that it is not enough to respond to Faust and those who think like him merely by drawing the distinction. We also have to show why one sort of good life—doing right—is preferable to the other—faring well. This means, as Plato saw, showing why, faced with the choice, we should prefer to suffer materially rather than do evil.

Kant and 'The Good Will'

This is in fact the task which the eighteenth-century German philosopher Immanuel Kant (1724–1804) set for himself. Kant was one of the greatest moral philosophers of all time. He developed and refined the very idea of 'the moral life' precisely to provide rational answers to these problems. Kant's most celebrated work in moral philosophy is entitled *The Groundwork to the Metaphysics of Morals*. As this title suggests, Kant aimed to lay out the fundamental, rational character of moral thought and action. He begins the book with an argument similar to that we found Socrates using against Callicles, the argument that material benefits and personal talents may be used well or badly and hence cannot constitute the fundamental principle of good and evil.

> Nothing in the world—indeed nothing even beyond the world—can possibly be conceived which could be called good without qualification except a good will. Intelligence, wit, judgement, and the other talents of the mind, however they may be named, or courage, resoluteness, and perseverance as qualities of temperament, are doubtless in many respects good and desirable. But they can become extremely bad and harmful if the will, which is to make use of these gifts of nature and which in its special constitution is called character, is not good. Power, riches, honour, even health, general well-being, and the contentment with one's condition which is called happiness, make for pride and even arrogance if there is not a good will to correct their influence on the mind and on its principles of action so as to make it universally conformable to its end. It need hardly be mentioned that the sight of a being adorned with no feature of a pure and good will, yet enjoying uninterrupted prosperity [i.e. anyone like Faust] can never give

pleasure to a rational impartial observer. Thus the good will seems to constitute the indispensable condition even of worthiness to be happy.

(Kant 1785, 1959: 9)

Kant's point is this: however wealthy or talented we may be, such benefits can be abused. Great wealth can deliberately be squandered on useless trivia, or used to corrupt and belittle others. Criminals and terrorists sometimes show a great talent for electronics, money laundering or strategic planning. Kant sees that, unless we are prepared to say that even in this sort of case these good things are unqualifiedly good, we must look elsewhere for the most basic standard of good and bad, right and wrong.

If material goods and natural talents cannot be the fundamental standard, what can it be? The examples just given of the abuse of good things might incline us to think that what is important is the purpose to which wealth and talent are put. But according to Kant this cannot be so because, however carefully we plan our actions, it is impossible to guarantee their outcome (the Scottish poet Robert Burns expresses the same thought in a famous line, 'The best laid schemes of mice and men, gang aft agley', i.e. go oft astray). If, Kant says, we have a good will or intention in what we try to do, but 'by a particularly unfortunate fate or the niggardly provision of a step-motherly nature' we are unable to accomplish the end in view, the good will that we had would still 'sparkle as a jewel in its own right, as something that had full worth in itself' (Kant 1785, 1959: 10).

An example may serve to make the general point. Suppose someone works for an international charity, collecting money and organizing supplies of medicines for refugee camps. In the wake of a great disaster, she makes a Herculean effort and manages to fund and to dispatch a massive quantity of much needed medicine. But through no fault of hers, the storage facilities fail, the medicines become contaminated. Unfortunately they are nonetheless administered in ignorance of their poor condition, and the result is that the death rate in the camps rises to a level far higher than it would have done if no medicines at all had been sent. This is of course a great tragedy. But even should the charity worker *feel* guilty, she would not actually *be* responsible for this terrible outcome. The real fault must be laid at the door of 'a particularly unfortunate fate or the niggardly provision of a step-motherly nature', and her efforts towards an end that failed to materialize, would 'still sparkle as a jewel … that had full worth in itself'.

Kant would make the same point with respect to the reverse kind of case. Suppose I see someone I regard as my enemy crossing a lonely road on a wild night when I am driving home, and try to run him down. As luck would have it, the sound of my sudden acceleration alerts him to a falling tree and he leaps into the ditch just in time to avoid being crushed beneath it. By this curious route, my evil intention has saved his life. Nevertheless, this good outcome mitigates none of the wickedness of my action.

Intention and outcome, then, need to be separated, with the result that it does not appear to be *successful* action that matters ultimately. This is because, in the first example, the unfortunate consequences did nothing to sully the fine nature of the intention, and in the second example, the beneficial results did nothing to alter its evil character. Thus it seems to be the intention behind an action (what Kant calls 'will'), rather than the success or failure of that action, that is all important.

About intention and will, however, more needs to be said, because intentions can themselves have differing motives behind them. The charity worker whose case was considered a moment ago can fail to bring about her good intentions and remain (so to speak) morally unscathed. But if we were to discover that her reason for attempting the relief work in the first place had nothing to do with the welfare of those involved but was rather a way of trying to win personal fame and glory, this would seriously undermine the moral merit in what she was doing. The same point is illustrated by the real case of bounty hunters in the American Wild West. These were people who aimed to do a good thing—bring violent and vicious criminals to justice. But often they themselves cared nothing for justice. They did what they did partly for monetary reward and partly because they enjoyed hunting down human beings. Such motives, on Kant's and on most people's view, completely destroys the moral worth of their actions.

But much more contentiously Kant also thinks that motivations of which we approve do not themselves carry moral worth. He says:

> There are … many persons so sympathetically constituted that without any motive of vanity or selfishness they find an inner satisfaction in spreading joy, and rejoice in the contentment of others which they have made possible. But I say that, however dutiful and aimiable it may be, that kind of action has no true moral worth.
>
> (Kant 1785, 1959: 14)

This is because it arises from *inclination*. Kant does not think, as some people have supposed him to, that you ought never to enjoy doing good. He does think, however, that there is an important difference between the actions of someone who spontaneously and with pleasure does what is right and the same actions on the part of someone who performs them, with difficulty perhaps, but solely *because* it is right. He invites us to consider the case of someone whose life has been easy and happy and who takes a great interest in others and attends to the needs of those in distress. Suddenly his life is clouded by some great personal sorrow. He finds that he can take no interest in the affairs of other people and is constantly overwhelmed by self-concern, though he still has the means to alleviate distress and the need to do so is as strong as ever.

> Now suppose him to tear himself, unsolicited by inclination, out of this dead insensibility and to perform this action only from duty and without any inclina-tion—then for the first time his action has genuine moral worth.
>
> (Kant 1785, 1959: 14)

The reason Kant thinks that true moral merit and demerit attaches to actions regardless of the feelings of those who perform them lies in his belief that 'inclination cannot be commanded' whereas action can. Since people can only be praised or blamed where they can be held responsible, praise and blame can only attach to action, not to feelings. You cannot make yourself glad to see someone, but you can nonetheless *welcome* them. You cannot help taking pleasure in the failures of people you dislike (what in German is called *Schadenfreude*), but you can, despite your feelings, act in a sympathetic way towards them. It follows, on Kant's view, that it is action not feeling that determines moral worth.

We must combine this conclusion with the earlier contention that success is not morally important either. What matters fundamentally is that people should aim to do what is right because it is right. Whether or not their natural inclinations support or oppose this, and whether their good intentions come off or not are both irrelevant; the first because we cannot command our feelings, and the second because we cannot completely control the world about us. The only thing wholly within our control, and hence the only thing for which we can be praised or blamed from a moral point of view, is the *will*. This is why Kant says that it is only a good will that can be unqualifiedly good, and that the unqualifiedly good will is doing your duty for duty's sake.

Suppose we agree with this (for the moment at any rate). There remains this important question. If the only unqualifiedly good thing is a good will, and if the good will is not good because of what it results in, how are we to determine or demonstrate its goodness? In what does its goodness *itself* consist? Kant's answer is that the good will is a purely rational will. To see what he means by this, however, needs a good deal of explanation.

David Hume and Practical Reason

Philosophers have often elaborated a distinction between theoretical reason and practical reason. The distinction they have in mind is that between reasoning which is directed at telling you what to think or believe, and reasoning that is directed at telling you what to do. In fact, however, the distinction is rather hard to draw; even the way I have just put it is open to objection since it is quite correct to speak of beliefs about what to do. But that there is some difference or other is fairly plain, because generally speaking a piece of theoretical reason, by which we mean appeal to evidence and argument, ends with a conclusion about what is the case—for example, 'Smoking is a contributory cause of lung diseases'. Practical reason on the other hand, which also consists in a review of evidence and arguments, ends with a conclusion about what ought to be done—for example, 'You ought to take a course in accountancy before you leave college'.

Some philosophers have thought that the difference between theoretical and practical reason is this: practical reason requires some desire or other on the part of the reasoner before the reasoning has any force. To see why they have thought this we need only take the example offered a moment ago. Imagine an argument designed to convince you that you should take a course in accountancy before you leave college. It might run like this:

> The best paid jobs for graduates at the present time are to be found in the financial
> and commercial sectors. Employers don't want to recruit people who think they

already know all about business. But at the same time, they want people who are not totally unfamiliar with business practice, and who can show that the intellectual abilities they have in history or philosophy will show themselves in ways beneficial to the company. So to have a course or two in accountancy is to make yourself a more attractive prospect in the job market than either a business graduate or a pure arts graduate.

As an argument, this has no doubt proved persuasive to many, but it is obvious that its strength is a function of two things. First, the facts it alleges about jobs in the finance sector and about company recruiters must be true. Second, the person addressed must want a well-paid job. If either of these conditions does not hold the argument loses its force. So, for instance, if the person I address this argument to has a private income and is thus not in search of a job at all, the conclusion 'You ought to take a course in accounting' doesn't apply.

In this respect the second example differs markedly from the first. If evidence and argument is mounted which shows that smoking contributes to lung disease, only the facts alleged need be true for the conclusion to follow and for me to be obliged to accept it. What I want or do not want does not come into the matter. Of course, people sometimes allow their desires to blind them to the truth, but the point is that when this happens their belief is irrational, contrary to reason. In the case of practical reason, on the other hand, your desire determines the applicability of the argument.

One way of putting this is to say that practical reason is hypothetical. That is, it takes the form 'If you want such and such, then you ought to do so and so'. If on the other hand you don't want such and such, nothing follows about what you ought to do. This means that practical reason, at least so far as the example we have been discussing goes, is not a very forceful guide to conduct, since we can escape its demands by abandoning or modifying our desires.

Some philosophers have in fact claimed that all practical reason is hypothetical and dependent upon desire in this way. The Scottish philosopher David Hume (1711–1776) [...] held this view. In a famous passage of his *A Treatise of Human Nature* he claims that 'Reason is, and ought only to be the slave of the passions, and can never pretend to any other office than to serve and obey them' (Hume 1739, 1967: 415). By this he means that the use of reason can only be practical in so far as it points the means to ends that we independently desire.

This view of Hume's has what some people regard as a curious consequence, namely that we cannot reason about desires and cannot therefore declare any desire to be irrational. Hume in fact accepts this.

'Tis not contrary to reason (he says) to prefer the destruction of the whole world to the scratching of my finger. 'Tis not contrary to reason for me to chuse my total ruin, to prevent the least uneasiness of an Indian or person wholly unknown to me. 'Tis as little contrary to reason to prefer even my own acknowledg'd lesser good to my greater, and have a more ardent affection for the former than the latter.

(Hume 1739, 1967: 416)

We need to be very clear about what Hume is saying here. He is not commending any of the attitudes that he describes. All three are abnormal, and may even be said to be unreasonable, if by reasonable we just mean 'what ordinary people would accept as sensible'. No doubt if we were to come across someone who thought so much of himself that he really did express a preference to see the whole world destroyed rather than have a scratch on his little finger, we would be appalled at his attitude. Similarly, anyone who sincerely preferred to go through agonies, rather than have someone quite unknown to him suffer the mildest discomfort, would no doubt be treated as odd to the point of madness. And those who are self-destructive, that is, those who seem positively to seek the things that harm them and belittle what is in their best interests are generally recognized as psychologically problematic. But none of these attitudes, according to Hume, is strictly irrational, since no intellectual error of any kind is being made. There is no fact of the matter, or mathematical-type calculation, or logically provable inference about which the person in question is mistaken. The difference between normality and abnormality lies entirely in the uncommon character of the desires these people have.

If this is true, it is clear that no appeal to reason could produce a conclusive ground for action because all such appeals come into play only in a subservient role to desire, and consequently Reason in the abstract is silent upon practical matters. This means that general principles like 'You ought not to murder' must sooner or later depend upon some desire or other, the desire not to rob others of their most valued possession (life), or the desire not to cause anguish and suffering to friends and relatives. But what if someone does *not* have any such desires? What if they are complete nihilists in the sense that they care for nothing? Does this mean that the principle does not apply to *them*? And is there here the further implication that the principle would cease to apply to me also, if only I could induce in myself a state of mind in which I too no longer cared about the lives and feelings of others?

On the face of it, this seems quite unacceptable. Most people would say of those who are callously indifferent to the feelings of others, not that they are free from obligations because they don't care, but that they *ought* to care? Yet if Hume is right, there is no further rational basis upon which this 'ought' is to be based. They don't care and 'tis not contrary to reason' that they do not. If Hume is right, how could feelings and desires be made subject to reason? You either have them or you don't.

Hypothetical and Categorical Imperatives

It was this question of practical rationality that caused Kant to try to provide an alternative account of practical reason to Hume's, although he does not expressly discuss Hume in the *Groundwork*. If we think of the conclusions of practical reason as imperatives (directives about what to do), these come, Kant argues, not in a single type, but in two different types. First of all there are those that Hume rightly identifies as hypothetical, which is to say, imperatives whose force depends on our having the appropriate desire. This can be seen from the following imaginary dialogue.

> 'If you want to run in the London marathon, you ought to start training,' (Hypothetical imperative).
>
> 'But I don't want to run in the London marathon.'
>
> 'Well in that case, you've no reason to start training.'

Hypothetical imperatives themselves fall into two kinds. This is an example of what Kant calls 'technical' imperatives, instructions that point to the technical means to chosen ends. Then there are assertoric imperatives. These imperatives also rest upon a desire, but not a desire that someone *happens* to have. Assertoric imperatives appeal to desires that human beings tend naturally to share—health and happiness, for example. Just because these are widely shared, their existence is usually assumed, and in the normal run of things this gives rise to the appearance of assertoric imperatives carrying more general force than hypothetical imperatives do. But despite this appearance, assertoric imperatives are not universally binding. For example the assertoric imperative 'You ought to give up smoking because it is ruining your health' is normally treated as a knockdown argument (assuming there really is a causal connection between smoking and ill-health). But in fact someone could reply 'I have no desire to be healthy', and though such a sentiment is highly unusual, when true, it is enough to dispel the force of the assertoric imperative. In cases like this the value we had reasonably supposed to be common to us—good health—is not in fact shared, and the recommendation to action fails to apply just as much as in the case of a technical imperative.

In contrast to both kinds of hypothetical, there are categorical imperatives. These have the very special property of resting upon no hypothetical condition whatever, and hence cannot be rejected by denying any conditional desire. It is imperatives of this sort that are supposed to block the move that Hume's account of practical reason leaves open.

> 'You ought to visit your neighbour in hospital, because you promised to.'
>
> 'But I don't want to.'
>
> 'Whether you want to or not, you ought to keep your promises.' (Categorical imperative.)

With the discovery of categorical imperatives, Kant thought, we have reached the heart of morality. Categorical imperatives transcend our wants and desires by presenting us with rational principles of action in the light of which those desires themselves are to be assessed. Philosophers usually express this by saying that such principles of conduct are overriding, that is, they take precedence over other sorts of consideration when we are deciding what to do.

In fact this idea of overriding principles of conduct fits rather well with a view that many people have about morality, namely that it is a more important dimension to human behaviour than any other. If we show that some proposal is likely to be unprofitable, or unpopular, we are providing reasons against it, but not overriding reasons, because considerations of profit and mere popularity (or so it is commonly thought) should not take precedence over what is morally required of us. The profit motive is a rational one to have, but it must take second place to honesty. Making people laugh is a good thing, but not when it involves telling slanderous lies about others. In short, moral uprightness requires us to give second place to popularity, profitablility, convenience and all other sorts of personal advantage.

This common belief about the overriding character of moral considerations is what makes Kant's conception of *categorical* imperatives appealing. Or at least it does so, if there are such things. So far, in fact, we have simply drawn a contrast between two basic types of imperative (the technical and the assertoric are fundamentally the same). As yet, we have no clear indication as to how categorical imperatives are grounded in reason.

Now there is a real difficulty about this just because it is so easy to see that hypothetical imperatives are grounded in reason *precisely in virtue of their being hypothetical.* 'If you want credit for this course, you must sit the exam.' If you *do* want credit, you can test the rational basis of this recommendation by checking the rules to see if it is true that credit is obtainable only by sitting the exam (and not by submitting an essay for example). The rationality of the recommendation is simply a function of its truth. Or again 'If you want clear skin, you ought to use perfume-free soap'. If you *do* want clear skin, it is open to you to test the truth of this recommendation by examining the effects of soap with and without perfume.

But in the case of a categorical imperative, there does not seem to be any truth to check. 'You ought not to steal, if you don't want to end up in jail' can be checked by looking into facts about detection and conviction rates. But what facts can we look into to check the categorical 'You ought not to steal'? Actually, it is no part of Kant's strategy to appeal to any realist moral 'facts'. Rather, he thinks that we can check the rationality of categorical imperatives by examining them in the light of what he calls 'pure practical reason'. Kant calls it *pure* practical reason because on his view it involves no appeal to matters of empirical fact or sensory experience but to principles of intellectual reasoning alone.

Pure Practical Reason and the Moral Law

Imagine a world of perfectly rational beings (for brevity's sake let us call them 'angels'). To say that such beings are perfectly rational is to say that they always *do* what we, being less than perfect, always *ought to do.* Kant expresses this by saying that what is *objective law* for angels (demonstrably the right thing to do) is also *subjectively necessary* for them (just what by nature angels are inclined to do). This is not true for us. What is objectively right is usually experienced by us as a constraint on action, something we ought to do, because our natural inclinations often lie in other directions.

By contrast, for a perfectly rational creature there is no sense of constraint, no sense of being bound or required, and from this we can see that in a world of angels the laws of rationality would be like the laws of nature are in this one. We could explain and predict the behaviour of the angels by appealing to moral laws, laws of right and wrong, just in the way that we can explain and predict the behaviour of liquids, gases and solids by appealing to the laws of physics. Angels do what is morally right as automatically as water runs downhill.

Now this supplies us, in fact, with a way of determining what the moral law is. Suppose I propose to perform an action for a reason (what Kant calls a maxim). I can now ask myself 'Could acting on that maxim be a law of nature in a world of perfect beings?' If it could not, I have shown that the proposed action is not in accordance with pure practical reason and therefore not morally right. Consequently it is contrary to a rational will to perform the proposed action for the reason given.

This is a formal statement of the principle, of course, abstracted from any particular case. Kant offers us four examples of the detailed application of his method of pure practical reason.

1. A man who has suffered a great deal and anticipates even more suffering before his life is over, wonders whether it would not be better if he took his own life. But he asks himself what his reason would be, and whether he could consistently will that people always act on this reason. His reason is that life holds out a greater likelihood of bad than good for him, and so the maxim under examination is this: 'Whenever the future promises more bad than good, kill yourself'. But immediately he sees (Kant argues) that this could not be a law of nature because it is precisely the fact of the future's looking bleak that provides us with a reason to work for its improvement. It is precisely because we have no food in the house (for example) that we have a reason to go out and get some. A world in which the would-be suicide's maxim held as a law of nature, would pretty soon destroy itself because everything that supplies good reason to work for the continuation of life would lead people to kill themselves. From this it follows, Kant thinks, that suicide is against the moral law.

2. A man is in debt. He has the opportunity to borrow money with a promise to repay, but knows that in fact he will never be able to repay it. He is nonetheless tempted to make the promise, a lying promise, but asks himself whether this would be morally right. Once again the categorical imperative is appealed to, and he sees that, were it to be a law of nature that those in dire financial circumstances always made lying promises, this would lead immediately to the collapse of the institution of promising since lenders would know that the money would not be repaid and would refuse to lend. It follows that lying promises are contrary to the moral law.

3. A man has a natural talent for something, but an inclination to idleness tempts him to ignore it and hence fail to improve it. He asks himself whether there is anything morally wrong in this. And immediately he sees, or so Kant claims, that though a world of essentially idle and pleasure seeking people is possible, it is impossible to will that such a world exist, since any rational creature will want to keep open the opportunities which different kinds of talent provide.

4. A prosperous man sees many others around him in poverty and hardship but says 'What concern is that of mine? I have no desire to contribute to the welfare of the needy. And, should I fall on hard times, I have no intention of calling upon others myself.' It is possible, Kant says, to imagine a world in which everyone takes that attitude, but it is impossible to will that, through your will, such a world come into existence. For then you would have robbed yourself of the help and sympathy of others which you are likely to want when times get hard.

These examples are meant only as illustrations of a general thesis about morality and it is to that thesis we must return. But it is worth remarking that most philosophers share John Stuart Mill's estimation of Kant's attempt to apply pure practical reason to particular examples—'when he begins to deduce from his precept any of the actual duties of morality, he fails, almost grotesquely, to show that there would be any contradiction' (Mill 1871, 1998: 51–2). None of the examples is convincing. Take the last. It depends upon the hardhearted man wanting precisely what he says he does not mean to claim—the help of others should he himself fall upon hard times. It is certainly open to Kant to doubt that anyone would continue to hold this view once hard times were actually upon him. But if so, this is a result of the very human nature that Kant thinks has no part in pure practical reason, and does not show that the principle 'Offer and ask no help' cannot be consistently maintained, even if, as a matter of fact, it is not likely to be consistently maintained by those who hold it. It seems that Kant is conflating logical impossibility and psychological improbability.

Or consider the first example. This is supposed to show that suicide is impossible for a rational being. But it does nothing of the kind. We can consistently maintain that it is rational to commit suicide when circumstances are *very* adverse without thereby agreeing that suicide is justified in the face of any adversity whatever. It is only by equating the two that Kant's conclusion follows.

Universalizability

Still, if Kant does the job of illustration badly, this does not necessarily mean that the basic philosophy at work is unsound. What is important is whether the method he proposes for deciding what morality requires of us is satisfactory. That method consists of applying a test to every reasoned action, a test that has subsequently become known in moral philosophy as 'universalizability'. This is the procedure of seeing whether your own reasons for action could apply to everyone equally or whether they amount to nothing better than special pleading in your own case.

There are many sophisticated twists and turns that can be given to the philosophical elaboration of this test, but in fact it is not far in spirit from what is a common enough way of thinking. When some action is proposed people often ask of themselves and others—'What if everyone did that?' This is thought to be an important objection, but it is open to two different interpretations. Sometimes the idea is that the consequences of everyone's doing the action in question is highly *undesirable*. For example, I might object to your walking on the grass on the grounds that if everyone did so, the cumulative result would soon be no lawn. However, an alternative interpretation of the 'What if everyone did that?' objection draws attention to the fact that there are some actions which it would be *impossible* for everyone to perform, with the result that any attempt to justify performing them must involve some special pleading on the part of the individual. For example, the advantage of cheating depends upon it's being the case that most people don't cheat, so any attempt to justify *my* cheating must involve special pleading.

It is in this second test of universalizability that Kant is interested, and he gives it its first formal elaboration. It is important to see, however, that in contrast to the first interpretation, he is not speculating upon what the general run of humanity would do, but rather what we could consistently will to be the behaviour of all humanity. We are not asking 'What *will* everyone do?' but 'What if everyone *were* to do it?', knowing of course that everyone will not. The test is about consistency not consequences.

Kant's illustrations offer us a number of categorical imperatives—you ought not to commit suicide, you ought not to make lying promises, you ought to develop such talents as you have, and so on—but Kant argues that these can all be derived from one basic imperative from which all the laws of moral conduct can be derived. It is this: 'I should never act in such a way that I could not also will that my maxim should be universal law' (Kant 1785, 1959: 18). What he means is this. If you want to know whether what you propose to do is morally right or not, ask yourself whether you can consistently will that everyone whenever they have the same reason as you do, should act in that way. Or to put it in philosophers' jargon, ask yourself if you can consistently universalize the maxim of your action.

Kant goes on, with an ever increasing degree of abstraction, to formulate two other versions of the categorical imperative. His argument is complex and the resulting claim is that the fundamental moral law is one which requires from us 'respect for persons'. He formulates this version thus: 'Act so that you treat humanity, whether in your own person or that of another always as an end and never as a means only' (Kant 1785, 1959: 47).

This formulation has become known as the ideal of 'respect for persons'. It has been more influential in Western moral philosophy than any other ethical idea, perhaps, and to understand it properly a great deal needs to be said about it. But it is not necessary here either to trace all the steps by which Kant reaches this ideal or to explore the ideal itself more closely. For what we want to know is not whether 'respect for persons' is a good moral principle, but whether the conception of the moral life in which it is one element is a conception that we have good reason to accept. And enough has been said about Kant's philosophy to allow us to summarize and examine this conception. First the summary.

Summary of Kant's Philosophy

When we ask questions about 'the good life' there is built into them an ambiguity. We can mean 'the happiest life' or we can mean 'the worthiest life'. It is the latter that is more important since the best a human being can hope for is to be worthy of happiness, and to attain such worthiness is to lead a moral life. This does not consist in doing good, however, because whether the good we try to do actually comes about is not a matter over which, ultimately, we can exercise control. Between aspiration and reality misfortune may well intervene. Neither does the moral life consist in having the right sort of attitudes. Whether we are cheerful, friendly, generous and optimistic, or solemn, withdrawn, thrifty and pessimistic is a matter of the nature with which we are born, and hence also something over which we can exercise little control. Consequently our temper, good or bad, is not something which can properly attract either praise or blame.

What can properly be examined from a moral point of view is our will, the intention behind the things we do and say, because this is wholly within our control as rational agents. Be we rich or poor, clever or stupid, handsome or ugly, jolly or sad, everyone of us can aim to do what is right just because it is right, and if we succeed in this we succeed in living a morally good life.

But how do we know what is right? We know it by considering what actions are categorically forbidden or required, not because of their consequences or outcome in any particular case, but on grounds of pure reason alone. These are all those actions which match up to the test of the most fundamental categorical imperative of universalizability and respect for persons.

Kant's moral philosophy has generated a huge quantity of comment, interpretation and criticism. A great deal of this has served to show that there are complexities in his thought of which even he was not wholly aware. Moreover, however impressive his attempt to delineate a clear conception of morality pure and simple and to give it a firm foundation in reason, it is widely agreed that Kant's philosophy fails. Some of the reasons for this failure lie in quite technical philosophical issues which are difficult to explain briefly or simply. But the larger part of the failure arises from features of Kant's conception of the moral life whose unattractiveness or inadequacy can be shown without too much complexity. There are in fact three main objections. These have to do with the separation of intention and outcome, the test of universalizability, and the idea of doing one's duty for its own sake. We will consider each of these in turn.

Act, Intention and Outcome

Kant holds that the moral worth of an action must reside in the will with which it is performed, or as we would more naturally say, in the intention behind it. This is, as we have seen, because people cannot be held responsible for nor can they claim the merit of outcomes over which they have very imperfect control. It is both pointless and wrong to praise and blame people for things that they could neither prevent nor bring about. 'An unfortunate fate' or a 'step-motherly nature' may bring our best intentions to nothing. It is to our intentions, then, that praise and blame must be attached.

Many people find this an intuitively appealing idea, and yet it is hard to see that it can be sustained for long. We may want to confine moral merit and demerit to the intentions behind an action, but it is very difficult to deny that actions and their consequences must also be taken into account. *Intending* to murder someone is wrong, presumably, at least in part because actually murdering them would be wrong, and whether I actually murder them is a matter of consequences. If I am to murder someone, it is not enough for me to pull a trigger or plunge a knife. My victim must actually die as a consequence of what I do. Similarly, intending to save someone from drowning is meritorious, presumably because the action of saving them is, and once more this is partly a matter of the actual consequences of my intention. It is not enough for me to have reached for their hand, or pulled them aboard; they must go on living as a result. If, then, we are to concern ourselves with the moral character of intention, we are at the same time obliged to take actions into account and cannot take as indifferent an attitude to success as Kant's way of thinking would suggest.

Someone might deny this, deny in other words that actions are morally important. They might claim that what matters from a moral point of view is not what we *do* but what we *try* to do. This is indeed a common thought. Many people think that moral right and wrong is not about accomplishing things or being successful but about trying hard and doing your best. 'At least you tried' is often offered as moral compensation for failure. ('It's the thought that counts' expresses the same sentiment.) But though the belief that trying is more important than succeeding is quite widely shared, at least one important objection can be brought against it. This objection arises from the fact that genuine attempts and intentions have to be *expressed in* actions. Trying to do something is not the same as doing it, certainly, but it is still the performance of some action or other. I cannot be accused of trying to murder you unless I have succeeded in some action or other—holding up a gun, firing it, waving a knife, putting a poisonous substance in your food. If none of these actions or others like them take place, there is no substance to the claim that I tried to murder you. And this means that *some* consequential actions must take place if we are to talk even of the moral assessment of attempts.

Similarly, I cannot claim to have tried to save a drowning child unless I have succeeded in doing something else—reaching out my hand, running for a life belt, pulling at his body. Were you to see me sitting perfectly still and accuse me of callous indifference to his plight, it would hardly do for me to reply that I had tried to save him but that an 'unfortunate fate' or a 'stepmother nature' had intervened in every one of my attempts and robbed my good intentions of any result whatsoever. I cannot reasonably say that I have attempted to do something, if absolutely none of my attempts have met with any success of any kind.

The upshot of this argument is really very simple. If we are to make a moral assessment of the lives of ourselves and others, we have to decide not only whether what we *meant to do* was right or wrong, but also whether what we *did* was right or wrong. Since doing anything whatever involves having *some* effect on the world, however small, this moral assessment cannot but be in part concerned with the success of our intentions. This means that success cannot be left out of the calculation in the way that Kant suggests. It is not enough, in short, simply to have a good will. A good will that accomplishes nothing whatever cannot 'shine like a jewel'.

The Universalizability Test

Of course, none of this shows that will and intention are not of great moral importance. Nor does it show that intentions do not matter. It is still the case that people who mean well, but whose good intentions do not come off for reasons quite independent of their actions, deserve moral commendation. From this it follows that at least some moral assessment is based upon considerations other than success.

It is here that Kant's most widely discussed contribution to moral philosophy comes into play, namely his formulations of the categorical imperative. Kant claims to offer us a test by which our actions and intentions can be assessed, a test quite independent of desired or actual outcomes. This is the test of universalizability. According to Kant we have to ask ourselves whether an action we propose to perform could consistently be performed by everyone similarly placed and with the same reasons. And, he argues, such a test plainly rules out many of the sorts of actions the moral consensus of his day condemned—suicide, lying promises, failure to develop one's own talents. We saw, however, that Kant's own illustrations of this principle are far from convincing. The fact that they do not work very well is not in itself conclusive proof that the test is a poor one, because it might be made to work better than Kant himself manages to do. But when we try to apply it more rigorously it turns out, in fact, that the test is *too easily* satisfied.

[...] the existentialist's 'ethics of authenticity'—the idea that good actions are made good by the sincerity with which they are performed—has difficulty in accommodating the case of 'the sincere Nazi'. This is the person who engages *sincerely* in behaviour widely recognized to be evil. Our intuitions suggest that this sincerity, far from making those actions good or even better than similar actions performed in *bad* faith, actually makes them worse. Indeed it is arguable that bad actions become truly evil when they are freely, deliberately and sincerely performed.

A similar objection to the Kantian ethics of intention can be found in what we might call 'the *consistent* Nazi'. Let us characterize Nazis as people who act on the maxim 'This person should be exterminated because he/she is a Jew'. Now according to Kant's moral philosophy we can put this maxim to the test by appealing to the categorical imperative—'Act only according to that maxim by which you can at the same time will that it should become a universal law'—and we might point out to Nazis that if it were a universal law of nature that Jews were regularly exterminated, then if they themselves were Jewish, they would have to be exterminated. Now as a matter of fact it was not unknown for enthusiastic Nazis to be found to have Jewish ancestry, and if such people were to engage in some special pleading, some argument which made theirs a special case, we could indeed accuse them of failing to judge in accordance with the categorical imperative. We could show, in other words, that the maxim 'This person should be exterminated because he/she is a Jew' was not being universalized.

But if these people were *consistent* Nazis, who not only conceded but positively endorsed the idea that were they to be found to be Jewish they too must perish, we could not find fault with them on these grounds. To be prepared to promote political ideals that taken to their logical conclusion imply your own destruction may be a *psychologically unlikely* attitude of mind for most people.

But it is certainly *logically possible* and displays consistency. However, if a policy of genocide is deeply mistaken from a moral (as well as every other) point of view, consistency in its application is hardly any improvement. And in so far as people are prepared to sacrifice *themselves* in a programme of genocide, this reveals not their moral rectitude but their fanaticism.

The same point can be made about one of Kant's own examples. Recall the man who prided himself on his independence and neither gave nor asked for charity. Kant says that such a man could hardly will that were he himself to fall on hard times it should nonetheless be a universal law of nature that no one assist him in his poverty. Now it may be psychologically unlikely that an individual in need could wish to receive no assistance (though surely we are familiar with people who are too proud to receive charity), but it is plainly not a logical contradiction. The opponents of charity can as easily apply their harsh doctrine to themselves as to others if they choose. Whilst we may remark upon their rather grim, almost inhuman, consistency, this does not make their action any better, because it does not make them any the less uncharitable. Once more, consistency does not seem to bring objectionable actions any nearer to what we recognise as moral right and wrong.

The 'consistent Nazi' objection is not merely a matter of comparing the results of universalizability with intuitive moral conviction. It can also be used to show that the test of universalizability is quite powerless when it comes to deciding between competing moral recommendations. Consider two, contradictory, recommendations. 'Never kill people just because they're Jewish', and 'Always kill people who are Jewish because they're Jewish'. The case of the consistent Nazi shows that the second of these recommendations, however loathsome, can be made to square with the demands of the categorical imperative, and it should be fairly obvious that the first can be made to satisfy it. But if contradictory proposals can both satisfy the test of universalizability, it follows that that test is unable to discriminate between good and bad recommendations. In short, it cannot tell us what to do. From this it follows that Kantian universalizability cannot provide the means by which to determine right from wrong.

The question of what Kantianism has to say about Nazism is not merely theoretical, but arises in at least one specific instance. Hannah Arendt, in her famous book *Eichmann in Jerusalem*, records how Adolf Eichmann, who was tried and executed for his part in the destruction of millions of Jews, astonished his examining officer when he suddenly claimed that throughout his life he had been guided by Kantian moral precepts.

> The examining officer did not press the point, but Judge Raveh, either out of curiosity or out of indignation at Eichmann's having dared to invoke Kant's name in connection with his crimes, decided to question the accused. And to the surprise of everybody, Eichmann came up with an approximately correct definition of the categorical imperative: 'I meant by my remark about Kant that the principle of my will must always be such that it can become the principle of general laws'. ... He then proceeded to explain that from the moment he was charged with carrying out the Final Solution he had ceased to live according to

Kantian principles. ... [But] what he failed to point out to the court was that in this 'period of crimes legalized by the state', as he himself now called it, he had not simply dismissed the Kantian formula as no longer applicable, he had distorted it to read: Act as if the principle of your actions were the same as the legislator or of the law of the land. ... Kant to be sure had never intended to say anything of the sort. ... But it is true that Eichmann's unconscious distortion agrees with what he himself called the version of Kant 'for the household use of the little man' [in which what] is left of Kant's spirit is the demand that a man do more than obey the law, that he go beyond the mere call of obedience and identify his own will with the principle behind the law—the source from which the law sprang.

Arendt then goes on to comment:

Much of the horribly painstaking thoroughness in the execution of the Final Solution that usually strikes the observer as typically German, or else as characteristic of the perfect bureaucrat—can be traced to the odd notion, indeed very common in Germany, that to be law abiding means not merely to obey the laws but to act as though one were the legislator of the laws that one obeys.

(Arendt 1963, 1994: 136–7)

We may indeed agree with Arendt that Kant had never intended to say anything of the sort, but the philosophical point this concrete example illustrates is that there is nothing in the logic of his universalizability test that rules it out.

Duty For Duty's Sake

So far we have seen that Kant's view of the good life as the moral life is marred in two respects. First, the emphasis he places upon moral goodness residing in our will or intention to do our duty and not in the good or bad consequences of our actions is mistaken since a complete divorce between intention, action and outcome is impossible. For this reason, there can be no question of judging an intention right or wrong without considering the goodness or badness of at least some of the consequences of that intention. This means that the moral quality of a life cannot be decided purely in terms of will and intention.

Second, even if we agree that intention must form a large part of our moral assessment, the idea of requiring the reasons upon which we act to be universally applicable, i.e. the requirement of universalizability, does not supply us with an effective test for deciding which intentions are good and which are bad. People can consistently pursue evil courses of action, and wholly contradictory recommendations can consistently be based upon the same reasoning. It follows that universalizability is not an effective test at all. Any action or mode of conduct can be made to meet it and hence no course of action can be shown to be ruled out by it.

But besides these two objections there is a third. Kant observes, with some plausibility, that it is not enough to *do* one's duty. Morality requires that we do it *because* it is our duty and for no other reason. In other words, a morally good life does not consist merely in acting in accordance with moral right and wrong, but doing so because of an explicit commitment to moral right and wrong. Those who do not steal because they never have the chance or inclination to, or because they are fearful of punishment, are to be contrasted with those who never steal because it is wrong to steal. This is what is meant by saying that they do their duty for duty's sake. And according to Kant, acting on this reason exceeds in value acting in the same way for any other reason. It is worth recalling the passage quoted earlier where he says:

> To be kind where one can is duty, and there are, moreover many persons so
> sympathetically constituted that without any motive of vanity or selfishness
> they find an inner satisfaction in spreading joy, and rejoice in the contentment
> of others which they have made possible. But I say that, however dutiful and
> amiable it may be, that kind of action has no true moral worth.

> (Kant 1785, 1959: 14)

Now if the moral life is the life of duty for duty's sake, and the best (in the sense of finest) form of human life is the moral life, we are led rather swiftly to the somewhat unpalatable conclusion that many happy and attractive human lives fall far short of the most admirable kind of life, and may even realize nothing of it at all. Consider for instance someone who is talented and clever and who, being naturally disposed to use these gifts for the health and happiness of others, works hard on inventing and developing an ingenious device that is of great use to the physically handicapped. The work is enjoyable, though not specially well paid; much good is gladly done, but without any sense of 'doing one's duty'. Is it really plausible to claim, as Kant does, that such a life has 'no true moral worth'?

There is, however, an even more implausible and uncomfortable conclusion to be drawn from Kant's conception of morality and that is that we must attribute high moral worth to deeply *unattractive* human lives, and hence prefer them to the sort of life just described. That this is an unpalatable consequence of the theory is brought out by the following description of one of Anthony Trollope's characters in *The Eustace Diamonds*, Lady Linlithgow.

> In her way Lady Linlithgow was a very powerful human being. She knew nothing
> of fear, nothing of charity, nothing of mercy, and nothing of the softness of love.
> She had no imagination. She was worldly, covetous and not unfrequently cruel.
> But she meant to be true and honest, though she often failed in her meaning;
> and she had an idea of her duty in life. She was not self-indulgent. She was as

hard as an oak post—but then she was also as trustworthy. No human being liked her;—but she had the good word of a great many human beings.

This rather appalling picture of rectitude which knows nothing of happiness but means to do its duty can hardly strike us as the model of the life we ought to lead. This is especially true when set beside that of happy hardworking lives in which a lot of good is done but where duty for its own sake plays little or no part. Of course, the defender of Kant's moral philosophy might use the same argument that has been employed at several other places [...]—it is not a good reason to reject a philosophy of value just because it conflicts with what we commonly think; after all what we commonly think about morality and the good life may be wrong, just as what people have thought about health and medicine has often been corrected by scientific investigation. Perhaps then Lady Linlithgow's life *is* to be admired as a good example of the sort of life we ought to lead.

But the conflict with common thought is not so easily ignored. Here we must return to the opening topic of this chapter, doing right and faring well. There a distinction was drawn between two senses of the expression 'the good life'. In one it meant 'living as we ought', what we may call 'the virtuous life', and in the other 'living as we would like to', what we may call 'the happy life'. Just as in the story of Faustus we find an attempt to abandon the constraints of virtue entirely in the exclusive pursuit of happiness, so in Kant's moral philosophy we find an attempt to divorce completely the concerns of virtue and happiness, in the belief that the most important thing is to lead a virtuous or moral life. It is this attempt at a complete separation that makes possible the construction of lives and characters like Lady Linlithgow which, though naturally repellent, we must regard as exemplary instances of the Kantian good life.

But in fact virtue and happiness cannot be held completely separate in this way. This can be seen if we consider once more the foundations of Kant's thought. His concern is to urge upon us an ideal greater than that of the happy life, namely a life worthy of happiness. There are two ways in which we might think of this as the greater ideal. On the one hand we might suppose that though a happy life is good, a deservedly happy life is better. This is, I think, the other side to our thought about the wicked who prosper—that they don't *deserve* to prosper. On this way of thinking, the good life has two aspects, virtue and happiness.

Kant takes it another way. The moral life is a superior mode of life because so long as we are *worthy* to be happy, there is a sense in which we don't need happiness itself. We have attained the most admirable life. Virtue is its own reward. This is how it is possible for those who are unhappy and unattractive to lead good lives on the Kantian model. The question arises, however, as to why anyone should aspire to such an existence. What, in other words, could motivate anyone to try to lead a moral life conceived of in this way?

To see how important this question is in the context, imagine a world in which an 'unfortunate fate' and 'a step-motherly nature' constantly held the upper hand, so that to act in accordance with the moral law was a sure-fire way of courting disaster. (There have occasionally been societies in which this condition seems to have prevailed.) In such a world virtue and happiness are not only separate but in constant competition, and people are regularly faced with the choice of doing their duty for its own sake at the cost of personal misery, or ignoring the call of duty and securing their own happiness and that of their families and friends. What should they do in such a world?

On the one side there is plainly reason to forget about duty—it will lead to misery. On the other side (if we ignore some of the objections considered earlier and assume that Kant's arguments are sound) there is the conflict with pure practical reason. But what does this amount to in the end? It amounts to this: if I act against the moral law, I will be acting irrationally, i.e. inconsistently, and contradicting myself in the reasoning upon which I act. Put like this, however, the demands of the moral law do not seem so very overpowering. While it is no doubt important to be rational and avoid inconsistency, contradiction or incoherence in what we say and do, if the cost of so doing is certain to be personal misery (as we are imagining), there is surely at the very least equal reason to abandon pure practical rationality.

Kant would probably have denied that there is a problem here. On his view, once our duty has been discerned, only those who are morally insensible will fail to 'reverence the law'. There is no further reason to be found or given for doing what duty requires of us. But what of the possible conflict between duty and happiness? If duty can require us to sacrifice our happiness, don't we need *some* basis to choose between the two? To appreciate Kant's answer here we need to see his philosophy in the context of its background belief that our duty is part of a natural harmony of purposes by which God ensures that there is no ultimate conflict between duty and happiness. Indeed, Kant thought that the best argument for God's existence arises from the fact that rational action is only possible if duty and happiness do not in the end conflict, and must therefore presuppose a God who can and will ensure this.

[...] Most philosophers, however, have not followed Kant along this theological path. They have tried to defend a non-religious conception of morality and for them the problem remains—why should I follow the dictates of duty at the expense of happiness? This is in fact the reverse of the problem that we encountered in the examination of egoism, hedonism and eudaemonism. There we saw that a reason is needed to persuade us to abandon all our customary scruples or sense of right and wrong in favour of what we want or what would give us pleasure. Here, on the other hand, we are in search of a reason to abandon all our natural concern with happiness in obedience to the demands of something called 'the moral law'. And the Kantian non-theological answer to this question—obedience to the moral law for its own sake is a requirement of pure practical reason—does not seem sufficiently weighty to override the natural considerations in favour of happiness.

It may well be argued, of course, that all the fault arises from focusing upon worthiness to be happy than upon happiness itself. In fact, some philosophers have thought that morality is centrally concerned with happiness; that the morally good person is *not* the sort of person Kant describes, who strives to obey an abstract, rational law indifferent to the welfare of human beings as we find them. Rather a morally good person is someone who seeks in all they do to bring about 'the greatest happiness of the greatest number of people'. This last expression is, in fact, the slogan of an alternative but no less influential school of moral philosophy—utilitarianism [...].

Suggested Further Reading

Original sources

David Hume, *A Treatise of Human Nature* Bk. II Pt III. Bk. III Pt I
Immanuel Kant, *Foundations of the Metaphysics of Morals*

Commentary

James Baillie, *Hume on Morality*
H J Paton, *The Categorical Imperative*

Contemporary Discussion

Christine Korsgaard, *The Sources of Normativity*
Phillip Stratton-Lake, *Kant, Duty and Moral Worth*

"Jokes Are Conditional" and "Taste, Morality, and the Propriety of Joking"

Ted Cohen

....

Jokes Are Conditional

W hen I first wrote about jokes,[1] I thought of dividing them into the pure ones and the conditional ones. A conditional joke is one that can work only with certain audiences, and typically is meant only for those audiences. The audience must supply something in order either to get the joke or to be amused by it. That something is the *condition* on which the success of the joke depends. It is a vital feature of much joking that only a suitably qualified audience—one that can meet the condition—can receive the joke, and the audience often derives an additional satisfaction from knowing this about itself. A pure joke would be universal, would get through to everyone, because it presupposed nothing in the audience.

It now seems clear to me that there is no such thing as a pure joke. It is a kind of ideal, but it doesn't exist. At the very least, the audience will have to understand the language of the joke, and probably much more. But even if all jokes are conditional, it is still useful to note just how strongly conditional a particular joke is, and just what kind of condition is presupposed.

When the background condition involves knowledge or belief, I call the joke *hermetic*. Perhaps all you need to understand my joke is a working knowledge of the English language. But you may need a good bit more, as the background information becomes ever more specific and arcane. Some of the most strongly conditional hermetic jokes are ones involving the topics

---

1   That was in a short essay, "Jokes," first published in *Pleasure, Preference and Value: Studies in Philosophical Aesthetics*, edited by Eva Schaper (Cambridge: Cambridge University Press, 1983). This piece was subsequently reprinted, in edited versions, in *Aesthetics: A Reader in Philosophy of the Arts*, edited by D. Goldblatt and L. Brown (Upper Saddle River, New Jersey: Prentice-Hall, 1997), and in *Aesthetics: An Oxford Reader*; edited by P. Maynard and S. Feagin (Oxford and New York: Oxford University Press, 1997). A few years before those reprintings it was published, curiously, in Finnish translation in *Kauneudesta kauhuun taide ja filosofia* 2, edited by Arto Haapala and Markus Lammenranta (Helsinki, 1993), where it is called "*Vitsi.*" I am unable to read any Finnish whatever, and I have been puzzled by the appearance in the Finnish translation of footnotes that are not in the original English. It is my guess and fear that those footnotes are explanations of the jokes in the essay.

and jargon of a profession. Some such jokes are not actually *within* the profession. For instance, this doctor joke:

> Four doctors went duck hunting together. Together in the duck blind, they decided that instead of all shooting away at the same time, they would take turns as each duck came by. The first to have a shot would be the general practitioner, next would be the internist, then the surgeon, and finally the pathologist.
>
> When the first bird flew over, the general practitioner lifted his shotgun, but never fired, saying, "I'm not sure that was a duck."
>
> The second bird was the internist's. He aimed and followed the bird in his sights, saying, "It looks like a duck, it flies like a duck, it sounds like a duck...," but then the bird was out of range and the internist didn't take a shot.
>
> As soon as the third bird appeared, flying up out of the water only a few feet from the blind, the surgeon blasted away, emptying his pump gun and blowing the bird to smithereens. Turning to the pathologist, the surgeon said, "Go see whether that was a duck."

Or this mathematician joke:

> To tell a mathematician from a physicist, it is enough to administer this test. Send the person into a cabin in the woods, telling him his problem is to boil water. If you have previously put a pot in the cabin, and arranged for the stove to be hooked up and for there to be a working sink, then both a mathematician and a physicist will proceed to run water into the pot, put the pot on the stove, turn on the gas, and bring the water to a boil. You cannot tell them apart. But if you fill the pot with water beforehand, then you can tell. The physicist will carry the pot to the stove, turn on the gas, and bring the water to a boil. The mathematician will empty the pot in the sink, thereby reducing this to the first problem, which has already been solved.

Or this philosopher joke:

> The president of a small college desires to improve his school's academic reputation. He is told that the best way to do this is to create at least a few first-rank departments. It would be good to work on the mathematics department, he is told, because that would not be too expensive. Mathematicians do not require laboratories or even much equipment. All they need are pencils, paper, and wastebaskets. It might be even better to work on the philosophy department. The philosophers don't need wastebaskets.

You need not be a doctor or a mathematician or a philosopher to appreciate these jokes, nor even know much at all about doctoring, mathematics, or philosophy. At most you need some acquaintance with the presumed proclivity of surgeons to cut first and then diagnose, of mathematicians' curious notions of elegance, and of philosophers' professional license to say anything they want because there is no way to prove them wrong, and so they are permitted to do anything they can get away with (like writing a book about jokes).[2] These three jokes do require something specific of their audiences, but they are only mildly hermetic. A slightly more intricate example is this:

> Early one morning a man awoke in a state of terrible anxiety because of the dream he had been having. He immediately called his psychiatrist, and after making a special plea because of his distress he was granted an appointment that morning even though it was not the day for seeing his psychiatrist. When he arrived in the doctor's office, he said, "I had the most awful dream you can imagine. In it I raped my mother, killed my wife, and seduced my daughter, and more things worse than those. I woke up shaking and sweating, and I called you immediately. Then I had a quick piece of toast and some coffee, and ran down here to see you."
>
> "What?" said the psychiatrist. "You call that a breakfast?"[3]

For this, one needs to know only two things, although one other thing deepens the joke. One needs to know the exceptionally high proportion of Jews among psychiatrists, and to know the commonplace about Jewish mothers that they are excessively concerned, especially about food. The joke is deeper for those who believe it an occupational hazard of psychiatry that its practitioners tend to look for deep and convoluted explanations when simple and direct ones would do, and, conversely, that they tend to look only at the surface in the few cases in which something hidden is at work.

Strongly hermetic jokes require audiences with at least some substantive knowledge of their topics, and such jokes do not always require the information and jargon of professions, but only some significant acquaintance with a specific subject, like this one, for which you need to know a little about drama:

> A panhandler approached a man on the street outside a theater. The man declined to give anything, saying, "'Neither a borrower nor a lender be.'—William Shakespeare."
>
> The panhandler replied, "'Fuck you!'—David Mamet."

---

2 But surely it is not only philosophers, and among philosophers it is not only Hegel, about whom it might be said, "He never had a thought he didn't publish."

3 David Malament, who has taught me many, many things, taught me this joke.

This one needs an audience with at least some knowledge of the history of formal logic:

> What did Lesniewski say to Lukasiewicz?
>
> "Logically, we're poles apart."[4]

Here is one only for those who know a common Yiddish word (which is not so improbable) and also a particularly arcane topic set by Nelson Goodman in the theory of induction:

> What is a goy?
>
> A goy is a person who is a girl if examined at any time up to and including *t*, and a boy if examined at any time after *t*.[5]

And this one needs hearers who know at least a little of problems of reference in the philosophy of language, along with some slight information about ancient Greek literature:

> One day a paleographer came into his classics department in great excitement. "There has been an earthshaking discovery," he announced. "The *Iliad* and the *Odyssey* were not written by Homer, but by some other Greek with the same name."

For jokes that are severely hermetic, deeply embedded in particular cultures, one finds some of the best and worst examples among mathematician jokes.

> What's round and purple, and commutes to work?
>
> An Abelian grape.

The audience for this joke first needs some acquaintance with grape jokes, and then it needs to know, at least roughly, what commutativity is, and what an Abelian group is. (I suppose the audience needn't already know that Abelian groups are commutative, but it is unlikely that it would know all the rest and not know that.) Sometimes the condition required is not especially arcane, but it is relatively complex.

> According to Freud, what comes between fear and sex?
>
> *Fünf*

Here one needs to know that Freud's language was German, that Freud wrote about things like fear and sex (and, of course, one has to understand 'fear' and 'sex' in English), and how to count up to six in German.

---

4 This classical composition is by Michael Slote.

5 When I first published this joke, I attributed it to my friend George Boolos, who later told me the joke had been created by Richard Jeffrey, who in turn told me it had been created by Sidney Morgenbesser. I recounted all this in a subsequent correction of the original publication, and sent the whole thing to Boolos. It was a great pleasure to me to know that Boolos had kept the correction posted in his office at M.I.T. When George Boolos died not long ago, we lost a fine friend, a very good philosopher, a man devoted to scholarly exactitude, and one hell of a good man to exchange jokes with.

With some hermetic jokes what is required is not knowledge, or belief, in the first instance, but an awareness of what might be called "commonplaces."

> A young Catholic woman told her friend, "I told my husband to buy all the Viagra he can find."
>
> Her Jewish friend replied, "I told my husband to buy all the stock in Pfizer he can find."

It is not required that the audience (or the teller) actually *believe* that Jewish women are more interested in money than in sex, but he must be acquainted with this idea. When jokes play upon commonplaces—which may or may not be believed—they often do it by exaggeration. Typical examples are clergymen jokes. For instance,

> After knowing one another for a long time, three clergymen—one Catholic, one Jewish, and one Episcopalian—have become good friends. When they are together one day, the Catholic priest is in a sober, reflective mood, and he says, "I'd like to confess to you that although I have done my best to keep my faith, I have occasionally lapsed, and even since my seminary days I have, not often, but sometimes, succumbed and sought carnal knowledge."
>
> "Ah well," says the rabbi, "it is good to admit these things, and so I will tell you that, not often, but sometimes, I break the dietary laws and eat forbidden food."
>
> At this the Episcopalian priest, his face reddening, says, "If only I had so little to be ashamed of. You know, only last week I caught myself eating a main course with my salad fork."

I do not know exactly where jokes come from (nor does anyone else), but it is my sense that clergymen jokes have often originated in New England, and whether or not that is true, it is almost certain that the earlier versions are of the interfaith variety just exemplified, and that the form was later adapted for intrafaith purposes, as in,

> Three rabbis, one Orthodox, one Conservative, and one Reform, are accustomed to playing golf together every Sunday. On one particular Sunday their play is going very slowly because the foursome ahead of them is playing very slowly. In annoyance, the rabbis send one of their caddies ahead to speed things up, to tell the foursome ahead to play faster or to let the rabbis play through.
>
> When the caddie returns he looks crestfallen, and he says, "I am so ashamed. The foursome ahead is playing slowly because all four of them are blind. Blind golfers have to play slowly. They must wait while their caddies find their balls and then align them to swing in the right direction. And there I was, complaining. As soon as I learned, I was so embarrassed. I apologized and left."
>
> "Oh my," says the Orthodox rabbi. "I am humiliated."

"Me too," says the Conservative rabbi. "I think we should pray for those less fortunate and remind ourselves, as the Torah says, not to put obstacles in the path of the blind."

"Right," says the Reform rabbi. "Yeah, fine. Why the hell don't they play at night?"

Jokes like these, besides being caustic and possibly unflattering, sometimes incorporate genuine profundity. For instance,

> After many days of hard, continuous rain, the river is in danger of flooding, and word goes out that people may have to abandon their homes. When the river crests, water pours through the town, inundating houses, and it continues to rise. Firemen are sent in a small motorboat to go through the streets to make sure everyone is leaving. When they come to the house of the rabbi, they find him standing knee-deep in water on his front porch.
>
> "Come on, Rabbi," say the firemen. "The river will go much higher, and you should leave with us."
>
> "No," says the rabbi. "God will protect me." And he sends them away.
>
> The river rises higher, the rabbi is forced to go up to the second floor of his house, and now the police come in a motor launch.
>
> "Come on, Rabbi," say the police, "there isn't much time."
>
> "No," insists the rabbi, "I will stay right here. God will look after me." And he sends them away.
>
> Now the river rises so high that the rabbi is forced to stand on the roof of his house. When the National Guard arrive in a large boat, telling him that the river is sure to go even higher, the rabbi says, "All my life I have been a man of faith, and I will stay now, and trust in God," and sends them away.
>
> The river rises, the rabbi is swept away, and the rabbi drowns.
>
> Forthwith the rabbi appears in heaven, where he angrily approaches the throne of God, demanding, "How can You have let this happen to me? For all my life I have kept Your *mitzvot*. I have done what You asked, and trusted in You. Why?"
>
> A voice sounds from the throne: "You shmuck. I sent three boats."

I suppose some hearers might find these jokes unflattering, but I doubt that the jokes are found very offensive. I doubt that New Yorkers or citizens of New Jersey object to either of these:

> A family from Nebraska went to New York City for the first time on a week's vacation. After being battered by New York and its citizens for the first few days, the entire family felt exhausted and humiliated, and they were nearly ready to cut their vacation short, but the father insisted on trying once more to have

an agreeable vacation in New York. The family walked out of their hotel in the morning, and the father went up to a traffic policeman and inquired, "Officer, would you tell me the way to the United Nations building, or should I just go fuck myself?"[6]

How is the alphabet recited in New Jersey?

"Fuckin' A, fuckin' B, fuckin' C...."[7]

It is difficult to say just when such jokes become genuinely offensive. What do you make of this one?

What does it say on the bottom of a Polish Coke bottle?

Open other end.

Understanding this joke certainly does not require believing that Poles are stupid or inept. It requires understanding something like "what a Polish joke is." This is not a difficult understanding, and it isn't essentially different from what is required to understand Irish jokes (made in England), Ukrainian jokes (made in Russia), Russian jokes (made in Poland), Newfie jokes (made in Canada), Sikh jokes (made in India), Iowa legislator and Texas Aggie jokes (made in the good old U.S.A., along with Polish jokes). And yet these jokes are not equally appreciated, however well they are understood. All things being equal, a joke in which a rabbi makes an ass of a priest is likelier to succeed with a Jewish audience than with a Catholic one, although the joke is completely understood on all sides. This is due to another kind of condition.

Conditional jokes that depend upon feelings in the audience, likes and dislikes, and preferences, I call *affective*. Typically, these jokes are understood by many people, but the success of the jokes—their capacity to amuse—depends upon the affective disposition of the audience. It isn't always simply a matter of succeeding, or not, but a question of degree of success. For instance,

The thing about German food is that no matter how much you eat, an hour later you're hungry for power.

This joke is largely unavailable to anyone who doesn't know the old chestnut about Chinese food invariably leaving one hungry soon after eating, whether one believes that about Chinese food or not. But then one must also know the commonplace about Germans that they long to control others, to have and to wield power. Now it makes some difference whether one only knows this commonplace, or whether one knows it and believes it to be true. And finally, it matters whether one has negative

---

6 My friend the learned and talented Nicholas Rudall tells this joke in a version in which a Pakistani approaches a bowler-wearing gentleman on the streets of London. I do not think either version is superior, but the New York version tends to work in both England and the United States, while the London version does not always succeed in the United States. There is no doubt, however, that Mr. Rudall tells his version far better than I tell mine: he does the Pakistani far better than I do the Nebraskan.
7 A few years ago the distinguished Chicago architect Michael Rosen supervised the construction of an office building he designed in New Jersey. Mr. Rosen tells me that this may not be a joke.

feelings about Germans on that count, or doesn't. If it offends one to have Germans represented in this way, then the amusement may be lost altogether.

It is not only affective jokes that can have this variable success. With hermetic jokes, as well, there may be levels of response depending upon just how much the audience can bring to the joke. For instance,

> Not long after the Six-Day War in the Middle East, a class was meeting in the Soviet Union, a class in the Russian War College. The problem under discussion that day was how the Soviet Union might fight a war against China. Some of the students were distressed and puzzled, and one of them said, "How could we possibly fight a war against China? We could put at most, what, 150 or 200 million soldiers in the field? The enemy would have an army of nearly a billion. It would be hopeless."
>
> "Not necessarily," said the teacher, a distinguished Soviet Army commander. "It is entirely possible for the smaller army to win. Just notice what happened not long ago in the Middle East. Israel can field an army of at most 2 or 3 million soldiers, while the combined Arab armies number 100 million, and yet Israel won that war."
>
> "Yes," objected the student, "but where can we find 3 million Jews?"[8]

Beneath the twist in this story, the idea that the Soviet officer-candidate did not see how to transfer the lesson of Israel to the Soviet Union, is the savage irony of the fact that at the time of the Six-Day War there were far more than 3 million Jews in the Soviet Union, many of them there only because they were not permitted to emigrate.

Here is another multilayered hermetic joke, this one less bitter:

> A musician was performing a solo recital in Israel. When he ended the last selection, a thunderous response came from the audience, including many cries of "Play it again." He stepped forward, bowed, and said, "What a wonderfully moving response. Of course I shall be delighted to play it again." And he did. At the end, again there was a roar from the audience, and again many cries of "Play it again." This time the soloist came forward smiling and said, "Thank you. I have never been so touched in all my concert career. I should love to play it again, but there is no time, for I must perform tonight in Tel Aviv. So, thank you from the bottom of my heart—and farewell." Immediately a voice was heard from the back of the hall saying, "You will stay here and play it again until you get it right."

This is a pretty good joke just as it stands, with no background conditions beyond some obvious knowledge of what music recitals are like, and in this respect it is one of those "Jewish" jokes that

---

8 I owe this to Amos Cohen, who not only told me the joke but also pointed out its bitter aftertaste. He credits the joke to Rabbi Elliot Gertel.

needn't be told or heard by Jews in order to succeed. But something is added for those who know of the extremely confident music audience to be found in Israel, especially the very sophisticated, self-applauding German Jews. And then there is more. The total riches of this joke are available only to those who know the Jewish religious requirement that on certain occasions the appropriate portion of the Hebrew Bible be read out, that those present make known any errors they detect in the reading, and that the reader not only acknowledge these corrections but that he then go back and read out the text correctly, and that he stay there and read it again until he gets it right. It is this last piece of information that makes for yet another level in the joke, and, so I think, makes it a better joke than the version I have often heard in which the performer is a tenor singing arias in Italy. In Italy, too, there is the presumption of a supremely confident audience, especially for singing, which is why it should be not a pianist but a tenor, but it is not there that there is the connection with a required public performance ordained on religious-legal grounds. Here is another salient point of comparison of jokes with works of art. Shakespeare's *Hamlet* certainly is accessible to those who know only one meaning of the word 'nunnery,' but for those who know that in Shakespeare's time the word was slang for a brothel, there is more in the play when Hamlet says to Ophelia, "Get thee to a nunnery."

If all jokes are conditional, at least to some degree, then what difference does it make that they call for a contribution from the audience? And why can't the joke-teller simply inform his audience in advance, tell them whatever they need to know in order to get his joke? Or, why can't the audience accept the joke conditionally?

Suppose you tell me that Noah Cohen could not now become president of the United States. I don't believe you. You tell me that he is only eighteen years old, and that one must be at least thirty-five years old to be president according to the United States Constitution. Suppose I don't know how old Noah Cohen is, and I don't know this constitutional provision. If I believe you about those things, then I will believe that he can't become president. But even if I don't believe you, I certainly can believe this: If a person must be at least thirty-five years old to be president, and if Noah Cohen is eighteen years old, then Noah Cohen could not now become president of the United States. That is, I can certainly believe the conditional statement without believing the if-parts. Can I do something like this with a joke?

Suppose I am not a mathematician, and I don't know about grape jokes, and so in order to tell me about the Abelian grape, you first tell me what I need to know. Grape jokes are like elephant jokes, you explain, those jokes in which the word 'elephant' is in the answer to a question.

> What's big and gray, and wrote gloomy poetry?
> T. S. Elephant.

> What's big and gray, and sang both jazz and popular songs?
> Elephants Gerald.[9]

---

9 Although some jokes are virtually impossible to write, like the Freud-fear-sex joke, some seem to me even more effective when written. This one, about Elephants Gerald (Ella Fitzgerald), works even better when seen.

Grape jokes are like that, except that the word 'grape' is in the answer to a question. Like

What's round and purple, and conquered the world?

Alexander the Grape.

Then you go on to teach me, superficially, enough elementary mathematics: I learn a little about sets, about groups, and about the relations of members of sets and groups one to another, including the relations of associativity and commutativity And then you give me the Abelian grape joke. Will this work? Will I now realize that if mathematical groups are like that, and there is this institution of grape jokes, then your joke is funny? Will I find the joke funny? Highly unlikely, but exactly why is this enterprise so misguided?

The first thing to note is that, so encumbered, the joke seems labored, and even contrived. Good jokes, and perhaps jokes in general, tend to be concise (which is not to deny that there are wonderful jokes of great length; "Berl-in-debate-with-the-priest" is an example [...]), and why is that? It may be that jokes are most appreciated when they are brisk and not weighed down, but I think it is a mistake to think that it is the concision itself that matters. What matters is what makes the concision possible. What makes it possible is that so much can go unsaid. And why can it go unsaid? *Because the audience already knows it.*

It is a general thesis of mine that a deep satisfaction in successful joke transactions is the sense held mutually by teller and hearer that they are joined in feeling. As I noted earlier, jokes do not *compel* a sequel, not in the way, say, that arguments do. Not only is the effect not forced on the audience, but there is nothing especially acute to say when one's joke fails. When one's argument fails to move someone, when it fails to elicit a belief, one may always write this off to the benighted condition of the audience. They have been unable to follow the argument, or they are too ignorant to accept the premises, perhaps. But with a joke that has gone flat, all the teller is entitled to suppose is that his audience doesn't share his sense of humor. He may be bold enough, and confident enough in his fine joke, as well as in his ability to tell it, to go so far as to deny that his audience has any sense of humor whatever. But he cannot *prove* that, not in the way in which one might prove that one's argument is valid, and thereby consign the unmoved audience to the ranks of the irrational, the inattentive, or the downright stupid. All you can say of the fellow who doesn't laugh at your joke, at least all you can say when it has been established that he understands you, that he gets the joke, is that *he is not like you*, at least not in regard to the dynamics of your joke. And even if the joke has worked with everyone else, even if gets a good laugh from everyone else you or anyone else has tried it on, still this unlaughing listener is, in the end, nothing worse than not like you. He is not less human, at least not in any demonstrable regard. He is like someone who isn't enraptured by Mozart's *Marriage of Figaro*, who doesn't swoon at a fabulous Rembrandt, or who doesn't care to turn his head to see the sun set behind a mountain, or to see the colors of the ocean change as the sun plays upon the water.

How important is that? Surely you can inhabit a world with this person, even though he is a kind of stranger to you. Later I will urge you to agree that this estrangement is very important indeed, and that it can represent a threat to one's conception of his own humanity, and I will be insisting that this infirmity shows in failed jokes just as surely as in failures to care for the same art, but until then I want only to note that what has failed is the effort to achieve an intimacy between teller and hearer. It is a failure to join one another in a community of appreciation. It is exactly this community that begins to be marshaled when conditional jokes are told. These are the jokes that require the audience to supply something, and it is essential in the effect of such jokes that the audience be allowed to supply this. In fact they are urged to supply it, virtually compelled to supply it automatically, without even considering whether they would like to be thus pulled in. You cannot do this to someone, you cannot capture him by playing on what he knows and feels, if you first have to instruct him. Instructing him leaves him passive; it does not pull him toward you in terms of what you already share, precisely because you do not already share it. Consider this joke, which is available to both Jews and non-Jews, but has a greater or a different kick for Jews:

> Abe and his friend Sol are out for a walk together in a part of town they haven't been in. Passing a Christian church, they notice a curious sign in front saying "$1,000 to anyone who will convert." "I wonder what that's about," says Abe. "I think I'll go in and have a look. I'll be back in a minute; just wait for me."
>
> Sol sits on a sidewalk bench and waits patiently for nearly half an hour, and then Abe reappears.
>
> "Well," asks Sol, "what are they up to? Who are they trying to convert? Why do they care? Did you get the $1,000?"
>
> Indignantly, Abe replies, "Money. That's all you people care about."

Think of trying to tell this joke to someone who is not only ignorant of the widespread idea that Jews care more about money than almost anything else, but also does not even recognize 'Abe' and 'Sol' as Jewish names. Of course you could begin by telling him about those names, and then go on to inform him of this idea about Jews, and you might do this at considerable length, mentioning the character of Shylock, mistaken histories of the practice of usury during the Middle Ages, and whatever else you think will fortify a rich sense of the idea. Do you think the joke will work then?

Certainly it won't work well, if at all. Why not? Because you need your audience to know something *in advance of the joke*, and you need them to know it without your telling them. In this respect it is not like the solution to a puzzle or a mathematical problem. Suppose the problem is how to ensure that a pie will be cut into six equal slices, when the pie is to be sliced by one of those who will be given a slice. The solution, assuming the rationality of the man with the knife, and assuming that he is skilled enough to cut a slice that will be any reasonable fraction of the whole pie, is to stipulate that after each slice has been cut, all those except the slicer will be given the opportunity to select the just-sliced piece. Thus the only way for the person cutting the pie to ensure that he will have a piece no smaller than one-sixth of the pie is to cut the pie into six equal pieces.

It is perfectly possible to give this solution to someone, and to have it fully appreciated by the recipient, even if he has no advance knowledge of the problem. You might simply explain the problem to him, and then offer the solution. You cannot do this with a joke, at least not without considerable cost to the joke-transaction, and the reason is that you need to begin with an implicit acknowledgment of a shared background, a background of awareness that you both are already in possession of and bring to the joke. This is the foundation of the intimacy that will develop if your joke succeeds, and the hearer then also joins you in a shared response to the joke.

And just what is this *intimacy*? It is the shared sense of those in a *community*. The members know that they are in this community, and they know that they are joined there by one another. When the community is focused on a joke, the intimacy has two constituents. The first constituent is a shared set of beliefs, dispositions, prejudices, preferences, et cetera—a shared outlook on the world, or at least part of an outlook. The second constituent is a shared feeling—a shared response to something. The first constituent can be cultivated and realized without jokes. So can the second constituent, but with jokes, the second constituent is amplified by the first, and this is a very curious and wonderful fact about jokes.

I may overvalue the intimacy available through joke-telling; after all, I am one of those who love and need joke-telling. But I am confident that it is an intimacy that should not be underestimated. When we laugh at the same thing, that is a very special occasion. It is already noteworthy that we laugh at all, at anything, and that we laugh all alone. That we do it together is the satisfaction of a deep human longing, the realization of a desperate hope. It is the hope that we are enough like one another to sense one another, to be able to live together.

When you have good reasons for believing something, you expect me to join you in your belief once you have given me your reasons. And if I fail, you may be troubled by my failure, but you will indeed consider it a *failure*, and you will consign me to the ranks of the cognitively defective. When you find a joke funny, you expect me to join you in your amusement once you have told me the joke. If I fail, then once you have determined that I understand the joke, exactly what *failure* will you attribute to me? You find the joke funny, I don't. It is not as if some argument or proof had been presented, with your following to the conclusion and my not. In that case, the conclusion is something *to be believed*. This is an objective matter. My failure to join you is an error, or a mistake, or a misapprehension. But with the unsuccessful joke, there is nothing to point to besides the joke itself. You cannot show that the joke is an instance of something that must be acknowledged as funny, as you might show that an argument is an instance of valid reasoning. So you point to the joke. In fact, you tell it. Why do you expect me to find it funny? And just what is it you want of me, in wanting me to find it funny? What is it you want beyond the satisfaction you get from succeeding—and succeeding at what?

I think what you want is to *reach* me, and therein to verify that you understand me, at least a little, which is to exhibit that we are, at least a little, alike. This is the establishment of a felt intimacy between us.

I have been making heavy weather of this *intimacy*, as I am calling it, this community of amusement we belong to when we are laughing at the same joke, and I had better say something about why it seems to me such an important human achievement, virtually indispensable despite being something no one can guarantee—indeed *because* it cannot be guaranteed.

There are two ways in which you and I might agree. We might both believe the same thing, perhaps for just the same reasons. And we might feel the same way about something. In the first case, say, we both believe that the coast of Maine in the summer is characteristically a warm but not hot place, with a rockbound shoreline, often with mountains nearby, and near the coast there is often a persistent fog. In the second case, we find Maine in the summer rather melancholy, with beauty no doubt, but a beauty that seems dim and fragile, and we feel sweetly blue to be there.

The climatology of Maine is an objective fact. I have learned it firsthand, and if you have not yet learned it that way, you can look it up, or you can listen to me and believe me, or you might sojourn up there to check it out for yourself. In the end, if you do not agree with me, I will have to suppose that you don't know how to observe, or you didn't check the right references, or you haven't adequate eyesight, or something else keeps you from latching on to the objective features of the world, or at least of Maine.

The *feel* of Maine in the summer, however, is another matter. If you don't feel about Maine as I do, then you may yet "understand my semi-sadness at being there by grasping my best descriptions of myself-in-Maine. (It is one of the great achievements of art to provide for this kind of communication.) But even if you have a thorough grasp of my state, you still do not agree with me *in feeling*. You do not have the feeling yourself. I am alone with my feeling, at least so far as you are concerned, and you and I are not in communion in this matter. So what? Well, let us try thinking of this with reference to a joke. Take this gem:

> What do Alexander the Great and Winnie the Pooh have in common?
>
> They have the same middle name.

I can say something about why that tickles me, how it calls up the question of just what a name is, and the memory of what a child takes himself to be doing when he learns someone's name, and Milne's cleverness in building a kind of name on the model of historical nomenclature, and things like that. And I'm sure you can follow that. But what if you are not amused by the joke? The thing amuses me and it doesn't amuse you, and that's that. Yes, but why is that that? It is because (and now you must indulge me) there is something in me that is reached by this joke, and this something is not in you. This doesn't mean you are deficient, that I am somehow more than you, any more than it would mean that if I had an ingrown toenail and you didn't. But it does mean that you are not *like* me, at least not in this inner something that is tickled by the idea of Winnie the Pooh's middle name. And why does that matter to me?

Why do we recommend these things to one another, anyway? Why point out the huge, bright new moon, the funny stuff happening on *King of the Hill* on television (calling me into the room to watch it with you), the gritty beauty of the waterfront in Gdansk? Why draw one another's attention to all that stuff? Because we wish one another well? Well, maybe, but at its core I do not think this is entirely a matter of altruism. I think it is a wish, a need, a longing to *share* these things, to feel them together. And it is not quite enough to explain this to say that we are, after all, communal creatures, although I suppose we are. The other component in the explanation is the fact that I need reassurance that this something inside me, the something that is tickled by a joke, is indeed something that constitutes an element of my humanity. I discover something of what it is to be a human being by finding this thing in me, and then having it echoed in you, another human being.

Of course I want you to like the one about Winnie the Pooh. I want you to like it because I like you and I want you to have something you like, and I want you to be grateful to me for supplying it. But I also need you to like it, because in your liking I receive a confirmation of my own liking. I put this by saying that the joke *is funny*, as if this were an objective matter, like there being damned little sand along the coast of Maine, but what I mean is that *I* laugh at it, and if everyone laughed at it, then it would really *be* funny (or as good as funny), and I do so want you to laugh at it.

It is one thing to worry over a version of eighteenth-century skepticism, and wonder whether green looks green to you the way it does to me, and what it would mean to inhabit a world in which we did not experience green the same way, and what it means that we seemingly do inhabit a world in which we can't be "sure" that we see green together. It is quite another thing to wonder what the world would be like for me if I never found the same things funny that you or anyone else find funny. I personally have no worries on account of the problem about green, but I worry and feel stricken every time one of my jokes does not reach you.

● ● ● ●

Taste, Morality, and the Propriety of Joking

Do I think we *should* joke about absurdities? Should we be laughing at the fact of death? Death is a bleak topic. Jokes about death can be bleak. But apart from all that bleakness, joke-telling about death has a special dark side, which it shares with much joke-telling. I am one of those who believe jokes and joke-telling are wonderful and can be very serious, but I am also aware of the danger in too much joke-telling and joke-telling when it is out of place. Whether joking is in place or out of place may depend upon who is telling jokes to whom. In this regard, at least in America, or at least in my part of America, there seems to be a difference between men and women. Although it is not true uniformly and universally, men are much more likely to tell jokes to one another than are women to tell jokes to one another. Men are probably more often joke-tellers than women, and when women do tell jokes, they are more likely to tell them to men than to women. Why is that? Perhaps women have other conversational devices for establishing and maintaining intimacy, while for at least some men, joke-telling is a primary device of this kind.[10] But joking is almost always out of place when it is a kind

---

10   I owe this point to Andy Austin Cohen, herself a joke-teller, and an excellent audience to tell jokes to, who tells many more to men than to women.

of avoidance. Telling a joke about death can be a way of dealing with death, even of grappling with it; but sometimes the only proper way to think about death is to try looking it straight in its morbid, mordant eye, and on those occasions telling a joke is exactly the wrong thing to do because it is a way of avoiding the real issue. People like me who tell too many jokes, and tell them too often and in too many kinds of situations, usually get away with it because the laughter and ostensible humor are taken to be good things, things worth having even at the cost of other things. But we shouldn't get away with it, because a laugh is not always worth it, not if it is a deflection from something else that needs to be done. Mark Twain knew a very great deal about these matters, but when he said, "Against the assault of laughter nothing can stand," he neglected to note that some things should remain standing.

When is it in order to joke about death, and when not? I cannot say. No one can say. There is no rule here. It is up to you every time, it is up to you and your own moral sensibility (which includes concern for the sensibilities of others) to decide whether to tell a joke or to get serious, or whether, perhaps, telling a joke is a way of getting serious. This is a fact about all joke-telling, whether the jokes are about death or about anything else.

Here are two principles: One, jokes cannot be the entire human response to death, or to anything else; two, any total response to death that does not include the possibility of jokes is less than a totally human response.

Sometimes a joke is exactly the wrong response, the wrong overture to make. But when is this? If those jokes about New York and New Jersey are acceptable and are not seriously offensive, this one is a bit different.

> When God was creating the world, when He was finishing Europe He realized that
> France had come out perfect, which was not His plan. So He made Frenchmen.

However you feel about these jokes yourself, I think you know this: it would be surprising if New Yorkers or New Jerseyites were upset about the man from Nebraska or the recitation of the alphabet, but it would not be surprising if Frenchmen (and maybe others) were annoyed by this joke. But what is the difference? If, as I think, there is no formula to tell us which jokes are offensive or when it is the wrong time to put forth a particular joke, it may be possible to say something about just what goes wrong when these transgressions occur. To start, it will be useful to take a look at almost everyone's favorite example of jokes that shouldn't be told, "ethnic jokes."

In one kind of so-called ethnic joke, the ethnicity of the characters is not essential to the joke, because identifying someone as a Pole, or a Sikh, or an Iowa legislator is simply to stipulate that the character is inept or stupid or benighted. There is no doubt considerable significance in the fact of just which groups are chosen to be used in this way, and there may be moral, political, or social objections to using these groups in this way, but their ethnicity itself does not function in the joke. In other jokes, also deservedly called ethnic jokes, the ethnicity itself (or the religion or the nationality) is a substantial element in the joke. Here is an Irish joke (which is also an English joke, to a degree):

> An out-of-work Irishman went walking around London until he found a construction site with a sign announcing that workmen were being hired. When he applied for the job it was his bad luck that the foreman in charge was an Englishman with a dismal view of the Irish.
>
> "So, Paddy, you think you can do the work?" asked the foreman.
>
> "Oh yes," said the Irishman. "I've been doin' construction for thirty years."
>
> "Then you really understand construction?" asked the foreman.
>
> "Of course," said the Irishman. "I can do it all—the plumbin', the electric, the carpentry."
>
> "Then you wouldn't mind if I gave you a bit of a test?" asked the foreman.
>
> "No, no. Test away."
>
> "Then tell me, Paddy, what is the difference between a joist and a girder?"
>
> "It's too easy," said the Irishman. "'Twas the former wrote *Ulysses,* whilst the latter wrote *Faust.*"

And here is a Polish joke (which is also a Russian joke, to a degree):

> In the days of the Cold War, long before the collapse of the Soviet Union, a Polish man let it be known to his friends that he kept his life savings, one hundred thousand zlotys, in his bed, under the mattress.
>
> In horror one of his friends objected, "It isn't safe there. You must put it in the bank."
>
> "Oh?" said the man, "and what if the bank fails?"
>
> "How could the bank fail? It is supported by the Polish government."
>
> "Oh?" said the man, "and what if the Polish government fails?"
>
> "How could our government fail? It is kept in place by the Soviet Union."
>
> "Oh?" said the man, "and what if the Soviet Union collapses?"
>
> "Wouldn't that be worth 100,000 zlotys?"[11]

---

11 I already knew this joke in 1985, when I was visiting my very good friends, a Polish colleague of mine and his wife, in Poland. During a splendid evening with my colleague, his wife, and various guests including his wife's mother, I told this joke. When I had finished, and the joke had been translated into Polish for general consumption, this older lady made a reply, also in Polish, that brought down the house, and I realized that my joke had been topped. My colleague translated for me, "She says it would be worth 200,000 zlotys." That was a rare moment. My colleague's mother-in-law has since died, but I will never forget her.

In jokes like these, the relevant ethnicities are essential. Commonplaces about the Irish (that they are exceedingly and excessively literary), about the English (that they don't care much for the Irish), and about the Poles (that they are given to marvelously intricate subtleties and indirections of logic, and that they don't like Russians) are relatively very specific—quite different from just a generalized presumption that they are smart or stupid or venal. And in fact even if it were wrong it would not be unreasonable to believe that these commonplaces are in fact truths, whereas it is unreasonable to the point of utter ignorance to believe that Poles or Sikhs or students at Texas A&M are stupid.

An intermediate example is the joke in which an Englishman hears a joke about a monkey and a martini. Of course it is not true that the English have no sense of humor or appreciation of jokes, but it is nevertheless a kind of commonplace about them, and so the appreciation of the joke requires knowing this relatively specific commonplace.

I confess to a fondness for the structurally simplest kind of ethnic jokes, like

> This year's Polish science prize went to an engineer in Warsaw who has developed a solar-powered flashlight.

But I have a deeper appreciation for ethnic jokes in which the ethnicity is *used,* even if as slightly as in this:

> A Polish man walks up to a counter and says, "I want to buy some sausage."
>
> "You want Polish sausage?" asks the clerk. "Kielbasa?"
>
> "Why do you think I want Polish sausage?" replies the man indignantly. "Why wouldn't I want Italian sausage, or Jewish sausage? Do I look Polish? What makes you think I'm Polish?"
>
> The clerk responds, "This is a hardware store."

Here there is at least a reliance on the fact that there is such a thing as Polish sausage, even if the main presumption of the joke is the artificially given obtuseness of some group.

Sometimes the established presumption is not that the principal character is stupid or inept, but that he is disagreeable—mean, nasty, vicious. And sometimes that is all there is to the presumption, as in a number of jokes about agents and lawyers. For instance,

> A man walked angrily into a crowded bar, ordered a drink, and then said to the bartender, "All agents are assholes."
>
> From the end of the bar a man spoke up, saying, "Just a minute. I resent that."
>
> "Why? Are you an agent?"
>
> "No. I'm an asshole."[12]

---

12 I owe this joke to Mrs. Billy Wilder, although she disclaims credit and says she heard it from someone, perhaps Jack Lemmon. I owe it to Mrs. Wilder because she told the joke to Karen Lerner, who gave it to me. I am further indebted to Ms. Lerner for working keen improvements in the versions of some of the jokes used in this book.

In that joke nothing whatever is made of what might be disagreeable about agents as such, nor is anything made of lawyers in this joke:

> You find yourself trapped in a locked room with a murderer, a rapist, and a lawyer. Your only hope is a revolver you have, with two bullets left. What do you do?
>
> Shoot the lawyer. Twice.

Some jokes of this kind manage to invoke something at least slightly more specific, as in

> One summer noontime two lawyers were walking together over the Michigan Avenue bridge when they passed a particularly good-looking young woman in a thin summer dress walking the other way.
>
> "Man, I'd like to screw her," said one of the lawyers.
>
> His companion answered, "Yeah? Out of what?"

This joke suggests at least that lawyers' main interest is in taking advantage of people, and that that ambition supersedes any other interest they might take in human beings. It is possible, however, for such jokes, ones that presume to take an ethnically or professionally or otherwise identified character as the principal focus to make much more of the putative characteristics of the person. I have a preference for jokes that do this, that make more of the presumed profession or ethnicity, and so I think that ethnic jokes like the one about the Irish workman who knows his Joyce and Goethe are, if not better, at least richer and subtler, and they are devices for achieving considerably greater intimacy. One reason is the same as the reason why I think color movies are better when the color is used for something, large-scale orchestral music is better when the extra instruments are used for more than simply increasing the volume, and fiction is better when all the characters have something to do with the story and are not added only as filler. I tend to have a better opinion of works of art, and to be further moved by them, when all their parts seem relevant. If the only point in making a character in a joke Polish is to signal that he will be inept, I have the feeling that some potential "material" in the joke has gone unused, and this seems somehow a waste.

Another reason for preferring a Polish or Irish joke in which it really matters that the character is Polish or Irish, is that such jokes require more of the hearer, involve him more intimately, and give him greater opportunity for self-congratulation in his appreciation of the joke. They invoke a bigger and richer contribution from the hearer. It is one thing to know, simply, that there are jokes in which Polish characters are found to do misguided things, even though such jokes can be very funny, and it is another thing, a more substantial thing, to know that Poles have a long-standing, historical distrust of Russia.

All of these jokes, the simpler and the more complex ones, feel innocuous, but they carry a hint of something unsavory.

It is a very widespread conviction, shared by me, that some jokes on some occasions, and maybe some jokes on all occasions, are, as we say, "in bad taste," and should be thought of as morally objectionable. But it is very, very difficult to say just what this moral defect is. First is the problem of finding a basis for any moral judgment passed upon fiction, and then there is the problem of establishing the impropriety of laughing at something, especially when the something is fictional. Fiction itself might be objectionable as such, for instance when one puts it forth in hopes of inducing a belief in something false, but surely this is not characteristic of jokes. I say this to you:

> A man was told by his doctor that to improve his health he should take up jogging, and he should run two miles every day. After a couple of weeks the man was to call the doctor to tell him how he was feeling. Two weeks later the man called and the doctor asked, "So how are you doing?"
>
> "I feel pretty good," said the man, "but I'm twenty-eight miles from home."

Would you object, and be angry with me because I had told you a falsehood? Ridiculous. (Of course even if there were such a misguided jogger, you might just find that funny.) Consider again this exquisite children's joke:

> What do Alexander the Great and Winnie the Pooh have in common?
>
> They have the same middle name.

Would you object to this that it is not true, that the word 'the' is not the middle name of either character, and, furthermore, that there is no such creature as Winnie the Pooh? Ridiculous. It cannot be an objection solely that the joke contains falsehoods. In fact, in many cases the entire joke is a falsehood. Actually, it is a *fiction*, and a fiction is not—simply—a falsehood. (And a joke is not—simply—a fiction.) Of course a fiction might be taken as a statement of fact, but the fiction is not itself accountable for that. And yet something disturbing appears in some jokes. Some people are bothered by this joke:

> A man calls home from his office one day, and his phone is answered by the maid, Maria. "Maria," says the man, "I'd like to speak to my wife."
>
> "I'm sorry, *señor*, but she cannot come to the phone. She is making love to a man in the master bedroom."
>
> "My God, Maria. Can that be true?"
>
> "Yes, *señor*. I am *muy* sorry."
>
> "Maria, I must ask a favor. You have been with me many years, and now I need something from you."
>
> "Yes, *señor*, what is it?"
>
> "Maria, are you in my study?"
>
> "*Sí, señor.*"
>
> "In the upper right drawer of the desk you will find a loaded revolver. Take it to the bedroom and shoot them both."

The phone goes dead for a few minutes, and then Maria's voice comes through. "It is done, *señor.*"

"Good, Maria. I am in your debt. Now take the revolver, wipe off the handle, and throw it into the swimming pool."

"*Señor*? We have no swimming pool."

"Is this 555–4694?"

And, probably, more people are bothered by this one:

This year's annual prize for Polish medicine went to a surgeon in Krakow who performed the world's first appendix transplant.

But many more people are bothered by this one:

How did a passerby stop a group of black men from committing a gang rape?

He threw them a basketball.

Exactly what is *wrong* with any of these three jokes, and why is the last one so much more disturbing? The first is from a short-lived genre of "Maria jokes" that came from Southern California, I think (all such jokes involving a Mexican maid named Maria). The second is a Polish joke, so called, and the third is a black joke (although that category seems to me less well defined).

Each joke says that something happened, and in fact it didn't. There was no man who called home for his wife, got the wrong number without knowing it, and commissioned the murder of two strangers. There is no annual prize for Polish medicine, and no Polish surgeon performed an appendix transplant. No group of black men was distracted from a criminal sexual assault by being given the opportunity to play basketball.

But none of the jokes says that these things really happened. The jokes are short stories, fictions, perhaps, although of a very peculiar kind, and one can no more sensibly object to them as falsehoods than one might object to *Hamlet* that in fact there never was a prince of Denmark who had a couple of friends named Rosencrantz and Guildenstern.

Is it that the jokes say that Mexican maids are obtusely obedient even to the point of murder, that Poles are so stupid that they do not understand the point in organ transplant, that black men are sexually violent and mindlessly committed to playing basketball?

But the jokes don't *say* those things, any more than they say anything at all. Do they somehow purvey stereotypes, and disagreeable ones at that? Do those who respond to these jokes either believe in advance or come to believe nonsense about Mexican maids, Polish scientists, and black men? I doubt this. And I doubt that one could show any connection between traffic in such jokes and negative beliefs about these groups of people. Even if there is such a connection, I have myself been amused by all three jokes, and I do not myself believe any of those generalizations about the relevant characters, and yet these jokes disturb me, especially the last one, the one about criminal black basketball players. Why?

There are two questions. First I would like to know just why these jokes disturb me, and then I wonder whether my personal discomfort and objection can be generalized and rendered "objective" so that a negative assessment might be made about the jokes themselves. It may be that my personal dislike is just that—personal. This does not mean that it is unreal, that you should persist in telling me such jokes on the grounds that is only a personal, subjective matter that they do not agree with me, but it would mean that my complaint that such jokes are in bad taste or unwholesome comes to nothing more than my wish to be free of them. That is pretty much how it is for me, for instance, with regard to the music of Wagner and some of Eliot's poetry. I do not claim that these works are poor or corrupt, but only that I do not care for them; and if you do care for them, then this may mark a significant difference between you and me, but it signals nothing I am prepared to say about the works in themselves.

Why am I made uneasy about the joke about the black men? I think it is because I am made uneasy by the idea that black men are criminals and mindless basketball players. But how can an *idea* do that to me? Is it that I think the idea is false, or that it would lead to a false proposition if one believed it? But I think that almost all the statements and ideas presented in almost all the jokes I know are false in the sense that they would lead to false propositions if one believed them. Is there something especially disagreeable or obnoxious in this particular idea's being believed? Yes, I think so. If I, or others, believed in this idea, then I and others might well treat people badly. But so what? As a matter of fact I don't believe the idea, and I don't think that your telling me this joke leads either of us to believe the idea, nor does it suggest that either of us already believes it.

It is possible that the existence of such jokes and commerce in them are symptoms of pernicious attitudes and beliefs, and perhaps the jokes even are causes of this perniciousness. If that were true, then of course that would be the basis of a moral objection to the jokes. I do not know that this is true, and I do not know that it is false. And neither does anyone else know about this, nor does anyone have any idea how to discover whether it is true. But this question—the question of what role such jokes may play in bad behavior—might be set aside, if we could agree on how to answer a different question.

If jokes about the uncontrolled animalism of black men or about the venality of Jews could be shown to have no effect whatever on people's beliefs about black men and Jews, then would the jokes cease to be troublesome? I think the jokes would still be disturbing. Why? And need there be an answer to this question? Let me restart this little moral inquiry by asking, again, just what is disturbing in these jokes, as well as in certain works of art.

I do not like the portrayal of the Jewish nightclub-owners in Spike Lee's movie *Mo' Better Blues*, and I do not like the ridiculous portrayal of Jews in Edith Wharton's novel *House of Mirth*. No doubt this is at least partly because I am Jewish, but neither do I like the portrayal of black men in D. W. Griffith's movie *Birth of a Nation*. And why don't I like those portrayals? Because they are inaccurate? Because they are stereotypes? These seem lame answers to me.

I am not much bothered by the portrayal of WASPs in the movie *Auntie Mame*, although that portrayal is at least as inaccurate and unflattering as the others. It must be relevant that I do not regard WASPs as vulnerable, not in the way that Jews and blacks seem vulnerable. Is it that I am worried that people will think that Jews and blacks are in fact as they are portrayed in these works, and that I have no worry on behalf of the WASPs? It is not that I have no concern for WASPs; it is that I think they have nothing to worry about. But is that true? Are they not as entitled as anyone to object to stereotypical representations of themselves? Incidentally, stereotypes can be annoying, just as such, without regard to whether they are negative. In "Concerning the Jews," Mark Twain offers an exceedingly flattering characterization of Jews, and it troubles me almost as much as the negative portraits offered by T. S. Eliot and Edith Wharton. A stereotype can rob you of your particularity just as surely if it is flattering as if it is negative. What about the stereotype of young black men in that basketball joke?

The fact that this joke works is a fact only because of some genuine truths—not truths about black men, but truths about how black men are thought of. These truths are, for instance, that young black men are associated with basketball, and they are thought to have a passion for basketball that takes them away, for instance, from learning mathematics or learning to read; and that is what is being insinuated in a joke in which they give up even violent sex—another of their putative passions—for the chance to slam-dunk. I know all that, that these are associations that go with young black men, and it is only because I know all that that I am able to respond to the joke. Do I, perhaps, dislike it in myself that I know these things? And do I then dislike my own laughter at the joke? Is the joke working its magical establishment of intimacy by forcing me to acknowledge something I don't care for in myself? Would I rather that I did not know these things? Of course I wish that these were not things to be known, but is it my fault that they are, and that I know them?

If I were to offer some resounding moral condemnation of this joke, no doubt I would have to invoke some "moral theory," and then show that an implication of the theory is that this joke is Bad. I will not do that. It would be inappropriate in this book to do that, but I have another reason for not doing it: I think it can't be done.

A common, sometimes useful device in analytical, conceptual moral theory is the idea of an ideal creature, sometimes called an ideal observer, or an impartial spectator, or a person of practical wisdom. First, such a creature is characterized (perhaps as being completely informed, disinterested, and so on), and then it is supposed that the right way to act, or to feel, or to judge, is to act, feel, or judge as this ideal creature would. Try thinking up such a person, and then ask whether this person would disapprove of these jokes, whether he would tell them or laugh at them, and how he would feel about anyone who tells them. What do you think? Would he damn these jokes? I don't know, and neither, I think, do you.

Among contemporary normative theories of morality, most would require that it be shown that traffic in these jokes produces genuine harm to someone, or at least that it reduces the moral character of those who traffic in them. It seems to me preposterous to suppose that anyone could show that either of these consequences obtains. One of the more ponderous and depressing features of large-scale moral theories is that they tell you what makes things right or wrong, good or bad, and then leave it to you to take a case about whose morality you feel strongly and try to outfit it with the theory's sanctioned reasons. Thus someone who hates that joke about the black basketball players is forced to give his reasons for declaring it morally disagreeable. It may be that a mammoth raft of literature, propaganda, fiction, poetry, religious writing and preaching, and casual conversation can produce or sustain a general opinion of things, including an opinion of kinds of people—surely it would be foolish to deny that; but it is farfetched to indict a movie or a novel or a joke on those grounds. And worse: when it turns out that you can find no convincing evidence to support this claim about the effects of such jokes, you seem obliged to give up your moral complaint. And you shouldn't do that.

Here is some friendly advice: When you feel strongly that some joke (or anything else) is no damned good, and especially when you don't like having that joke told, and it seems to you that the thing—either itself or the telling of it—is morally defective, hold on to that feeling, and continue to express the feeling in terms of moral condemnation. When someone demands a moral-theoretical reason for your condemnation, ask them why they think you need one. You don't have to prove that a joke is funny, or that it is unfunny (good thing, too, because you couldn't do it), and surely you don't have to prove that it seems to you to be immoral. Do you have to prove that it is immoral? I don't think so. If your opponent thinks so, then ask him to supply the theory, the apparatus that would allow a claim that something is morally objectionable. When he does, then either you will be able to fit this joke to his theory, or you won't. If you can't make the theory work in support of your conviction, then try telling your philosophical opponent that you now have good reason to disbelieve his theory, namely that it can't account for the immoral character of this joke you hate. But before you do that, perhaps you should expand your categories. Not everything you dislike is illegal, or should be. Not everything you dislike is immoral. But something's being legal and morally acceptable doesn't mean you have to think it is OK. Nor does it mean you have to put up with it.

Don't like it, and don't put up with it when someone commits murder. Or when someone commits adultery. Or when young men don't give their seats to burdened women standing on the bus. Or when someone picks his nose. Or when people don't write thank-you notes for parties you have given or gifts you have sent. You don't have to put up with any of these. But don't suppose that there should be laws forbidding them, at least not all of them. And don't imagine that your dislike must be grounded in some stupefying Moral Theory.

You can avoid people who tell jokes you hate, or at least insist that they not tell them to you or when you are present. You can tell strong young men that they should give up their seats to pregnant women (although before doing this, you might well consider just what bus you are riding on).

Clarify these matters for yourself, and choose your words carefully—and above all be sure that they are *your words*—when you express your disapproval. This requires asking yourself persistently *why* you don't like something, as I tried to discover why I don't like the one about the black basketball players. Then notice whether you have felt a need for moral vocabulary.

I wish you good luck in thus maintaining your feeling of disgust—moral disgust, if that's how it feels to you—at the joke, but I insist that you not let your conviction that a joke is in bad taste, or downright immoral, blind you to whether you find it funny.

When an obnoxious portrayal is in a joke, it is likely to be upsetting in a special regard. Jokes are humorous, amusing, fun. It is ponderous and obtuse to object to the fun. The offended person who takes issue with a joke finds himself doubly assaulted, first by the offensive portrayal in the joke, and then again by the implicit accusation that he is humorless. But the offended person may make the reflexive mistake of denying that the joke is funny More than once someone has demanded of me that I explain exactly why anti-Semitic jokes are not funny. I have come to realize that if there is a problem with such jokes, the problem is compounded exactly by the fact that they *are* funny. Face that fact. And then let us talk about it.

A young, earnest, white college student confesses his guilt at his own reactions when walking big-city streets after dark. He finds that he is more worried for himself when a stranger appears on the street when that stranger is black than he is when the stranger is white. He feels guilty for having this feeling, and he wishes he didn't feel that way. He is right to wish he didn't feel that way, if that is a wish that the world were different, but he is not wrong to have the feeling. Given the world as it is, there is nothing wrong with having the feeling, and it might well be a practical error not to have the feeling. As a matter of fact, given the neighborhood he walks in, it is enormously more likely that he will be set upon by a black stranger than by a white one. And that is a God-damned shame. But it is a fact. By all means, wish that it were not a fact. Weep because it is a fact. Try to change the world so that it will cease to be a fact. But don't turn away from the fact, don't force yourself to deny it.

Wish that there were no mean jokes. Try remaking the world so that such jokes will have no place, will not arise. But do not deny that they are funny. That denial is a pretense that will help nothing. And it is at least possible, sometimes, that the jokes themselves do help something. Perhaps they help us to bear unbearable affronts like crude racism and stubborn prejudice by letting us laugh while we take a breather.

What do you think of this joke?

> The Secret Service has an opening in its ranks, needing to recruit someone to join those who guard the President of the United States. They post a notice in bulletins for government workers, and soon they receive three applications, one from an F.B.I. man, one from an agent from the Bureau of Alcohol, Tobacco, and Firearms, and a third from a Chicago city policeman. Each of the three is given a qualifying examination, beginning with the F.B.I. man.
>
> The F.B.I. man is given a revolver and told to go into the adjacent room and shoot whomever he finds there. When he has been gone only a few minutes, the F.B.I. man returns, saying, "You must be out of your minds! That's my wife. I'm not shooting her."

"Fine," say the examiners. "You must be a good family man, but you're not cut out for the Secret Service."

Next the A.T.F. agent is sent in with the revolver, with the same instructions to shoot whomever he finds in the next room. He too returns in minutes, exclaiming, "That's the mother of my children, you lunatics."

"Good for you," say the examiners. "Enjoy your career in the bureau and continue looking after your wife; but we can't use you in the Secret Service."

Finally, the Chicago policeman is given the same test. When he has been in the adjacent room for about ten minutes, sounds are heard, the sounds of struggle and muffled groaning. A few minutes later the cop reappears, looking somewhat mussed, and says, "Some moron put blanks in the gun; I had to strangle her."

Now consider this: this marvelous story was told to me by my wife. She learned it from a Chicago policeman.[13] I do not know where the policeman came by it, but I do know that he and his fellow officers have had a good time telling it to one another. Do you think that is a bad thing? I don't. I don't know just what to make of it, but I do know that the dynamics of joking—including the intimacy sought and achieved, the relief gained from unpleasantness, and the moral dimensions of all this—depend absolutely upon who tells the joke and who hears it. Do you think this story *says* something about Chicago cops? If it does, it may well not be the same thing said when cops tell the joke to one another as it is when civilians tell the joke, and it is yet different when cops and civilians exchange this joke.[14] I think that Chicago cops' telling this joke to one another is a very good thing, a hopeful sign in a difficult world.

---

13 This was her good friend John Berry, a sergeant in the Chicago Police Department, an Irish-American, and the bearer of many a fine story.

14 It is remarkable, I think, that Officers Golonka and Berry tell my wife, Andy Austin Cohen, the same jokes they exchange with other policemen.

CPSIA information can be obtained
at www.ICGtesting.com
Printed in the USA
LVHW112105071221
705534LV00004B/19

9 781793 517166